Discovering West Lothian

Discovering
West Lothian

WILLIAM F. HENDRIE

JOHN DONALD PUBLISHERS LTD
EDINBURGH

ISBN 0 85976 162 2

Exclusive distribution in the United States of
America and Canada by Humanities Press Inc.,
Atlantic Highlands, NJ 07716, USA

Phototypesetting by Newtext Composition Ltd., Glasgow
Printed in Great Britain by Bell & Bain Ltd., Glasgow

Acknowledgements

My thanks to John Doherty for supplying many of the pictures which illustrate this book; to Guthrie Pollock for providing the map; to the Royal Commission on the Ancient and Historical Monuments of Scotland for permission to reproduce pictures of buildings in their care; Livingston Mill Restoration Group and Livingston Mill Farm for photographs and information; Livingston Development Corporation for the use of photographs; Livingston Oil Museum for information; West Lothian District Library Headquarters, Bathgate, for help with research; The Bo'ness Sea Box for information and photographs; and Hopetoun House Preservation Trust for supplying an illustration.

Contents

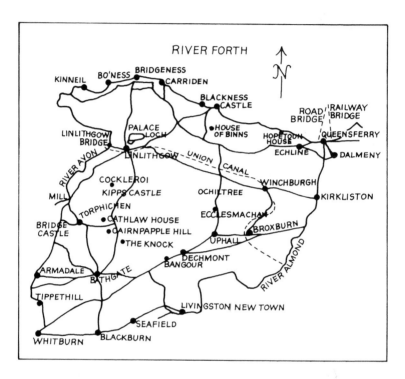

Introduction

Before the re-organisation of Scottish local government with the creation of the two-tier system of regions and districts in 1975, West Lothian was the second smallest of Scotland's mainland counties, only Clackmannanshire having a smaller land area.

Situated on the southern shore of the River Forth, right in the middle of Central Scotland, West Lothian was often described as 'Corridor County' because its valleys running straight across it from east to west have since the times of stage coach and canal, through the coming of the railways to the motorways of the present day, always formed the main routes between Edinburgh and Glasgow and Stirling and the North.

West Lothian has therefore always been a county to pass through rather than a place to visit in its own right. But it is a pity that the thousands of motorists who speed each day along its busy motorways never stop to really discover this compact little county. For the lands which are sandwiched between the M9 to the north and the M8 in the south are stuffed full of ingredients which make up a rich filling, well worth stopping to taste.

In one small bite, West Lothian takes in a great deal of Scottish history from the birth of the royal house of Stewart to the birth of its most famous member, Mary Queen of Scots, because as a result of its close proximity to Edinburgh it always had many royal connections giving it a heritage of castles, with Linlithgow Palace as its crowning glory.

West Lothian was always rich in trade as well, because its setting on the Forth ensured that it got its full share of business with Europe in those days when Scotland had closer links with the continent than with its neighbour England, to such an extent that the now tiny village of Blackness was once Scotland's second most important seaport, second only to Leith.

The Forth also brought West Lothian its first links with the oil industry through the cargoes of blubber brought home by its whalers; and through the Victorian shale-oil bonanza it has maintained these connections right down to its present involvement with the North Sea oil industry.

1

The mining of shale, and before that coal and even silver, has naturally left its mark on the West Lothian landscape, but while it is the ugly black pit bings and massive pink plateau of shale waste which are immediately visible to the hurrying motorist on the motorways, West Lothian is also a county of great beauty, as can be discovered by driving up the quiet country roads into the Bathgate Hills. For here lies hidden a veritable miniature Trossachs, complete with hills, lochs and forests; and the views from the top of Cockleroi or Cairnpapple right across the narrow waist of Central Scotland from the Isle of May in the east to the Isle of Arran in the west are truly panoramic.

At just over a thousand feet high, Cairnpapple used to give West Lothian the claim of being the Scottish county with the lowest highest point, but much more importantly it is the site of one of Scotland's richest archaeological sites and one of the earliest places of organised worship in the country. That worship continued into Christian times at neighbouring Torphichen, where the world's oldest order of chivalry, the Knights of St. John, built the castle-like Preceptory as their Scottish headquarters. Linlithgow, Abercorn, Dalmeny and Queensferry each also have historic churches which are all equally well worth discovering.

Officially Queensferry and Dalmeny are no longer part of West Lothian, because they were ceded to the Edinburgh District of Lothian at the same time as Bo'ness and Blackness were transferred to Central Region in 1975, but *Discovering West Lothian* still deliberately includes them, as it looks at the county as it was originally designated with the Forth and its tributaries the Avon and Almond as its natural boundaries.

West Lothian – or Linlithgowshire as it was known in past centuries – has never previously attracted the same amount of attention as many other Scottish counties such as Perthshire, Fife or even East Lothian. *Discovering West Lothian* aims to rectify this by introducing readers to this county of contrasts, from the mining of silver in the Bathgate Hills to the golden crown of thorns atop St. Michael's Church, and from the royal revels and feasts of the 'Daft Days' of Christmas at medieval Linlithgow Palace to the present-day fun and frolics of Scotland's most spectacular children's summer celebration, Bo'ness Fair.

CHAPTER 1

Bo'ness, Burgh Town on the Point

'Dirty Bo'ness!' That's how West Lothian's old sea port of Bo'ness or Borrowstounness, to give it its full name of the Burgh Town on the Point, was often described, and it is still a matter of argument amongst its older inhabitants whether the epithet was more justified by the grime of its many coal bings or by the tactics of its football teams.

Over the years Bo'ness on its somewhat isolated nose of land sticking out into the River Forth did indeed build a reputation for coal and football, but while its football team, Bo'ness United, still repeatedly puts up a strong challenge for the Scottish Junior Cup, its last links with coal were smashed in January 1984, when despite an underground sit-in by its miners, the last of its dozens of pits, the famous Kinneil Colliery, was closed as uneconomic by the National Coal Board.

This was a cruel blow for a town which was literally built on coal, as subsiding roads, disappearing gardens and collapsing homes still bear testament to the honeycomb of mine workings which provided it with work and wealth for all of eight hundred years, ever since the monks of Holyrood Abbey are credited with hewing the first coal in Scotland there in the twelfth century. The monks who in those days led the way not only in matters of religion, but also in agriculture and industry, loaded the coal, which they dug from the hillside overlooking the Forth to the east of Bo'ness at Carriden, into boats and shipped it downriver to Leith, and it was this immediate access to sea transport which gave Bo'ness its headstart in the coalmining industry.

It was to be over five hundred years before West Lothian's other coalfield only ten miles inland around Armadale, Bathgate and Whitburn was to be developed, because of the impossible state of Scotland's roads throughout the whole of the Middle Ages and beyond, but for Bo'ness with its coastal position no such difficulties impeded its progress, and soon fleets of small sailing ships were carrying cargoes of coal across

When one looks at this turn of the century picture of the miners' row at Kinneil, it is not hard to understand why Bo'ness was often described as 'dirty'. Courtesy of John Doherty.

the North Sea to the Scandinavian countries, which had no supplies of their own, and south to London. This was why the term 'sea coal' was used in the English capital and not, as has sometimes been suggested, because it was scavenged on the shores of the Tyne.

Much nearer at hand one user of Bo'ness coal was the royal palace at Linlithgow, despite the protests of the ladies of the court that this cheap substitute for the traditional wood fires would undoubtedly ruin their complexions with its black soot.

While the nobles at Linlithgow Palace enjoyed the warmth of their coal fires, the miners of Carriden had to work hard to dig it from the hillside above the Forth. At first the coal was simply dug from outcrops, but soon the surface measures were exhausted and it was necessary to dig shallow mines. These were nicknamed 'Ingaun E'es', because as the miners worked on into the night, their flickering candles made the workings look like eyes staring out across the Forth from the dark hillside.

As demand for coal increased still further, the sloping 'In-Going Eyes' were replaced by the first proper pits, and they too in their turn gained a nickname – 'Bell Pits' – because their

4

steep straight shafts resembled the handles of old-fashioned handbells while the limited circular workings at the foot of each shaft were indeed bell-shaped. As soon as the available coal around the base of each shaft was exhausted, the miners simply sank another shaft a few hundred yards away and repeated the process again and again until hundreds of years later during the latter half of the eighteenth century the growth of the Industrial Revolution in Scotland increased the demand for coal and made it economically worthwhile to develop the underground workings, which grew into a labyrinth beneath the town.

At first many of the workings were very near the surface, and it was claimed that the miners working below Carriden Brae could hear the clip clop of horses' hooves on the road above, and this lack of depth and the method used to construct the underground passages both contributed to the many modern problems of subsidence in Bo'ness today. For the method adopted was that of Stoop and Room, or Stack and Room as it was sometimes called. This meant that large pillars of coal were left untouched at regular intervals along the whole length of the seam and these were the stacks, while the coal dug out around them formed the rooms. In itself this would have been reasonably safe, but when the seam was exhausted using this method, the colliery owners, seeking to maximise profits, ordered their men to dig out the coal in the supporting stoops with the result that 'sits' or collapses occurred.

Most famous of these 'sits' took place right beneath the original Bo'ness Town Hall and resulted in the demolition of the clock tower, which was somewhat of a coincidence as the crash took place during a Sunday evening prayer meeting in the year 1883, when the well-known local lay preacher Mr. Hope just happened to have taken as the text for his sermon the downfall of the Biblical Tower of Siloam.

The collapses caused by the Stoop and Room method resulted in the deaths of many local miners trapped under-ground, but it was not for religious or humanitarian reasons that the mine owners abandoned it in favour of the Shropshire Method as it was known in England or the Long Wall Method as it was generally called in Scotland. Long Wall describes it well for, using this much more efficient system, whole seams of

Bo'ness' interest in the sea remained strong throughout Victorian times, as can be seen from the crowds who lined the harbour on this Regatta Saturday, which was a great annual summer event in the town until the First World War. Courtesy of John Doherty.

coal were worked and removed, but this created the problem of how to support the roof and interestingly resulted in one of the many ancillary industries which Bo'ness gained as a result of its involvement in coalmining.

'This palace of Kinneil' was how West Lothian's earliest historian, Sir Robert Sibbald, described Kinneil House, a home of the Dukes of Hamilton, which overlooks the River Forth between Bo'ness and Grangemouth. This view was taken at the beginning of the century.

Timber supports were the obvious answer, and to begin with full-length tree trunks were purchased by the colliery owners and at the start of each shift the miners had to saw up the number of props of various sizes which they reckoned they would require during the day. This method was very wasteful, because the miners never bothered to calculate how to make the best use of each tree, and many short lengths of timber were often left over, quite possibly deliberately, as the miners collected the scrap and took it home to burn on their own fires.

This continual waste was noticed by the young cashier at the Grange Colliery, George Stewart, whose watchfulness resulted in his becoming one of the richest men in Bo'ness as well as one of its best-known provosts and the founder of the town's famous Children's Fair Festival. For Mr. Stewart resigned his job at the pit, went into partnership with Mr. James Love, a Glasgow businessman, and imported cheap ready-cut pit props from the softwood coniferous forests of Norway, Sweden, Finland and Russia. Their new business proved so successful that they were soon able to buy their own forests in Scandinavia and their own ships, including the *Lovart*, which they named after themselves, to bring the cargoes of pitprops to Bo'ness, as soon as the Baltic ice melted each spring. From one small yard on land recently reclaimed from the Forth by the dumping of colliery waste from the Grange Pit where George Stewart had started his career, Stewart and Love spread right along the shores of the river until they had a veritable forest of pit props stacked high from Kinneil in the west to Carriden in the east, and in summer the sweet cloying smell of resin as the propyard women in the Newhaven fisherwives-style sriped dresses ripped off the bark became so pervasive that it was said that visitors to the town always smelt it before they saw it.

Bo'ness because so associated with its pit-prop trade that the town became known as 'Pitpropolis', and in 1881 the old harbour was vastly expanded by the opening of a large new dock with 2400 feet of quays to cope with the business which the prop boats brought. Even with this increased capacity and the extension of the East and West piers of the old outer harbour to take extra vessels, during the busiest season at the start of each summer many of the prop boats with their deck cargoes piled high on top of the hatch covers had to queue patiently in the roads out in the river off Bo'ness waiting for a berth as the dockers and the mechanical coal hoists used to refuel the ships worked day and night to cope with the traffic.

These latter years of Queen Victoria's reign and the first years of the present century up to the First World War saw Bo'ness at its bustling best with a fine new stone-built custom house which can still be admired impressively by the dockside, an equally solid new stone-built post office and telegraph office just round the corner overlooking the harbour,[1] and substantial stone villas, panelled inside with the best of Baltic timber, crowning the braes behind to provide fitting homes for the merchants, shipowners and other businessmen who had brought the town its prosperity.

Their workers had to be content with equally solid but simpler sensible homes in the stone tenements of Man O' War Street and Hamilton Lane and Corbiehall crowded into the narrow strip of land between the Forth and the hills, which rose behind in distinct levels like a large wedding cake. On the whole masters and men lived tolerably together, each dependent on the other, but in May 1910 there was a decided rift which ended in the Battle of Slaghill.

That spring the heavily laden prop boats arrived as usual, but instead of their usual welcome for the work they brought

Sunday best was the order of the day on this quiet Sabbath morning amongst the railway sidings below Fountain Park in Bo'ness. Courtesy of John Doherty.

they were greeted with hostility and strikes, because the propyard bosses had cut their workers' wages from sixpence to only fivepence an hour, alleging that trade was depressed. The Bo'ness labourers were even angrier when they learned that similar workers in propyards upriver at Grangemouth and Alloa were still being paid the whole sixpence and, encouraged by their newly formed trade union, they downed tools.

By evening their union organiser had arrived by train from Glasgow and at a crowded meeting in the Market Square inflamed the situation still further by announcing that he had news that he had heard on his journey at Queen Street Station that the employers intended to break the strike the very next morning by laying on a special train from the city to import hundreds of blacklegs. Enraged, the propyard men, their wives and bairns marched up the School Brae, along Braeside and on up through Craigallen Park to surround 'Elmpark', the home of the Harrower family who owned one of the largest of the yards. For a time the situation looked very nasty as the strikers catcalled and jeered as they pressed against the black wrought iron railings, but as darkness fell on that long May evening, they dispersed, vowing to be up at crack of dawn to greet the Glaswegians.

Forewarned, all six Bo'ness policemen were already on guard long before the special train bringing the Glasgow workers came into sight, steaming down the single-line track from Manuel Junction near Polmont on the main Glasgow to Edinburgh line, just before six o'clock. Jeers and shouts greeted the incomers, but they were all allowed to proceed unmolested as they made their way from the little platform at Kinneil Halt across into the propyard to start work.

It looked indeed as if the police had been called out unnecessarily as the strikers made their way back along Corbiehall, into the centre of Bo'ness. But this was only the lull before the storm, because the strikers had only returned to the town to gather reinforcements. For the next three hours they marched round all the other works in the town, and as news of the forthcoming battle spread they were joined by several hundred foundry workers who all stopped work for the day to support the propyard men. At nine o'clock many a schoolboy defied the bell at Bo'ness Academy and joined the Bo'ness army as, led by a piper, it marched back to Kinneil and the fray.

Inside the yard the Glaswegians stopped work and watched anxiously. As the first ranks of strikers advanced upon them the constables drew their batons. For a second the strikers halted, then urged on by the shouts of their womenfolk they let fly a hail of stones and bricks and charged the police, who stood no chance. As they entered the yard the strikers grabbed pit props and, thus armed, began the battle. All over the yard skirmishes broke out as the Bo'nessians fell upon the Glasgow men. Seeing that they were very clearly outnumbered, the Glaswegians did not wait to fight, but sought cover under the long rows of railway waggons and in the yard bothies. Relentlessly the Bo'ness labourers hunted them down and, despite pleas for mercy, battered them with the heavy props.

As the battle raged the yard clerks, who had not stopped work along with the men, barricaded themselves in their office, but the strikers were not interested in them. They wanted the blood of the Glasgow invaders. Suddenly they heard that a

Members of the Bo'ness Sea Box in 1899 posed for this group photograph on the steps of Rondebush, the former family home of the society's present president, Mr. William J. Cochrane, whose grandfather, John Cochrane, is the bearded gentleman seated on the extreme left of the front row. Courtesy of W. Cochrane.

group of Glasgow men were hiding between two of the long high lines of stacks of props. The incomers could not have chosen a worse refuge and the strikers knew it, for the far end of the narrow gap was blocked by another huge pile of pit props and once in there was no way out. Led by their leader, nicknamed 'Showman Bill', one group of strikers guarded the entrance, while the others climbed up on top of the piles of props and pushed down the long heavy round pieces of wood on top of the terrified blacklegs. As the avalanche of tree trunks crashed down on them the trapped men yelled their surrender and were dragged out by the victorious Bo'ness men. 'A veritable Khyber Pass', wrote one reporter, who covered the battle from the frontline for that afternoon's *Edinburgh Evening News*.

In other parts of the yard, the battle continued with fierce bursts of fighting as group after group of the enemy was ferreted out. Some of the Glasgow men tried desperately to escape by fleeing out of the far side of the yard onto the shores of the Forth, but they found themselves cut off by the river. Mercilessly they were pursued out onto the oozing black

Bo'ness is famed in musical circles for its three brass bands, Bo'ness and Carriden, the Salvation Army Brass Band and Kinneil Colliery, some of whose earliest players are shown in this picture. Courtesy of John Doherty.

mudflats, where the fight continued. Others found themselves trapped on the steep crumbling black slopes of the huge Slaghill coal bing which dominated the scene and which gave the battle its name.

Just as the battle looked like turning into a massacre, the employers announced that they would meet the strikers' representatives and try to reach a settlement. As quickly as they had entered the yard the Bo'ness men withdrew and marched triumphantly back into town leaving behind them a trail of havoc among the prop stacks and over fifty Glasgow men seriously injured. Another two hundred suffered from minor cuts and bruises. As one of the propyard clerks, young Fred Farquharson, noted down their names and the extent of their injuries, one of the local G.P.s, Dr. Fischer, made them as comfortable as possible before they were carried back aboard the special train, which had been hurriedly summoned. When it left at 1 p.m., many of the Glaswegians could not be found, but they boarded the train later at Polmont to which they had walked across the fields and through Kinneil Woods, rather than remain any longer in Bo'ness.

In the meantime another special train was rushing towards Bo'ness from Waverley Station, Edinburgh, carrying police

Bo'ness Fair procession passes through the shows or fun fair which was set up each year in Corbiehall to mark the town's big event of the year. Courtesy of John Doherty.

reinforcements from the city. By the time they arrived the battle was of course all over, but many of the Bo'ness men, including a future provost of the town, were arrested and carted off by rail to the city's Calton Jail. Most were released again next morning for want of actual evidence against them, but several were charged and subsequently tried and imprisoned for up to six months.

At the same time negotiations dragged on until at the end of the summer, with the winter slack period approaching; the men were forced to accept only half what they had struck and fought for and settle for an hourly rate of 5½ pence.

It was not the first time that workers in Bo'ness had to accept less than satisfactory working conditions. One of the town's place names is still Thirlstane Terrace, and this is a lasting reminder of the long years during which many of the towns-folk were thirled, that is tied or bound to their work, and this applied not only to the colliers and the salters themselves, but

13

to their wives also and to any children borne by them so that this Scottish serfdom was self-perpetuating.

Serfdom amongst Scottish miners and their families is already well documented, but in a way it was even worse for the salters, for they were even paid in salt. Saltmaking was another of the industries which Bo'ness gained as a spin-off from its coalmining. There was always a demand for the best coal for export, but not for the small coal or dross. This was never wasted at Bo'ness, however, because by a fortunate coincidence it could be used as 'panwood', the fuel to feed the fires which burned day and night beneath the shallow iron pans to evaporate the sea water from the Forth to produce salt.

Salt was manufactured at many places around the Scottish coast where carboniferous coal measures provided cheap fuel from Saltcoats in the west to Prestonpans in the east, but nowhere more so than at Bo'ness, where at one time there were almost a hundred pans.

To produce three tons of salt it was necessary to evaporate one hundred tons of water, and the task of transferring all the water from the river to the pans fell to the women and children, using a huge wooden seesaw-like contraption called a wand pump. Built on the shore right at the water's edge, on one end of the long beam was fixed a large wooden bucket which the women and bairns dipped below the surface. When it was full, they pushed with all their might on the other end of the long plank which raised the bucket into the air, in which position it was then shoved around until it was clear of the river.

The contents of the bucket were never emptied straight into the salt pan, because even in those days the Forth was not the cleanest of rivers and it was found better to let the water settle in small reservoirs for a day or two to allow the mud and grit to settle. Even this precaution did not keep all of the impurities out of the pan, so once the water was boiling they were removed by couping a bucket of sheep or cow's blood into the steaming solution. The albumen in the blood thickened in the boiling water, forming a scum, just like the one which forms on home-made strawberry jam, and as it rose to the surface it carried with it all the other impurities in the pan. It was then once again the womenfolk's unenviable task to lean out over

The Queen's horse-drawn open landau in an early Fair procession reaches the East Partings. The head of the mounted boy Champion can be seen at the bottom of the picture. Courtesy of John Doherty.

the bubbling, steaming boiling water and, using long-handled wooden rakes, to skim off the scum, thus leaving the rest of the solution perfectly clear, and it was possibly this unpleasant job which gave rise to the local legend of the 'Bloody Witches of Cuffabouts', who were alleged to haunt one of the sets of pans at Carriden, for it is easy to imagine how horrific and ghostly must have been the appearance of the salters' wives as they emerged from the swirling steam of the pans, their clothes, faces and arms streaked red with the blood of the scum.

Once the scum was removed, the evaporation of the water continued, fifty tons of coal being necessary to produce every three tons of salt, and the only time that the fires beneath the pans were damped down was on Saturday nights, for the kirk sessions at both Carriden and Bo'ness parish churches strictly

forbade any work on Sundays. But even this delay in production was turned to advantage by the wily saltmasters, for the
slower rate of evaporation resulted in larger grains of salt being
formed, and these were sold as a more expensive table delicacy
called Sabbath Salt. Even the ordinary salt was considered dear
by the housewives of the Middle Ages, for the Scottish
Parliament cashed in on the fact that it was a vital commodity
which every family had to buy, and put a tax on it. Officially all
salt produced had to be stored in bonded warehouses called
girnels, but the tax resulted in a flourishing salt-smuggling
business. The price of Scottish salt was also forced up throughout the sixteenth century by constant demand from London,
the Low Countries and Scandinavia, which lacked the coal to
produce their own.

Saltmaking continued to be an important Bo'ness industry
throughout the seventeenth and eighteenth centuries, but at
the start of the nineteenth century it suffered two blows. The
Agricultural Revolution resulted in the introduction of root
vegetables for winter fodder so that sheep and cattle could be
kept alive all year round, thus removing the need to salt away
mutton and beef, thus leaving only fish to be salted: fortunately
the Norwegians, Swedes and Danes continued to love their salt
herring. The second and even worse blow was that while the
Scandinavians' tastes remained constant, Scottish tastes began
to change, with a preference for the newly imported rock salt
from Cheshire and Germany which was much more refined.

The fire beneath the last pan at Bo'ness was allowed to go
out in 1890, and the chapman knocked no more at the doors of
the salters to exchange their salary, which like the Roman
soldier's *solarium* had always been paid in kind, for food and
clothing.

While the chapman in turn traded the salt which he gathered
at Lanark market, of which the Salter's Way, just beside the M8
motorway slip road between Bathgate and Whitburn is a last
reminder of his route, most Bo'ness salt, like the town's coal,
was marketed by sea, and so shipbuilding was also a flourishing
industry from the time that the Port of Bo'ness was first
officially recognised at the start of the 1600s until Victorian
times. At the end of the seventeenth century two of the ships

for the ill-fated Darien Expedition were fitted out at Bo'ness, and after the Union of the Parliaments of England and Scotland in 1707, which partly resulted from the economic disaster of the Darien Scheme, the Bo'ness shipbuilders again cashed in by obtaining orders for the tobacco trade in which Scottish merchants were now able to indulge, thanks to their newly gained access to the former English colonies of Virginia and the West Indies from which they had formerly been excluded by the English Navigation Laws.

And so Bo'ness-built ships carried their rich cargoes of tobacco to the Clyde, where the Glasgow tobacco lords had it loaded into panniers strapped to horses' backs and carried across Central Scotland to the Bo'ness tobacco warehouse which is now the town's stylish public library in Scotland's Close, whence the still raw tobacco leaves were in turn re-exported to the Netherlands, where they were manufactured into top-quality Dutch cigars.

The tobacco trade ended as suddenly as it had begun when in 1776 the former American colonies declared their independence, but seven years later when peace was declared the Scottish merchants soon sought other merchandise ranging from sugar to West Indian cotton, and so there was still a demand for Bo'ness-built ships, even Greenock merchants ordering these sturdily built 300 to 350-ton wooden-hulled sailing vessels, before the coming of steam and steel brought their own Clyde shipbuilding industry to prominence.

The names of three Bo'ness shipbuilders survive. One was Thomas Boag, another Robert Hart and the third a Mr. Shaw. But the best-known name connected with Bo'ness shipbuilding was that of Henry Bell of *Comet* fame, who walked the seven miles from his native village of Torphichen to serve his apprenticeship in the by then combined yard of Shaw and Hart. Bell must have been suitably impressed by the training which he had received, because although the *Comet*, the world's first practical seagoing steamship, was indeed Clyde-built, it was to Bo'ness that he brought her for her first annual overhaul in the year 1813, thus providing the town with its second important link with the new steam age.

For it was at Bo'ness that Scotland's other famous steam

innovator, James Watt, also did much of his work on his new improved steam engine, having been summoned there by a fascinating English industrialist, 'The Indefatigable Dr. John Roebuck', as he is described on his tombstone in Carriden Churchyard.

The intriguing Dr. Roebuck first pioneered the manufacture of sulphuric acid by the new lead chamber method at his so-called 'Secret Factory' on the banks of the Forth at Prestonpans and while there met the Cadells of Cockenzie, a successful Scottish merchant family importing iron and steel from Russia. Suddenly in 1756 the outbreak of the Seven Years' War with France cut off their overseas supplies just at the very time when there was of course an enormous increase in the demand for metal for the munitions needed to win the war. Roebuck and the Cadells decided to seize the opportunity by building Scotland's first large-scale ironworks for which they found the ideal site seven miles west of Bo'ness on the River Carron.

It was to Bo'ness, however, that both families came to establish their new homes, because there they could exploit coal and iron ore reserves to supply their new Carron Works which, with a flare for publicity long before its time, commenced production with an all-night party on New Year's morn 1759. From then on the pressure was on both the Cadells and Roebuck to maintain supplies of vitally needed fuel and raw materials. The Cadells bought all of the coal pits at the east end of Bo'ness, while Roebuck leased all those at the west end of the town from the Duke of Hamilton. As both Roebuck and the Cadell brothers demanded higher and higher production from their miners, they were forced to go lower and lower to get it, and as their workings were sunk deeper and deeper, they both ran into the same dreaded problem, flood water from the Forth.

While the Cadells used the traditional horse-powered gin engine, Roebuck on the other hand decided to employ a new-fangled steam engine and had one shipped north from the tin mines of Cornwall, but this Newcomen engine proved no match for the floods from the Forth. It was then that Roebuck heard about Greenock instrument maker James Watt and his experiments and invited him to come and work at stately Kinneil House, which he had leased from the Duke of

Well known Bo'ness barber Willie Wilson looks out over the heads of the crowd lining the pavement outside his gents' hairdressing salon at the West Partings on a Fair Day in the late 1940s.

Hamilton along with his troublesome coal pits. At first Watt was reluctant to come to the big house and pled ill health to excuse him from the twenty-seven mile ride from Glasgow, but in the end mounting debts forced him to accept Roebuck's offer of financial aid and he arrived at Kinneil clutching a model of his new steam engine in front of him on his saddle.

The two men met in the dining room of the big house, which is at present being restored, and there Watt set up the little model on the large table. It worked beautifully, but when it came to building the full-scale engine in the little workshop, the ruins of which can still be seen in the grounds of the house, Watt soon ran into difficulties. For not even Roebuck's new Carron Works could make parts accurate enough to make Watt's new idea of a separate condenser cylinder work. The first of the new improved engines was however at last erected at the Burn Pit, Kinneil in 1768, but every time the pressure was increased the steam escaped in clouds around the piston, where it came through the cylinder head. Desperately Watt and the Doctor tried to find some way to cut off the escape. Suddenly Roebuck pulled off one of his top boots, whipped out his knife and cut off a ring of leather from round the top. It fitted like a glove and stopped the loss of pressure, but there were still so many faults in Watt's early prototype that it was not until he left Scotland and moved south to work with Birmingham engineer Matthew Boulton that it was perfected.

In the meantime as water continued to cascade into the pits at Kinneil, Roebuck, faced with bankruptcy, was forced to give up his lease and even sell his shares in Carron, but while tragic for the Doctor, it proved fortunate for Bo'ness, because with his last remaining funds he turned another of his ideas into reality by building Scotland's first large-scale commercial pottery on the shores of the Forth at Bridgeness, between the town and Carriden. Just as he had used his skills to choose an ideal site for Carron, Roebuck reckoned that Bo'ness was definitely the right place for a new pottery because it could provide a supply of local clay, plenty of coal to fire the clay in the kilns, and lots of miners' wives and daughters to provide cheap female labour. The availability of the little harbour right beside the new pottery at Bridgeness was also a vitally important factor, because not only could it be used to import finer clay from Devon and Cornwall when it was required, and other raw materials such as flints from northern France and large stones needed to grind them from Argyllshire, but it could guarantee comparatively safe transport to get the finished pottery to market, whereas a road journey would have smashed it to smithereens. This same problem of bad roads forced the English pottery owners such as Josiah Wedgwood in the Black Country of Staffordshire to invest in canals, but by careful siting Rosebuck had the Forth on his doorstep.

At first, however, it must be admitted that Bo'ness ware was rough, compared with the fine bone china of the English potteries, but after Roebuck's death several owners, including especially James Marshall, greatly improved the quality of the product by persuading skilled craftsmen to come north from Staffordshire, and during Victorian times many impressive dinner service designs and tea sets were produced. All the time, however, the Bo'ness potteries' main market continued to be the families of local miners and other industrial workers across Central Scotland. They shaped their products to their particular tastes, and so arose the peculiar local specialities of wally dugs, wedding jugs and surprise mugs.

The 'wally dugs' were officially classified as 'chimney piece ornaments' and the Bo'ness potters also produced wally cats, lions, hens, parrots and even fish, but the dogs were undoubtedly their speciality. They were made from a very thick coarse china ware known as 'wally' – a term also used to describe the thick white tiles used to line the walls of the closes of Glasgow tenements – and they were always manufactured as pairs, one facing right and the other left so thay they could sit at either end of a kitchen dresser or fireside mantlepiece, from which they could look down and survey all that was going on with the same rather supercilious grins on their flat pug-like faces. Where they differed was in their decoration, no two pairs being exactly alike as they were all handpainted. Among the most popular were the glossy white ones, with their gleaming black, or for those prepared to pay a wee bit extra, gold collars and chains.

Wedding jugs were another of the Bo'ness potteries' specialities. They were tall two-pint jugs, usually white with colourful patterns of flowers and leaves entwined around the names of the bride and groom and the date and place of their wedding. Later the wedding jugs on the kitchen dresser were joined by miniature versions known as christening jugs, which recorded the birth of each successive child.

Another favourite novelty produced by the Bo'ness potters was surprise mugs, which were a popular Victorian party joke. From the outside the surprise mugs looked perfectly normal, but inside on the bottom lurked a very realistic little china 'puddock', and the idea was to fill the mug with beer, present it to an unsuspecting guest, and watch the look of surprise on his face as he downed the beer and saw the frog appear.

Pottery making continued in Bo'ness, with contracts mainly for hospital ware, until the early 1960s, when Bridgeness Pottery, which was owned by the McNay family, was gutted by fire and never rebuilt.

While its founder Dr. Roebuck gave up his shares in Carron Iron Works, iron making did continue in Bo'ness as it does until today with two foundries including the famous Ballantines whose speciality products range from ornate lamp standards for the palaces of Arab princes to replacement cannon for the battlements of Edinburgh Castle and from reproductions of copies of the panels of the famous Elgin Marbles to a tall decorated pedestal for the new Bo'ness Town Clock near the site of the original opposite the Market Square.

In Victorian times the Bo'ness iron workers were particularly proud of another speciality, for they were responsible for forging the sharp barbed tips for the long harpoons on which the whole summer season's success of the town's famous whaling fleet depended.

By tradition all the Bo'ness whalers set sail on the same day each spring, because company was welcome on the long monotonous voyage north to the Arctic 'fishing' grounds, as they were always known. On the chosen day the quayside and harbour wall were thronged with crowds of local folk and especially with the wives and sweethearts of the crews, because they would not see their menfolk again for several months. Each of the sailors had a new rigout of thick navy blue handknitted jerseys, black waterproof oilskins, high leather sea boots, handmade and oiled with goose grease by the 'snabs' of neighbouring Linlithgow, and fisherman-type bonnets. When all the whalers were ready to put to sea there was a tremendous bang as they all fired off the little cannon which they carried on their stern decks, and this was the signal for the crowd to break and run up the braes behind the harbour to watch the procession as first the *Jean* and then *The Home Castle* and the *Ratler* and the famous lucky *Success* nosed out of the harbour and sailed away down the Forth and out of sight into the North Sea.

On the voyage north the little three-hundred-ton whalers, with their specially strengthened bows to withstand the ice which they were soon to meet, usually put in at Lerwick for their last chance to take on provisions before the long lonely summer ahead. For once they reached whaling waters it was very much a case of each ship to itself. A constant watch was kept from the crow's nest in the hope of being the first to shout 'Whale Ho'. Immediately the signal was given, the whaler launched her six or eight small boats, each with a crew of six made up of four oarsmen, the all-important harpooner poised

Thirty former Fair Queens came together to mark the 75th anniversary Fair in 1972. Courtesy of John Doherty.

in the bow, and the coilsman at the ready in the stern. As the name suggests, it was the coilsman's duty to make sure that the line attached to the eight-foot long wooden harpoon with its barbed tip ran free when the harpooner made his vicious throw.

These primitive harpoons lacked any kind of explosive charge in their tips, and so it was necessary to be at very close range before they had any effect on the huge sixty to eighty-foot whales which were often caught. Usually several strikes were necessary and there was always the danger that the enraged whale would capsize the small boat as it threshed in agony or tried to escape by swimming under the nearest ice floe. One blow from a whale's tail was enough to splinter a small boat like a matchbox, and once in the freezing water there was little hope for any man. It was always claimed that the Bo'ness whalers deliberately never learned to swim. It was quicker that way.

When a harpooner was successful in making a kill, all the other small boats from a mother ship raced to his aid, to help tow the catch alongside. Even when the whale was safely back at the mother ship, there was no time to be lost, for the carcass would float for a limited time only. No matter how exhausted the crew, they had to begin the flensing immediately. For this they swapped their sea boots for others with metal spikes on the soles, and wearing these, clambered over the side and down onto the slippery back of the whale. There, using specially shaped knives, they cut through the flesh and ripped it back to reveal the all-important six to twelve-inch layer of oily blubber. This was cut into brick-sized oblongs which were tossed on deck, to be stowed in the ships' holds, because unlike Dutch and Danish whalers the Scots never processed the blubber in the Arctic, but always brought it back home to be boiled in Scotland's earliest oil refineries, which existed in all the East Coast whaling ports such as Bo'ness. Each whale caught was carefully noted in the ship's log and indicated with a drawing of a whale's tail in the margin, as can be seen in the ships' logs carefully preserved in the Scottish Fisheries Museum at An-struther in Fife.

However, it was not only battles with the whales which were recorded in many of the ships' logs, but fights amongst the crews as well. Only the captains and harpooners had their own small cabins, and for the other sailors the long months of being cooped up in one communal cabin, where they lived, ate and slept, inevitably took their toll of frayed tempers, and knives normally used to carve whale bones and teeth into penguins and other little souvenirs to take home to their children and other loved ones were suddenly turned on crewmates.

The other battles which the whalers were often called upon to fight were against the ice, because it only needed a bad season, a poor catch and a decision to linger one day too long to leave a whaler trapped for the whole of the long dark bitter Arctic winter. Most of the Bo'ness boats did return, however, and as the last days of summer turned into autumn, the townsfolk made more and more frequent pilgrimages to the top of Tidings Hill, which got its name from the fact that it was from there that the whaling fleet was usually first spotted heading home up the Forth.

Even once they reached home, the whalers found it hard to forget their long season spent at sea and adapt to life on land again, and it is said that many of the skippers, who had their homes in the old Wagon Row, then a very fashionable building, insisted on having their living rooms on the first floor and their bedrooms on the ground floor, so that they could still go down to their bunks at night, just as they were accustomed to doing aboard their ships. The whalers and especially the harpooners were of course also in demand always to spin their yarns about their adventures and the excitements of life in the Arctic, but the winter was not one long holiday, for most of the men worked in the industries which depended on their catches.

First, within days of the fleet's return to port, came the public roup or auction of bones, for the long flexible whale bones were in great demand for a variety of uses, as varied as making furniture, producing waist-pinching stays for fashionable ladies and – even more painful – 'pandy-bats', the long leather-covered instruments of punishment with which Irish schoolmasters chastised their erring scholars. The pandy-bats, for which the most supple of the whale bones were carefully selected, took their names from the master's Latin command to the pupil, 'pande manum' meaning 'hold out your hand', which was also the origin of the Scottish term 'pandies' meaning strokes of the strap, but whether the local Bo'ness dominies ever experimented to see if the 'pandy-bats' were more effective than their traditional tawse is not recorded.

While bones were a profitable sideline, it was of course the profits from the processed oil which were the mainstay of the fleet. The largest cargo of blubber ever landed in Scotland came ashore from the *Resolution* of Peterhead, which caught forty-four whales in the year 1814. When this was processed it yielded oil to the value of £10,000 but the Bo'ness whalers considered themselves fortunate to earn half as much. The main whale-oil works in Bo'ness belonged to John Anderson, the town's most prosperous merchant, who also owned several of the whalers and who was often called the 'Uncrowned King of Bo'ness'. The works stood on the hillside on the west side of the Wynd, the steep road which, as its name suggests, twists and turns its way from sea level to the heights of Panbrae, Braeside and Braehead. For many years the site has been occupied by a garage selling oil rather than producing it, but whale bones and the large cinders of the coal used to fuel the fires to boil the blubber to obtain the oil are still often dug up around the yard. Fire was of course a constant danger at this early oil refinery, and one bitterly cold January the worst happened when one of the barrels of highly inflammable oil caught alight. As the fire raged, one of the large tanks which contained pure oil burst and a broad river of fiercely burning oil flowed down the Wynd, while the local part-time firemen who had been summoned to the scene were forced to stand by helpless, as the water supply was frozen. The oil works were rebuilt by Mr. Anderson in partnership with seven other local and Edinburgh businessmen, but only operated for a short time as ironically the large catches and high profits of the 1860s sounded the deathknell of the Bo'ness whaling industry as without any form of protection the Arctic whales began to die out.

With such dangerous voyages to make, it is not surprising that from early days the Bo'ness skippers and their sailors sought to band together to protect themselves and their families, and so it is that Bo'ness can claim the second oldest Sea Box society in Scotland, second only to one in Aberdeen.

Founded in 1634, the General United Sea Box Society of Borrowstounness took its name from the fact that all the shipmasters and their men agreed that at the end of every successful voyage they would put 10% of their profits into an old chest or sea box which should be 'double lockit', so that no money could be taken out again except at one of the society's regular quarterly meetings with at least two members and later the Box Master in attendance. At these regular meetings all cases of sailors and their dependants were carefully considered, and those requiring help because of accident, illness, old age or loss at sea duly received appropriate pensions from this local forerunner of the Welfare State.

The Sea Box did not just help its own members and their families, and amongst its most interesting records are details of assistance provided for shipwrecked mariners or other sea-farers from as far afield as St. Malo and Dublin. Its own members also got into trouble in many far-flung places, as is recalled by the grim entry, 'Given to William McPherson and two others, whose tongues were cut out by the Turks of Algiers. All three in a melancholy state', and by another for 7th April 1748 which reads, 'Given to James Campbell taken by the Algerians in a vessel called the "Swallow". After three years slavery released by a Maltese ship of war'.

In addition to helping individual cases the Sea Box also gave a great deal of help to the whole town of Bo'ness, by ensuring 'free schooling for all bairns of this burgh' and by providing all the timber, slates and other building materials for the construction of the new parish church in Corbiehall when it was moved there from its original site near the village of Kinneil in the middle of the seventeenth century.

This same intense community spirit was also to be found amongst the town's other main group of inhabitants, the miners and their families who, because of the unpleasant nature of their work and the shame of the thirldom which tied them to their pits, formed a very close-knit inward-looking group. Any stranger who ventured into the long low lines of miners' rows was viewed with deep suspicion, and it is said that all the families were alerted by a knock hammered out on the interior walls of the rows so that eyes were soon staring out of every window.

Marriage outside the mining community was frowned upon, with the result that much inbreeding took place, and the surnames of Snedden and Sneddon, Robertson, Grant and Hamilton became so common that until recent years mail used to be addressed with nicknames, and the last Provost of Bo'ness, Charles Snedden, O.B.E., Convenor of Central Region, was paid by his by-name when he worked as a youngster at Kinneil Colliery.

It was the miners who gave Bo'ness its most famous day of the year, the Fair Day, when to mark the Act of Parliament which emancipated them from their thirldom to their pits they took an annual one-day holiday and marched through the streets of Bo'ness. For their day they chose the date of the existing Bo'ness Fair or market granted to the Duchess Anna of Kinneil, when she succeeded in persuading King Charles II to grant Bo'ness burgh status in 1668. Thus it was on the first Friday after the second Thursday in July each year that the miners downed tools and had the audacity to knock on the big front door of Kinneil House, which was opened by the Duke of Hamilton's factor who presented each man with a glass of whisky toddy. From Kinneil, led by their deacon mounted on horseback and carrying a sword, the miners then proceeded to the other end of the town to the old Grange, home of the

Cadell family, where the 'maister' himself handed round the whisky and, it is said, even condescended to smile on this one day of the year. The rest of the day was then spent in more drinking and going to the races which Robert Burns once watched on the foreshore of the Forth; more drinking and visiting the funfair in Corbiehall; more drinking and whooping it up until dawn at the 'penny dance' in the Town Hall where there was no admission charge but a payment every time a miner took to the floor, if he was still able.

The amount of drinking at Bo'ness Fair came to shock and scandalise the more douce and sober Victorian members of the local community, until in 1894 Provost Ballantine and the Police Commissioners, forerunners of the Town Council, agreed to ride at the head of the procession and add an air of dignity to the, until then, somewhat shambolic proceedings. This however was nothing compared with the changes which Provost Stewart wrought three years later in 1897, when to mark Queen Victoria's Diamond Jubilee, he changed the whole Fair into Scotland's most spectacular Children's Festival complete with the very impressive coronation of a schoolgirl 'queen' elected by her own school fellows.

The first ever 'queen' was Grace Strachan from the old Anderson Academy, named after merchant John Anderson, and since that July day in 1897 a Bo'ness Fair Queen has been crowned annually with the exception of the war years and the years of the Depression in the 1920s. Today the big event has been moved to the last Friday in June or the first in July to tie in with the last day of the school term. Excitement is still as electric as ever as a crowd of over 20,000 including hundreds of returned exiles packs into the Glebe Park to watch as the hands of the Town Hall clock touch eleven and yet another Bo'ness Fair Queen receives her home town's highest honour as she is crowned. Then, led by one of the town's two championship-class brass bands, Bo'ness and Carriden or Kinneil, she is serenaded by a mass choir as all Bo'nessians join in singing their Fair songs, 'Our Festal Day' and 'Hail to Our Queen', which are also sung each time Bo'ness United wins the Scottish Junior Cup at Hampden Park and indeed wherever Bo'nessians meet around the world.

Today these same Bo'nessians have a new-found pride in their old grey town beside the Forth which has survived the closure of its dock in 1961 and the closure of its last pits to go on to become one of the most attractive dormitory towns in the Forth Valley. As pleasant new housing areas climb the hills to the south at Borrowstoun and Deanburn, the town centre itself has been restored, with the seventeenth-century Tolbooth, the eighteenth-century tobacco warehouse and the buildings of local architect Matthew Steel, who was strongly influenced by Charles Rennie MacIntosh, all well worth looking at, while the Victorian villas of Grange Terrace and Grahamsdyke have been declared a conservation area.

Grahamsdyke is one of the most historic place names in the town, because it comes from the local folk hero, Pictish leader Grime or Graham who is claimed to have overwhelmed the Antonine Wall, the Romans' outermost line of defence of their whole empire, when the legionaries were finally withdrawn. Today it is still possible to follow the line of the wall from the shores of the Forth where the Roman galleons docked with supplies, and up the slope behind to the crest of the hill where it turned west to run thirty-five miles right across the narrow waist of Central Scotland to Bowling on the River Clyde.

The Antonine Wall, which was erected about 140 A.D., during the Governorship of Lollius Urbicus and in the reign of the Emperor Antoninus, after whom it was named, consisted of a rampart made up mainly of earth and turf, varying in height from ten to twelve feet, with a ditch approximately forty feet wide and twelve feet deep, stretching in front of it. As far less stone was used in the construction of Antonine's Wall than in Hadrian's Wall to the south, far less remains to be seen, but recently a mile fort has been excavated at Kinneil, which means Wall's End, as in Victorian times it was believed that the wall ended there to the west of Bo'ness. Later excavations in 1868 by Henry Mowbray Cadell of Grange proved that it did in fact stretch on to Bridgeness, and now there are suggestions that a spur may have run on along the coast for another mile or so to Carriden, which means the fort on the hill.

Most interesting of the carved stones unearthed by Mr. Cadell bore an inscription which, translated, reads, 'To the Emperor Caesar Titus Aelius Hadrianius Antoninus Pius, Father of his Country, the Second Augustian Legion dedicates this, having completed 4652 paces of the Wall'.

Like a Roman altar found nearby, it is a prized exhibit in the

Royal Museum in Queen Street, Edinburgh, and only a copy of the inscription can be seen on the site, but now as Bo'ness looks to the future and begins to appreciate the benefits from developing its tourist trade there is local pressure to have it returned and displayed in the town.

In the meantime tourists are already coming in considerable numbers to visit the Scottish Rail Preservation Society's Steam Railway Museum, which has been established on the foreshore, where the old shunting engines used to chug to and fro hauling long rows of wagons from the ships discharging in the docks and returning with equally heavy loads of coal to be loaded from the busy coal hoists into the ships' bunkers. Sadly the town's own Victorian station was demolished twenty years ago after the withdrawal of passenger services on the single-line track which linked Bo'ness with the main Glasgow to Edinburgh line at Polmont, but now a very similar station has been brought all the way from Wormit in Fife and carefully rebuilt as the centrepiece of the steam museum. From it the track is also being steadily relaid all the way along the shore of the Forth to Kinneil and on over the Crawyet Bridge through the woods to Birkhill Clay Mine, which is also to be re-opened as a tourist attraction with trips below ground to tour the underground workings.

Back on the foreshore of the Forth plans are also being made to open a maritime museum in the old dock, and it already has its first major acquisition in the huge shape of the original boiler from the world's last seagoing paddle steamer, *Waverley*, while further along the coast Bridgeness Harbour is destined to become a yachting marina.

Thus from its industrial heritage Bo'ness is now developing its tourist future. The noise of the shunting engines in the sidings at Kinneil Colliery has long since been silenced, but now it is being replaced by the shrill whistle of the Steam Railway Preservation Society's summer excursion special as the many visitors discover that the old image of 'dirty' Bo'ness has happily been replaced by the new one of Scotland's 'Costa Forth'.

CHAPTER 2

Linlithgow, Home of the 'Black Bitches'

As far as many visitors are concerned Linlithgow means the royal palace overlooking the loch, the grassy parklands of the Peel and St. Michael's Kirk with its golden crown of thorns, which is such a landmark both for passengers on the high-speed trains on the Edinburgh to Glasgow line and to motorists on the M9 motorway which sweeps past to the north of the town.

But there is much more to discover about this Royal and Ancient Burgh, which gained its regal status from King Robert II in 1388. Linlithgow is said to mean the place in the hollow beside the loch, and this well describes its beautifully sheltered setting in the valley between the Erngath Hills, which lie between it and the River Forth three miles to the north, and the Bathgate Hills, which as the name suggests separate it from Bathgate and Torphichen to the south. This elongated valley was formed in the Ice Age, and as the temperature rose again and the ice retreated, it is said that a massive chunk fell off and melted, forming Linlithgow Loch. Other evidence of glacial moraine, the débris of soil left by the receding ice sheet, can be found to the east of the town, where large-scale housing developments are transforming Barons' Hill and the Spring-field area of the town.

Evidence points to the first settlement at Linlithgow having been a crannog, with a cunningly concealed causeway leading to these early homes, which were built on stilts in the waters of the loch. The coming of the Scottish kings and the building of the royal palace encouraged the building of houses in its immediate vicinity in the steep Kirkgate and in the area at its foot around the Cross Well. When he made Linlithgow a Royal Burgh, King Robert at the same time leased its customs and those of its port at Blackness to the burgesses for the sum of £5 per annum, and with all the trade connected with the palace the town soon flourished, so that by the end of the Middle Ages it stretched the full length of the south shore of the loch from the West Port at one end to the Low and High Ports at the other, with the long narrow crowded High Street in between.

At this time Linlithgow was a walled town and the lieges slept sounder in their beds at night thanks to the knowledge that the big heavy gates at the three ports were all barred and bolted, but this meant that travellers had to wait for them to be opened at dawn. This gave rise to the story of Katie Wearie's Tree. According to some versions of the tale, Katie was herself a cattle drover and to others she was one of the lassies who loved to follow the drovers, but either way it is said that each week when she came to market in Linlithgow she washed her feet in the cattle trough were the beasts were watered and then settled back to enjoy a rest below a leafy green tree just outside the West Port gate, where young saplings from the original tree are still carefully cultivated to this day.

Katie at least was always welcome at the West Port, which is more than can be said for the people of Bo'ness, with whom Linlithgow has always engaged in a rivalry to equal even that between Edinburgh and Glasgow. At one time in fact the Provost and Magistrates of Linlithgow gave orders for a gallows to be erected at the West Port and warned that any Bo'nessian who dared come over The Flints and down into the Royal Burgh would be hanged on this gibbet. Officially the reason for this action was that foreign ships had brought the plague to the port town and that this extreme measure was needed to ensure that it did not spread to Linlithgow, which always boasted that it was a particularly healthy place, but the people of Bo'ness have always claimed that this was only an excuse and that the gallows were a true sign of their neighbours' feelings for them. Even today there is a distinct edge to relationships between the two towns and argument as to whether Bo'ness Fair or Linlithgow Marches is the premier summer celebration; when their two junior football teams, Linlithgow Rose and the B.U.'s, Bo'ness United, meet, a fiercely fought derby match is assured. The report of the game is always carried by the local weekly paper, *The Linlithgow Journal and Gazette,* which mergers have forced the two towns to share, but Bo'nessians always buy a Journal, while in Linlithgow readers always ask for a Gazette!

The viaduct constructed in 1840 to carry the main Edinburgh to Glasgow railway line across the valley of the River Avon to the west of Linlithgow. Courtesy of John Doherty.

When Bo'nessians did venture over the hills and down into Linlithgow they were often taunted with the cry, 'Bo'ness for bleathers' to which they always retorted 'Aye and Linlithgow for leathers' and pointedly held their noses, for it was indeed the case that the latter was, along with Perth, one of the two most important tanning centres in Scotland, and the process did have a distinctive smell. Tradition has it that the art of leather making was brought to Linlithgow by Oliver Cromwell's soldiers during the 1650s. They taught it to the local inhabitants who became the first members of the town's Guild of Cordiners, whose badge, surrounded by oak leaves, can still be seen carved on the facade of the house at number 125 High Street. The presence of the oak leaves is a reminder of how the bark of the oak tree was put in the water in which the hides were steeped in order to supply the all-important tanning. The oak-leaf emblem of the cordiners also appears again next door carved on the wall of number 123 High Street, which the 1871 census records as the home of four shoemakers and one leather worker. Further west along the High Street more of the cordiners lived in Tanners Wynd, but the actual tanneries were situated on the opposite side of the street, between it and the loch, whose water was readily available for all the leather-making processes. Leather making no longer takes place in Linlithgow, but in one of the long dark closes, which led down from the High Street to one of the lochside tanneries, can still be seen the hook with which the heavy loads of raw hides were swung off the carts bringing them from the slaughter house at the west end of the town, as well as the metal runners which made it easier to drag them down to the leather works. There, the long laborious process of scraping all the hairs off the skins began and continued until the hides were transformed into the various grades of leather required from calfskin to the strongest harness leather.

A principal use for Linlithgow leather was the production of handmade shoes and boots by families such as the Stobies and Morrisons, who still own shoe shops in the High Street, but now import all of their products from places as far apart as Northamptonshire in England and Italy. Originally, however, they employed all of their own 'snabs', as the Linlithgow cobblers were always known, and the customers had their own lasts so that it was not necessary to measure their feet each and every time they wanted a new pair of shoes. Even in those days there was some mass marketing, and a mainstay of the Linlithgow shoemaking business was army contracts for thousands of boots. One such contract dated 1793 was placed by the Earl of Hopetoun who ordered 700 pairs of boots for the men of his regiment.

Another, possibly even more painful, use for Linlithgow leather, apart from these ill-fitting, official issue army boots, was the production of school straps. Long before Lochgelly in Fife became the tawse-making capital of Scotland, the Linlith-gow cordiners were so famed for their prowess at making these instruments of punishment for Scottish dominies that a whole page is devoted to the town and its multi-thonged products in a Victorian publication, *The History of the Rod*, according to which, apart from selling the three, five and even seven-thonged tawse to the teachers for whom they were intended, the cordiners were often tempted to use them on their young apprentices. The boys accepted their masters' right to beat

The massive stone pillars and arches of the Avon Aqueduct carry the Union Canal in a cast-iron trough over the river below. Courtesy of John Doherty.

them, but protested vigorously when one of the cordiners' wives took to leathering them as well.

Protests such as theirs would have been heard by the Guild of Cordiners, which like the other craft guilds in Linlithgow met weekly under its chairman, or deacon as he was always called, to debate such matters as prices for their goods and rules for their apprentices. With so much talk, these were often drouthy occasions, and so the habit grew up of each craft guild adopting an inn or pub in the town as a headquarters in which to hold its meetings, and in the case of the cordiners their sign of the oak leaves surrounding one of the sharp tools with which they cut the leather still hangs outside the Masonic Arms.

Further along the High Street at the West Port, the oldest inn in Linlithgow, the Black Bitch, today has a sign depicting the sleek black greyhound which bravely swam out across Linlithgow Loch to carry food to its master, who had been chained to an oak tree and sentenced to starve to death on one of the islands, and from which the people of Linlithgow adopt the name the Black Bitches of which both men and women born in the town are so proud. Originally, however, the sign outside the Black Bitch Inn was far less picturesque as it consisted of a butcher's slab and cleaver, to denote that it was the headquarters for the Guild of Fleshers, who supplied the cordiners with all their hides. While the cordiners gladly took all the leather, hooves and horns were left behind, and so a glue works was established behind the slaughter house in Preston Road. The Thistle Glue produced at the Gowanstank Works, which stood on the site now occupied by St. Joseph's Primary School, gained such a reputation for strength the Queen's Bodyguard in Scotland, the Royal Company of Archers, insisted that it be used in the manufacture of their bows and also to stick the feathers to their arrows. As well as bringing Linlithgow this little touch of fame, however, the glue works also produced such a dreadful smell that it gained for the town the title among railway passengers of the place that was smelt before it was seen and M.C.S.'s famous Scottish recitation 'The Boy In The Train', could apparently just as well have been written about the West Lothian town as about Kirkcaldy.

Another aspect of life in Linlithgow which gave the town a bad reputation was the constant presence in and around the High Street of the tinkers. Whereas in other Scottish towns they came and went as they mended the pots and pans with the tin which gave them their name, in Linlithgow they were always to be found, because they knew that there was always a ready demand for the millions of nails, which they produced, from the High Street snabs who needed them not only in their shoemaking but also to produce 'tackity boots' for everyone

Linlithgow Bridge carries the main road from the town to Falkirk across the River Avon and marks the western boundary of West Lothian with what was Stirlingshire and is now Central Region. On the other side is the Bridge Inn. Courtesy of John Doherty.

from schoolboys to farm labourers and the soldiers mentioned earlier. The tinker tykes therefore established their headquarters in the little red pantile-roofed crowstep-gabled stone cottage which can still be seen in Whitten Lane. All would have been reasonably well if the tinks had just worked away producing their nails in the ground-floor room of the cottage and sleeping in the tiny attic in the eaves above, but the cottage is situated immediately behind what is now the Armoury Inn and what was then the Swan Inn, as the mosaic of a white swan on its doorstep reminds us and it was here that the trouble began. For the Swan was officially the headquarters of the Guild of Wrights, and these carpenters, joiners and wheelwrights all objected strongly when, as frequently happened, the tinkers slipped in the back door to cadge a pint. According to the Guild of Wrights, these nailers had no right to drink in their pub, and if such disreputable folk had the right to drink anywhere, then as metal workers they ought to join the Guild of Hammermen.

The Hammermen's headquarters was, however, in the Red Lion at the other end of the High Street, and if the distance from the tinkers' cottage was not sufficient to deter them, then the various metal workers amongst the Hammermen made it clear that with members including the town's gold and silver smiths, such a guild was no place for workers in tin. The Guild of Hammermen did of course also include blacksmiths working in iron and farriers making horseshoes, but they were accepted as possessing skills, which the poor tinkers were alleged to lack, although the handmade nails which were, until quite recently occasionally picked up around their old cottage workshop would seem to indicate that they did not produce as inferior an article as was always alleged at the time – a good excuse to pay them poorly.

The Red Lion, whose sign still hangs proudly in the High Street, on the north side near Lowport, was in any case considered to be one of the poshest pubs in the town, because it was originally the family home of the Kae family, who were Linlithgow's surgeon barbers. In addition they were what was known as King's Sergeants and were responsible for collecting local taxes, and it was while the townsfolk queued patiently to pay their dues that they took the opportunity to make more money by selling ale and other drinks. Thus the Lion became an inn, but at some point during its long history it changed colour, because while it was originally always referred to as the Golden Lion it later, and without any explanation, became the Red Lion.

Perhaps the explanation was simply that one year before the town's annual riding of the marches the local painters found that they had no gilt paint and rather than abandon the tradition that every inn must be spruced up for the big day, they painted it red instead. Painting the town is still a Marches tradition, and it is also on that day each year that the guilds are recalled by the appearance of the deacons. Linlithgow's original eight Incorporated Trades in the order in which they are recorded as Riding the Marches in 1687 were the Hammermen, the Tailors, the Baxters or bakers, the Cordiners, the Weavers, the Wrights, the Coopers, and the Fleshers, who took over the place of the Guild of Walkers (which was the official name of the cloth fullers) when they died out in 1639.

The chemist's shop where David Waldie produced the first sample of chloroform is now a restaurant in Linlithgow High Street, but a plaque commemorates its former use and the important discovery made there. Courtesy of John Doherty.

Originally the deacons of these incorporated trades, as well as holding their own craft courts, were also always elected town councillors, and today the Deacons' Court remains as Linlithgow's defiant answer to the local government re-organisation which robbed the Burgh of its Town Council; and it still maintains the office of Provost. Its main business is now the annual organisation of the Marches. This popular event originated when King Robert granted the town its royal status, as the local inhabitants led by the Provost and Magistrates found it very necessary to make an annual inspection of the boundaries of the lands which had been entrusted to them, in case in these strife-torn days any rival had tried to annexe them. Little is known about these early inspections, except that they were made on foot and that this was almost certainly dictated by the state of the roads, which were little more than tracks.

The first actual *riding* of the Marches appears to have taken place in 1541 on Easter Tuesday, a choice of date which seems to have been influenced by both the weather and religion. The weather appears to have persuaded the Provost to wait long enough for spring to promise a reasonable day, but not too long so that any damage which the winter might have done could be put right without too much delay. The religious element appears to have been that, like the Rogation Day ceremonies in England, part of the Marches ceremonies included the blessing of the bounds by a priest, hence the choice of the Tuesday of Holy Week. Unfortunately this of course meant that the first Marches fell during Lent, and as this was a time for fasting, this must have inhibited the feasting and drinking which became such a feature of the event in later years. Perhaps therefore this accounted for the subsequent change of date to the Tuesday after Whitsun. Finally in 1767, the Provost, Magistrates and Councillors decided that the town's Whitsun Fair should be moved to the second Thursday in June and that the Riding of the Marches should be held on the following Tuesday. In those days few of the inhabitants possessed diaries or calendars and so they committed the date of the Marches to memory by remembering that from then on the big day would always fall on the now famous 'First Tuesday after the Second Thursday in June'. Thus a tradition was born, and with the exception of the years during the First and Second World Wars and the year of the General Strike in 1926, when celebrations were limited by law, it has continued to be honoured in this fashion ever since.

The excitement begins on the Saturday night preceding the date itself when the High Street is crowded to cheer the traditional ceremony of the chairing of the deacons. As the old guilds have disappeared, workers in the town's new industries and offices keep up the old custom by electing one of their number to represent them and, accompanied by his right-hand man, who is known as My Lord, each Deacon is carried shoulder high the full length of the High Street then back to the Cross Well, where his supporters carry him round the traditional three times. During recent years each newly installed Deacon and My Lord have then been received on the steps of the Town House by the Provost in his scarlet ermine-trimmed robes and invited to partake of the Loving Cup. Amongst scenes of great excitement and cheering from the large crowds who always gather, the new Deacon is then chaired once more and led by the Linlithgow Reed Band or one of the other local bands, and returns with his supporters to their headquarters which – again keeping up tradition – is always in one of the High Street Inns, where they enjoy a night of revelry to ensure that they get into the true Marches spirit.

The main ceremony in preparation for the day itself is the Crying, which takes place at one o'clock in the afternoon of the preceding Friday. As originally there was a local by-law which stated that the lieges could be fined if they did not take part in the Riding of the Marches, it was very important that they should all be reminded of the forthcoming event, and so at lunchtime on the Friday, Linlithgow's town crier, who is the only town crier in Scotland, makes his way right along the High Street from outside the Star and Garter Hotel at Lowport to West Port at the other end of the town. At intervals, at time-honoured spots along the route, he halts and, introduced by 'tuck of drum', announces 'O Yez, O Yez, O Yez, The burgesses, craftsmen and whole inhabitants of the Royal Burgh of Linlithgow are hearby warned and summoned to attend my Lord Provost, Bailies and Council at the ringing of the bells on Tuesday 20th June curt, for the purpose of riding the Town's Marches and liberties according to the use and custom of the ancient and honourable Burgh and that in their best carriage, equipage, apparel and array and also to attend all diets of court held and appointed on that day by my Lord Provost and Bailies and that under the penalty of One Hundred Pounds Scotch each. God save the Queen and My Lord Provost'.

As well as the drummer, the town crier, in his black velvet jacket and knee breeches and his distinctive plummed hat, is always accompanied by his bodyguard of two uniformed halberdiers. Equally traditionally he is also accompanied by the town's schoolchildren, who follow the little entourage all the way along the flag-bedecked High Street, past the freshly painted shop fronts and newly whitewashed closes, to the final crying at the West Port, which now takes place in the nearby playground of Linlithgow Primary School. One former pupil who clearly remembered these annual Friday escapes from the classroom was David Morrison, an exiled Black Bitch who wrote home as follows from the United States: 'I see myself again as a Burgh School pupil longing for the Friday preceding the great event, when the town herald, Jock the Blackie, attired in his new velvet suit, with red stockings and buckled shoes and cocked bonnet and feather, gathered us all around him for the Crying. Like a great orchestra leader he would direct and time us with his drum stick in the opening "O Yez O Yez O Yez" of his proclamation. Again I am in step to the "Roke and Wee Pickle Tow" played by flautist Muir and drummer Bowie as I find myself marching along the High Street with my school mates. I leave the crowd at the Cross and return to the Burgh School, realising that if I were late "Baldie" or "Bull Dog" Walker or "Coal Jock" Forrester would greet me with his tawse'. Now the pupils of Linlithgow Primary have no need to fear being punished when they return to class, for lunchtime is officially extended and the school's young brass group and the headmaster both welcome the town crier to the playground.

Four days later on the Tuesday the children are all on holiday and up at crack of dawn, because festivities begin shortly after five when the flautists parade through the streets. At six o'clock they are joined by the burgh piper and drummer as they march to the home of the Provost where they play before moving on to the houses of other well-known townsfolk. The reason for such an early start to Marches Morn was that in days gone by it was considered necessary for all of the burgh's financial accounts to be balanced and placed before the Provost at his breakfast to prove that all was well with the town before the actual riding could begin. Today the Provost's Breakfast is the most important event in the town's social year, and he is joined by two hundred guests in the Burgh Halls where the meal is served as the Town Clock strikes nine. In the past the breakfast always included salt herring on the menu to ensure a healthy drouth, but today guests are pleased to settle for bacon, eggs and freshly baked morning rolls. While the Provost welcomes and entertains his guests, the Fraternity of Dyers hold a similar event further along the High Street at their headquarters in St. Michael's Hotel. Even at such an early hour both of Linlithgow's Marches breakfasts are famed for the wit and eloquence of their speakers, who always set the standard for the rest of the day's many toasts and replies. Speakers and guests at the breakfasts often include exiled Black Bitches who have returned specially for the big day from places as far apart as New Zealand and Nigeria, Australia and America, South

This old view of the Cross Well and the Town Hose at Linlithgow shows the Town House, which contains the Burgh Halls, before the fire which destroyed its attractive arcade.

Africa and Saudi Arabia, and thoughts always turn to those who are still abroad but would very much like to be home for the Marches. Often their greetings are read out after the breakfasts and form one of the most sentimental moments of the whole Marches Morn.

After the breakfast the Provost leads his guests up the Kirkgate to the forecourt of the Palace, to which they are followed shortly afterwards by the members of the Fraternity of Dyers in their morning suits and grey silk toppers and the members of the Forty-One Club in their tweeds and deer-stalkers. Once they are all assembled the traditional fraternising takes place during which they all shake hands and wish each other 'Happy Marches'.

Back down at the Cross as the old town clock strikes eleven the equally traditional fencing of the court takes place, and as soon as the proclamation is finished the actual riding begins with the procession moving off west along the High Street towards Linlithgow Bridge. Nowadays, apart from the Provost's open landau, most of the floats in the procession are pulled by tractors, and many people feel that the parade has lost much with the disappearance of the horses which were such a feature of old-time Marches. Another feature which has disappeared over the years is the banners and flags, which each of the guilds and fraternities carried proudly in front of their ranks. As well as its banners, each guild also took pride in designing its float to reflect its particular craft by including tools of its trade and examples of its products, which its members turned out during the course of the year. The Hammermen's decorated cart, for instance, always bore a huge anvil and a massive hammer, while the Wrights' pony trap was covered all over with curly wood shavings and carried a work bench at which toiled cut-out figures of joiners whose arms sawed away, powered by elastic bands pulled to and fro by the youngest apprentice in the town. It was also the youngest apprentice's job to gather all the shavings needed to decorate the float, and this job began weeks before the Marches and went on nightly in the lofts of Brock's and Ritchie's joiners' shops. Traditionally the shavings were of yellow pine boards, as this wood was particularly suitable for the purpose, being almost knot-free. Long shavings were gathered to loop from one end of the cart to the other, while short light curly shavings were used to make tassles to hang between the loops.

Cheered all the way by the crowds which line the whole length of the High Street and West Port, the procession makes its way out to Linlithgow Bridge, where the bridge across the River Avon marks the most westerly of Linlithgow's marches. There, instead of the beating of the bounds which characterised similar ceremonies in English towns at which the local schoolchildren were whipped with canes to make sure that they would always remember the extent of their territories, the lieges of Linlithgow have always found it much more civilised to refresh their memories by drinking a series of toasts. Today these are proposed from the top of the foresteps in front of the old black painted and white harled Bridge Inn, where the silver Waldie Loving Cup, donated to the Marches in 1922 by the Deacon of the Dyers, Alexander Spence, waits, filled to the brim with whisky.

The procession then makes its way right back through the town and all the way down to the most easterly point of Linlithgow's jurisdiction at its port at Blackness. It was always considered a great honour to be the first carriage into the Square at Blackness, but on the last lap all carriages tradition-ally make a brief, but very necessary, stop at the top of the brae leading down into the village, at what is claimed to be the fastest-growing hedge in Scotland because of the annual watering it receives. Down the hill the procession stops a second time to enable a wreath to be laid at the little war memorial in front of the church, and then round the corner in the Square all the participants led by My Lord Provost are welcomed by the Baron Bailie whose role is described in the chapter on Blackness.

After the final ceremony at Blackness, which is the fencing of the court on the site of St. Ninian's Chapel on the hillside above the castle, the various parties adjourn for a late lunch, after which more speeches and fraternising take place, before everyone returns to Linlithgow, ready for the whole procession to re-assemble at the Lowport at five o'clock. By then the crowds have also returned to the High Street after family lunches at which steak pies traditionally feature, and an afternoon is passed meeting old friends and listening to the bands in the Peel and the Rose Garden, then cheering the procession to the echo as it makes its way three times round the Cross Well, as My Lord Provost on the steps of the Burgh Halls presides over the successful conclusion of yet another Marches.

The present well is an exact replica of the original erected by King James V in 1520. Topped by Scotland's original heraldic beast, the white unicorn, and with Linlithgow's Black Bitch on the south side, all of its ornate figures including the little town drummer were carved in 1805 by Edinburgh master mason, Robert Gray, who must have been quite a craftsman, consider-ing the fact that he had lost one of his hands in an accident several years earlier and worked with a mallet fixed to his arm. Behind it Linlithgow's Town House forms an impressive backdrop. It was originally erected in 1668 and built in an Italian style, complete with a covered arched piazza which ran the full length of the frontage and provided welcome shelter for the town's market stall holders. From the outset the Town House with its Burgh Halls served a wide variety of uses, not just as a meeting place for the Provost and Councillors of the

Burgh, but as a court, a jail and even a fire station, and there is still evidence of these former uses to be found around the building, the ground floor of which today houses the head-quarters of the Forth Valley Tourist Association, whose information office is kept busy with Linlithgow's ever-increasing number of tourists.

Many are curious to know about the murder of the Regent Moray, which was the first murder in Scotland committed with a firearm. The murder took place in 1570, when James Stewart, Earl of Moray, half brother of Mary Queen of Scots, was gunned down in the High Street, just west of the Cross. This was very much a political assassination, and it was planned with every bit as much detail as any modern crime of this kind. The murderer was James Hamilton of Bothwellhaugh, who as a loyal Catholic had supported Mary at the Battle of Langside two years earlier in 1568. He had consequently been punished by Moray, who had ordered the confiscation of all of his lands.

Hamilton learned that the Regent was to leave Linlithgow on either January 22nd or 23rd and persuaded the Roman Catholic opposition party to allow him to hide in the town house of the Archbishop of St. Andrews from where he could shoot Moray, thus satisfying his personal grudge and at the same time greatly furthering the Catholic cause. The Archbishop's Linlithgow residence could not have been better situated for Hamilton's purpose, as it was on the south side of the High Street at one of its narrowest points, on the slope leading up to the Cross, which would force Moray to slow down as he rode by and thus allow more time to take careful aim. Every possible precaution was taken to avoid Hamilton being discovered before he could carry out the deed. The room in the Archbishop's home, where Hamilton hid, was draped in black, so that there was no chance of even his shadow giving away his presence, while the wooden balcony overlooking the High Street was hung with white linen sheets, leaving only a small hole for the barrel of the gun. A matress was laid on the floor to ensure that Hamilton's footsteps would not be heard.

Outdoors, precautions were equally thorough, with a good mount supplied by the Abbot of Arbroath all ready harnessed and waiting for Hamilton's escape, while the lintel was removed from over the garden gate so that once in the saddle he could

Thrice round the Cross Well was the way, then as now, to end every Marches Day, after returning from Blackness.

ride straight through. Obstructions were even placed in the lane leading in from the High Street to hinder any of Moray's entourage who might try to give chase. Hamilton's vigil must have been a long and weary one, because it was not until lunchtime on January 23rd that Moray and the members of his party left their lodgings to begin their journey to Edinburgh. Then at last the Regent was within range. Hamilton raised his heavy gun and fired.

'The murderer shot him with a lead bullet below the navel', recorded George Buchanan at the time, but recent evidence unearthed by Patrick Cadell in his detailed study of the crime, entitled 'Sudden Slaughter', suggests that Moray was actually shot in the back and that the wound beside his navel was where the bullet came out after passing straight through his body. In any case Moray was so badly injured that he died that night, while Hamilton was already making good his escape to France, where he went on to make a career as a paid 'hit-man' carrying out several other assassinations.

Today the murder is recorded on a plaque on the wall of the Sheriff Court House, which stands on the site of the

Archbishop's House. While Hamilton escaped, the Linlithgow courts ensured over the years that many other wrongdoers did not. During the Middle Ages penalties, as in all Scottish towns, were physical, ranging from being placed in the stocks or the jougs at the Cross to being scourged through the town by the Burgh Executioner or, worst of all, branded on hand, cheek or shoulder with the town's mark, the letter 'L', and being banished from the town under pain of death. By the eighteenth century Linlithgow had acquired a town jail, and in 1843 the Second Statistical Account of Scotland described it as follows: 'The state of the prison here has been materially improved within these last few years, under the inspection of the Prison Board. The number of prisoners confined during the last year was 125. This, however, includes the county, and affords no criterion by which to judge the amount of crime in the parish. The prison is well secured, and every attention is paid to the health and even the comforts of the prisoners. Each cell is heated with a stove and lighted with gas, regularly cleaned and as well ventilated as the situation of the prison will admit. Each prisoner when brought in is washed and clothed in prison dress. The diet is excellent, consisting of six ounces bread, and a portion of vegetables, each alternate day, pease, or a pint of butter milk. Dinner, ox-head broath, four ounces barley, four ounces bread and a proportion of vegetables, each alternate day, pease brose, fish and potatoes. Supper is the same as breakfast. Provision is also made for the religious instruction of the prisoners. In addition to the services of a chaplain, each cell is also provided with a Testament. Mr. Alison, the governor, instructs the male prisoners, who cannot read or write and his wife, the female prisoners. Many of them appear to value the instruction they receive and some of them make considerable progress. A new jail is to be immediately erected, in which greater facilities will exist for the exercise of the improved prison discipline'.

In addition to the Burgh Halls with their multiplicity of uses, in December 1887 Linlithgow also acquired a Town Hall situated further east along the High Street. Very appropriately in view of the year in which its foundation stone was laid, it was decided to call it The Victoria Jubilee Town Hall, 'out of a desire to show loyal regard for her majesty in the jubilee year of her reign'. An elaborate building with fairytale turrets, it was completed in 1889 and officially opened by the Earl of Rosebery. In 1956 it was sold to Caledonian Associated Cinemas and before opening as the Ritz its ornate frontage was greatly altered. For several years now it has been closed to the public, but moves are afoot to re-open it as the large public hall which a flourishing town like Linlithgow so badly needs to provide suitable premises for its dramatic society and its recently formed musical society Lamp as well as for the monthly meetings of its Arts Guild, Civic Guild, History and Amenity Society and many other local associations.

On the opposite side of the High Street to the Victoria Hall, on the wall of the Four Marys Restaurant, is a plaque which details another of Linlithgow's many claims to fame. For it was in these premises in the days when they housed the local chemist's shop that pharmacist David Waldie carried out his experiments on anaesthetics. After months of experiments Dr. Waldie felt sufficently confident to send a small phial of gas to West Lothian's other famous medical pioneer, Sir James Young Simpson, who had by then established a flourishing practice from his home in Edinburgh's Queen Street. Simpson inhaled the gas and slid unconscious below the table, the first man to be safely anaesthetised using choloroform, which Simpson immediately recognised as being far safer and effective than ether and which he went on to use to make both childbirth and operations less dangerous.

Further along the same side of the High Street past the impressive turreted Victorian building of the Royal Bank, which was erected in 1859, lies the equally impressive Victorian frontage of the St. Michael's Hotel built in Linlithgow's nineteenth-century heyday, when it was confidently hoped that, with its loch and beautiful surrounding countryside and proximity to the coast at Blackness, the town would become an inland holiday resort similar to Crieff, Dunblane and Bridge of Allan. All of these towns had their waters, and Linlithgow too, although it never aspired to being a spa, was famed for its wells as the old rhyme, 'Glasgow for bells, Linlithgow for wells', reminds us. Situated in front of St. Michael's Hotel was the most famous of the town's wells, St. Michael's Well. Although no longer operational, the old well can still be seen to this day with its carving of the town's patron saint, St. Michael, and Linlithgow's famous motto, 'Linlithgow Is Kind to Strangers'. Linlithgow is in fact one of the few towns in Britain with two official coats of arms, the alternative one to the familiar Black Bitch tethered to an oak tree being one depicting the saint with the same motto as on the well.

Other wells, evidence of which can still be found along the High Street, in addition to St. Michael's Well and the Cross Well, include the Lion Well, the Dog Well and, furthest to the west, the New Well. To the east of St. Michael's Well another spring broke surface in the middle of the street and formed the famous Whitten Fountain, named after the owner of the Star and Garter Hotel in front of whose premises it stood, where the roundabout is now more prosaically situated. It was here around the Whitten Fountain that the members of the Linlithgow and Stirlingshire Hunt used to drink their stirrup cups provided by mine host of the Star, when they met in Linlithgow prior to hunting over the Erngath or Bathgate Hills. The Star and Garter with its stables was originally a coaching inn, but it was equally well situated to cater for passengers who arrived from 1842 onwards by the new railway, as the station is situated just behind it, a fact which also gave rise to the Palace Hotel opposite. It has long since gone out of business but its name still remains visible on the facade for all to see.

Now Linlithgow is eager to revive its short-lived Victorian tourist boom and is determined to build it into the town's biggest industry. Already it has become the first town outside Edinburgh to develop an official link with the annual International Festival, with a whole week of activities ranging from the re-enactment of a battle on the Peel to *son et lumière* in St. Michael's and from strolling players to a canal boat rally at Manse Basin. Medieval open-air markets are held each month during the summer, local schoolchildren in period costume provide conducted tours of the Palace, and it is planned to re-introduce boat trips on the loch, which already provides excellent opportunities for bird watchers, trout fishers and dinghy sailers and canoeists for whom Lothian Education Authority has built a well-equipped residential centre to complement the existing accommmodation available at Laetare, Scotland's only international youth holiday centre, which is beautifully situated overlooking the loch.

Laetare is Latin for 'Be Joyful', and that sums up the aim of its founder and moving spirit, local Roman Catholic parish priest, the late Father McGovern, who started the whole idea of encouraging teenagers from different countries to mix and meet by providing them with a small whitewashed cottage on the shores of the loch. The idea proved so successful that the original building proved too small and Father McGovern took over the premises occcupied by the Polish soldiers who had been billeted in Linlithgow during the Second World War, which adjoined St. Michael's Roman Catholic parish church, of which he was priest. Over the years the premises have been updated to provide comfortable twin and four-bedded rooms, along with a spacious dining room, comfortable lounge and facilities in St. Margaret's Hall for discos and dances. Outside the grounds offer room for tennis, putting and volleyball, while besides the attractions of the loch, Laetare's young visitors, like others to the town, can seek opportunities for sports and outdoor activities in Beecraigs Country Park, situated on the edge of the Bathgate Hills just behind the town.

Beecraigs started life as a reservoir dug by German prisoners of war during the First World War, and now houses a trout farm instead, as well as providing facilities for dinghy sailing and canoeing, while the surrounding forest provides excellent countryside for the Swedish sport of orienteering or 'cunning running' as it is often nicknamed, cross-country running, jogging and hillwalking. Beecraigs is also the site of the best field archery courses in Britain, where the European International Field Archery Championships have been held. Field archery is similar to golf in that competitors walk round a set course with a range of targets of different sizes at different distances. Normal target archery is also available at Beecraigs, as is rock climbing, but the pleasantest aspect of this beautifully wooded country park is the opportunities it provides for families simply to relax together, whether by watching its herd of red deer, or by following one of the nature trails laid out by its staff of fully trained rangers who often lead special nature walks, or perhaps by enjoying a barbecue at one of the fully equipped sites.

Beecraigs Country Park now takes in more pleasant country-side at neighbouring Balvormie, and its walks and trails lead all the way west to Cockleroi, Linlithgow's strangely shaped hill on whose summit, which is just below 1000 feet high, the Automobile Association has provided a viewfinder so that those who climb to the top can identify other hills and mountains right across Central Scotland as well as for miles to north and south. There are many arguments about Cockleroi's name and even its spelling, but the most popular theory is that it means the King's hat or crown and was so named in honour of the town's royal associations. Whether or not this is correct the runners in the annual Linlithgow Hill Race to the top of Cockleroi and back down again never have time to debate, but the interest taken in this yearly event is typical of the lively involvement in sport which Linlithgow has always demonstrated and which now helps to attract so many new families to choose it as their home town.

As well as being the home of Linlithgow Rose, the well-known junior football team, Linlithgow is also headquarters for the West Lothian County Cricket Team, whose pitch at Boghall is now adjoined by equally good tennis and squash facilities, while the town's rugby team has its headquarters at the other end of the town at Mains Park.

With all of these facilities, together with its excellent transport links both by road and rail, it is natural that Linlithgow has in recent years become one of the most popular commuter dormitory towns in Central Scotland with new housing estates spreading out all around the town at Riccarton, Springfield and almost all the way to the M9 motorway at Blackness Road. Now more houses are to be built on the site of the former paper mill on the banks of the River Avon and at the Beech Wood to the south of the town. To cater for all these new residents who have swollen the population from its three thousand just after the Second World War to around twelve thousand today, shopping facilities have also been greatly expanded with the new Regent Shopping Centre occupying the site of the former Nobel Explosives Factory.

The Nobel Works, whose arched redbrick Italian piazza-style frontage was a familiar landmark at the Lowport end of the town, until it was demolished to make way for the new shopping development, was opened in 1901, the same year that the Nobel Peace Prize was awarded for the first time as instructed in the will of the company's founder, Swedish chemist and engineer, Alfred Nobel, who had died five years earlier in 1896. As well as patenting processes for the manufacture of dynamite and for combining nitroglycerin with guncotton to make blasting gelatin, Nobel was also responsible for discovering how to make safety fuses so that his explosives could be detonated safely, and to begin with it was these detonators which were manufactured at his company's Linlithgow factory. Somewhat ironically however, considering that Nobel had left his huge fortune to further peace, when the First World War began in 1914, production at Linlithgow's Regent Works was soon switched to making munitions for the front. Later the works were converted for the manufacture of pharmaceutical goods and were acquired by Imperial Chemical Industries – I.C.I.

During demolition of the Regent Works a time capsule buried as part of the opening ceremony in 1901 was discovered. After examination of its contents, which included coins and local and national newspapers of the time, it was buried again, this time along with a second capsule detailing what life was like in Linlithgow at the start of the 1980s.

Opposite the Regent site is the lovely old sandstone building of Linlithgow Academy, which since that school's move to modern premises as part of the Preston Road education campus, has been occupied by Lowport Primary. Behind the Regent site to the south rises the tall chimney of the now disused St. Magdalene's Distillery, which took its name from the Knights of St. John's St. Magdalene's Hospital, which occupied the site until the time of the Reformation. In the other direction to the west the road bends sharply and leads steeply up the hill to the railway station, which was entirely redesigned and rebuilt in 1985 with a colourful and very lively mural entitled 'Happy Marches' as its most interesting feature. The mural is the work of local artist, American-born Mary Colouris, and this, the largest of the many pictures which she has produced of life in West Lothian, captures exactly all the verve and vitality of Linlithgow's annual celebration.

Further up the hill above the line of the railway runs the

Union Canal, whose Manse Basin, named after the original St. Michael's Manse, which was situated at the top of the hill, is a hive of activity as soon as winter gives way to spring. For this, the town dock on the old Union, is now the headquarters of both the Linlithgow Canoe Club and of the Linlithgow Union Canal Society whose members have converted the old stables into Scotland's only canal museum and whose immaculately painted replica nineteenth-century steam packet *Victoria*, complete with striped awnings, makes her one of the most photographed subjects in the town.

A vivid picture of the canal at this point in the 1820s is given by the essayist Alexander Smith, who spent his final years living in the town before his death in 1829 and who gave it its much beloved title of 'Dreamthorp'. He wrote, 'Such a secluded place is Dreamthorp that the railway does not come near and the canal is the only thing that connects it with the world. It stands high and from it the undulating country may be seen, stretching away in the grey distance, with hills and woods and stains of smoke, which mark the sites of villages. Every now and then a horse comes staggering along the towpath, trailing a sleepy barge filled with merchandise. A quiet, indolent life these bargemen lead in the summer days, one lies stretched at his length on the sun-heated plank; his comrade sits smoking in the little dog hutch, which I suppose he calls a cabin. Silently they come and go; silently the wooden bridge lifts to let them through. The horse stops at the bridge-house for a drink and there I like to talk a little with the men. They serve instead of a newspaper and retail with great willingness the news they have picked up in their progress from town to town. We are great friends, evidence of which they occassionally exhibit by request-ing me to disburse a trifle for drink money. This canal is a great haunt of mine of an evening. The water hardly invites one to bathe in it and a delicate stomach might suspect the flavour of the eels caught therein; yet to my thinking it is not the least destitute of beauty. A barge trailing up through it in the sunset is a pretty sight; and the crimsons and purples sleep quite lovingly upon its glossy ripples. Nor does the evening star disdain it, for as I walk along I see it mirrored therein as clearly as in the waters of the Mediterranean itself'.

Dreamthorp has certainly wakened up since Smith described

it over a century and a half ago, but much of its very special charm can still be found by leaving behind the tourists at the Palace and the traffic in the High Street and wandering along the towpath and returning past the late Georgian and Victorian houses of Royal Terrace and Friars Brae. Above them stretch many of Linlithgow's new developments at Priory, Deanburn, Clarendon, Oatlands Park, Laverock Park, Carmilaws and Riccarton, where atop the hill in its carefully landscaped grounds is situated the town's new industry, Racal Defence Radar and Displays Ltd., which as the name suggests manufactures the most intricate electronic and computerised defence equipment. Now it is hoped that other high technology firms will follow its lead and establish themselves in Linlithgow, thus ensuring for the town a future as rich as its historic past.

CHAPTER 3

St. Michael's and 'The Palace of Pleasure'

There can be few more beautiful churches than Linlithgow's St. Michael's. Situated on the same hilltop as the town's famous palace, St Michael's is reached up the steep narrow Kirk Gate or Kirk Gait. The first spelling of this age-old place-name fits in best with the other 'gates' to be found around Linlithgow, at the West, Low and High Ports and at the Water Yett, the entrance from the loch, halfway along the High Street, but many local people insist that the second spelling is correct, as in the Lang Gait or Long Stride or Walk as Edinburgh's Princess Street was originally known.

No matter the spelling, however, it is undoubtedly worth while to climb up from the High Street to admire St. Michael's, which was first consecrated as long ago as 22nd May 1242, by David de Bernham, Bishop of St. Andrews. But this act of consecration, early though it was, did not mark the start of the history of this ancient church, for worship is believed to have taken place here since long before written records were first kept. Evidence of this is the fact that by the time King David I gave St. Michael's to his friend and churchman, Robert of St. Andrews, it was already a powerful and wealthy mother church with, as the words of David's gift indicate, 'chapels and lands'. Among its daughter churches were St. Giles and St. Cuthbert's in Edinburgh.

When King Edward I, the Hammer of the Scots, garrisoned Linlithgow Palace during his long and wearisome campaign against the Bruce, he incorporated 'the Great Church', as it was described, within his strongly fortified peel, and to this day St. Michael's still has castellated battlements on its south side overlooking the town. In 1305 the Prior and Canons of St. Andrews prayed King Edward, 'seeing that he has made a camp and a fortalice of their old church, that he would build to them at his own expense, a new church'. Edward informed them that he would defer a decision until his next parliament, but then died. Later the same year, although Bruce was king by then, it appears that St. Michael's was still in the hands of the

The Queen's 60th birthday was marked in 1986 by the creation in St. Michael's, Linlithgow of the new Queen's Aisle side chapel on the south side of this historic building with so many links with Scotland's earlier monarchs. Crown copyright, Royal Commission on the Ancient and Historical Monuments of Scotland.

English, for there is on record a plea from the Knights of St. John at Torphichen, who were always pro-English, that they should be given refuge there. Apart from this there is little evidence of how St. Michael's fared during the reign of the Bruce.

Fifty years after Bannockburn, in 1363, Adam, Vicar of Linlithgow, was given £10 a year from the custom duties levied within the burgh of Linlithgow. By the reign of Robert II, St.

Michael's was badly in need of repair and the tower at the west end was either built or rebuilt, the King giving the princely sum of twenty-six shillings and eight pence towards its cost. Early next century, in 1424, a fire broke out in the church, started perhaps by a candle carelessly dropped, because damage was concentrated in the nave where the altars were situated in the bays between the thick stone pillars. According to tradition the equally impressive nave of the present church was built during the reign of James III, but there is no written evidence for this, and if the king contributed to the cost this would run against his usual reputation for meanness.

Where James III was mean, James IV was generous, and this generosity extended to St. Michael's, where masons worked for the whole of his all too short reign, which was a golden age for Scotland. Apart from gifts from the King, money for the work at St. Michael's came from many sources, including contributions from fines levied in the town. In particular all fines from chimney fires were paid to the church, so this was truly a case of holy smoke. Work on St. Michael's progressed so well that by the time King James attended his famous final service in the church on the eve of his departure for the Battle of Flodden in 1513, it was complete apart from the apse at the east end. According to tradition it was late afternoon when James crossed from the palace to attend evensong. The king was kneeling in prayer in St. Catherine's Aisle on the south side of the church when suddenly he was startled by the appearance of 'ane figure of ane blue man', who warned of the ill luck which would befall James if he went to war against his English in-laws. Before the King or any of his courtiers could react the blue man disappeared, but whether this was truly a ghost as believed at the time or merely a palace servant disguised and in the pay of Queen Margaret, who knew full well her husband's belief in magic and wanted to prevent his going, will never be known. No matter which, on this occasion James IV paid no heed and next morning departed for ill-fated Flodden field, leaving Margaret to 'weep away the weary hour' as Sir Walter Scott later romantically expressed it in his poem 'Marmion'.

Another of James IV's connections with St. Michael's might have inspired Sir Walter to poetry, for it was at the Linlithgow church that the King performed his Scottish version of the

Linlithgow Palace has a decidedly rural aspect in this early print. Today the Palace is enclosed within the Peel, Linlithgow's Royal Park which, like Holyrood Park in Edinburgh, has its own police force, known as the Peelies.

English Maundy Money ceremony. This took place each Easter and was described as 'the giening o' the Skire Siller'. 'Skire' was probably a corruption of the English 'Sheer Thursday', which took its name from the acts of purification carried out on the day prior to Good Friday, and the 'Siller' consisted of small silver coins produced specially by Linlithgow's royal mint, which stood on the site now occupied by the railway station on the hillside overlooking the High Street. These were handed out by King James to the old and the deserving poor, but he went on to carry his act of penance much further. For as the beggars and paupers made their way up the Kirk Gate to St. Michael's to where the king sat waiting at the top of the steps leading to the west door, the royal servants prepared basins of hot water and clean linen towels. Sweet perfumed herbs were sprinkled on the surface of each bowl of water and the King must have welcomed this thoughtful act, because as each of the old men and women appeared before him, he was expected to imitate the actions of Jesus at the Last Supper and painstaking-ly bathe their feet. Once their feet were washed and dried, James then presented them with the 'siller', but in addition he also gave each a new gown of blue or grey 'Holland cloth', a pair of shoes or boots made by Linlithgow's famous cobblers, and a wooden bowl and wooden platter from which to eat and drink during the coming year.

Next morning, on Good Friday itself, James continued his royal religious observances by rising at daybreak to make his way along the reed-strewn, stone-flagged passages of Linlithgow Palace, where he liked to spend this spring holiday, to the chapel where he received the sacraments, but later in the morning, accompanied by his young queen and all of his courtiers, he always crossed the courtyard and entered St. Michael's by the north door to attend a second service, and if, as often happened, this mass was celebrated by a young newly ordained priest, the King always marked the occasion by giving an especially generous offering.

James IV's generosity may also have contributed to the installation of the oldest of St. Michael's three bells, for it bears an inscription stating that it was placed there 'in the reign of the august Lord James IV, 1490'. As it was traditional to install a bell to mark the completion of a church, it can be assumed that St. Michael's was finished by this date, with the exception of the apse, work on which continued into the reign of James V. It was at this time also that the oak roof was installed in the nave and chancel, and it is known to have borne the initials and coat of arms of the then vicar of St. Michael's, George Crichton, who later became a bishop. Unfortunately this fine wooden ceiling had to be replaced in 1812, when the present plaster one was erected. It was always considered a poor substitute, but during the recent restoration work in St. Michael's during the early 1980s its appearance has been greatly improved by picking out and decorating its bosses, and interest was added by the discovery of two angels carved in the stonework.

Some church historians believe that at the same time as the apse was finished and the oak ceiling completed, James V also erected a throne for himself in St. Michael's together with a stall for each of his Knights of the Thistle. Others, including Sir Walter Scott, who adds banners to the scene, claim that this was the work of King James IV, while others write off the whole story as nonsense and claim that the Knights of the

This rustic scene by J. Clark shows Linlithgow Palace seen from across the tranquil waters of the loch. Today houses have replaced the fields, but the beauty of the scene survives.

Thistle were not created for another century and a half, until the reign of James VII of Scotland and II of England, the son of Charles I.

Whether or not St. Michael's was adorned with the stalls of the Knights, it is clear that by the end of James V's reign in 1542 it must have been looking at its most magnificent, both inside and out, with its new apse, its ceiling of solid oak, its tower adorned with its imperial crown, its candlelit altars in every alcove between the massive pillars of the nave, and statues of the saints filling every niche.

It was probably in this setting that James V's baby daughter Mary Queen of Scots, who was born at Linlithgow Palace only days before he died across the Forth at Falkland in Fife, was baptised, and the old stone font at St. Michael's, in accordance with ancient tradition, is still situated at the entrance to the church so that the baby can receive his or her Christian name before going into the church proper for the first time. It is a pity that the lives of the priests of St. Michael's, like those of other churchmen in Scotland at this time, did not live up to the beauty of their church, for their dissolute ways were to lead to the religious strife which was to wreck Mary's reign and finally lead to her execution.

Many of the complaints which led to the Reformation during Mary's reign are carefully listed in the records of the magistrates of Linlithgow, because as St. Michael's was from the outset a parochial church it was the Provost and the Bailies who appointed and disciplined the priests. The Magistrates' complaints ranged from the fact that the priests could not apparently summon up enough energy to light the stipulated number of candles on the altars to the much more serious one that they were breaking their vows of celibacy. Local tradition maintains that the discreetly screened clerestory, which runs the full length of both sides of the nave of St. Michael's, provided the priests of the church and the monks of the town's Carmelite and Augustinian monasteries with a place to do their courting and that the liaisons formed with the nuns of Emmanuel Priory on the shores of the River Avon, which gave nearby Manuel its name, resulted in many small unmarked graves in the churchyard.

One man who tried to reform the church from within was the rector of Linlithgow Grammar School, whose buildings were adjacent to the kirk, Ninian Winzet. It is claimed that he once debated the issue of reform with John Knox; in the end he had to flee to Germany, where later he became Roman Catholic Bishop of Ratisbon. Despite the efforts of men such as Winzet, the Roman Catholic Church failed to put its own house in order, and so in 1559 the Reformation got into full swing and the Lords of the Congregation, the leaders of the movement, reached St. Michael's on 29th June of that year. They emptied all the niches of their saints, smashed the holy water stoup, destroyed the altars and rid the church of everything which they deemed 'Popish'. Only one statue remained, and that was the one of St. Michael, which can still be seen on the south-west corner of the church, and it survived not because he was the church's patron saint, but because he was so well built into the exterior fabric of the building that to have removed him would have resulted in extensive damage.

Although the altars had all been swept away, the magistrates of Linlithgow decided that the trade guilds, which until then

A falcon's-eye view of Linlithgow Palace and St. Michael's Church. Even in the ruined state in which it has lain since it was destroyed by fire in 1746, the Palace remains one of the most impressive medieval buldings in the country and its sheer scale shows why it took over two hundred years to complete. Crown copyright, Royal Commission on the Ancient and Historical Monuments of Scotland.

had each been responsible for providing candles for the various Masses, should still ensure that St. Michael's was well lit by now assuming responsibility for the church windows. But glass was still an expensive luxury and many of the guild members were furious at this new imposition, the Hammermen going so far as to attempt to fill in the window allocated them, until swiftly ordered by the magistrates to replace the stone with glass.

A second major change after the Reformation was the introduction for the first time of pews. Until then it had been the custom for the worshippers simply to stand in front of the altars or to bring their own little folding stools of the kind which Jenny Geddes is said to have thrown at the preacher in St. Giles in Edinburgh, while the old and the ill who were unable to stand or not strong enough to bring their own stools could always sit on the stone seat round the sides of the church, thus giving rise to the saying, 'Let the weak go to the wall'.

After the Reformation, however, all that changed, and possibly because of the new-style Protestant services with their lengthy sermons or possibly simply because of the space created by the removal of the altars, it became the fashion for the wealthier members of the congregation to install their own pews, which they had built for themselves by the local wrights. The result was that there was no uniformity either of size or design, the magistrates being especially irate about the pew installed by the Incorporation of Tailors, whose members considered themselves of such importance to the burgh that they had their pew specially constructed so that it was higher than any other in the church. Later they annoyed the magistrates still further by adorning their pew with the emblems of their guild which consisted of a large smoothing iron and a huge pair of scissors.

In 1646 the magistrates decided to regularise the matter of the pews by installing benches of a standard design, and eighty fine trees were carefully selected in Kinneil Woods on the hillside above Bo'ness. After felling they were hauled by horses over Flints, the steep hill between the two towns, and down to the church beside the loch. The old pews were ripped out, but just as the joiners were beginning to install the new seats, all work was halted. Plague had broken out in Edinburgh. Unlike Scotland's other three universities of that period, Edinburgh University was a 'tounis college', so the regents, as the professors were known, appealed to the Lord Provost and Magistrates of Edinburgh to organise the evacuation of all of the students, and so it was that an urgent message was sent to the councillors of Linlithgow asking them to 'supply the college, regents and students with accommodation, until the judgement to be removed'.

The Linlithgow councillors replied to the city fathers stating that 'they were well pleasit to assist them and condescended to gie them fyne schoolis in the Kirk, dividit and made ready by themselves'. The trees from Kinneil were therefore used to erect partitions in the nave instead of being turned into pews as originally intended. Possibly because few of the students could afford to hire horses to ride the eighteen miles over the rolling Lothian countryside from Edinburgh to Linlithgow and so had to walk all the way with their books and clothes bundled under their arms or tied in packs on their backs, all was ready to receive them when they arrived at St. Michael's, but although they had a guarantee of accommodatiion for their lectures and classes, places to stay were not so easy to come by. For the students and their professors were not the only people to crowd into Linlithgow at this time, because the Committee of Estates – appointed by Parliament and in effect the government – also decided to evacuate its members to the West Lothian town, which was famed for its good fresh air and its healthy record. So great was the concern of the Linlithgow councillors that this sudden increase in the demand for lodgings might tempt their fellow townsfolk to charge exorbitant rates that they quickly issued the following order: 'It is ordainit that the following be observit be the haill inhabitants and no contravenit; viz., the price of the noblemen, chamber, cole and candle with twa bedis, for twenty four hours, 20 shillings; and of gentlemen and Commissioners of Burghs, that space, 13 shillings and 4 pence; and the price of the rest of the lodgers resorting to the said burgh for cole, candle and bed for 24 hours, 6 shillings and 8 pence and the grooms and footmen for their bed, 3 shillings'.

The Edinburgh students were not allowed to lie abed overlong, however, because they had to make their way along the High Street and up the Kirk Gate to St. Michael's shortly after dawn, in order to be in time for the start of their first lectures at six o'clock. Work then went on for three hours until 9 a.m., when the students were allowed a one-hour break for breakfast, before returning to the church for a further two hours' classes from ten until noon. But from then on the day was their own to practice archery at the bow butts below the Palace, to try the new Dutch game of golf on the smooth grassy lawns of the Peel or perhaps, it can be imagined, to flirt with the local lassies beside the loch.

With all of these country pleasures to enjoy, the students may well have been sad when word came from Edinburgh that the worst of the plague was over and the professors judged it safe to return to the city. Before doing so, however, they expressed 'their gratitude to the council for their great favour and courtesy', and presented them with 'the haill deallis brough into the Kirk in making up the schools for the University, to be employed by them to such purpose as they shall consider most convenient'. As a result the installation of the long-awaited pews was delayed, the magistrates apparently deciding that the congregation could make do with the rough wooden benches quickly knocked together for the students, and it was not until 1672 that proper pews were at last installed. When they were, the congregation had to pay for them, because seat rents were introduced for the first time, and these had to be paid quarterly. It was at this time decided to divide the church and to use only the nave for services, while the chancel and transepts on the other side of the partition were used for burials.

This arrangement continued throughout the eighteenth century, and it must therefore only have been the nave of St. Michael's which Robert Burns saw when he visited Linlithgow, which may help to account for his comment that although it was 'A pretty good old Gothic church, what a poor business is a Presbyterian place of worship, dirty, narrow and squalid'. Probably as a result of his own earlier personal experience, the poet also added that, 'The famous stool of repentance, in the old Roman way, is in a lofty situation'.

Another famous visitor to St. Michael's who was equally critical was the poet Wordsworth's sister Dorothy, who wrote that 'The shell of a small ancient church is standing, into which are crammed wooden pews, galleries and pulpit . . . very ugly and discordant with the exterior'. During the nineteenth century much restoration work was carried out, but it is a pity that while well intentioned, it resulted in the fine old oak ceiling being replaced, as mentioned earlier, by the present plaster one, the beautiful chancel arch being destroyed and – worst of all – the stone crown removed from the tower because it was feared that it was too heavy and would cause the stonework to crack.

Now St. Michael's once again has a crown atop its old tower, not a copy of the original imperial one, but a modernistic crown of thorns, made from equally modern materials consisting of prelaminated timber covered with aluminium sheeting, specially treated to ensure its golden finish will never tarnish. Twenty years after it was erected during the ministry of the Very Rev. Dr. David Steel, former Moderator of the General Assembly of the Church of Scotland and father of the equally controversial leader of the Liberal Party, it is still very much a

This carving of Mary Queen of Scots graces the famous Queen's pulpit in St. Michael's Church, which also bears carvings of Queen Margaret, wife of Malcolm Canmore and Queen Victoria. One space remains and many members of the congregation hope that some day it will be filled with an equally fine carved figure of the present Queen.

talking point amongst townsfolk and visitors alike, drawing comments ranging from 'Is it really finished?' and 'Looks like a misguided space missile' to 'The finest piece of new church architecture in Scotland this century'. Certainly it has put Linlithgow on the map, as it is probably the best-known landmark on the main line between Glasgow and Edinburgh and, seen from a distance and especially with the sun's rays slanting down upon it, it is strikingly beautiful. It is interesting to wonder whether in the future it will come to be admired just as much as the centuries old treasures in the church beneath it are today.

Directly below it in the belfry hang St. Michael's three bells, St. Michael, St. Mary and Wee Meg Duncan. In a way, St. Michael is both the oldest and the newest of the bells, because although it was, as already mentioned, the first to be hung to mark the completion of the fabric of the church, in 1773 it was found to be cracked. Inquiries were made in Edinburgh to discover if any craftsman could repair it, but none was sufficiently skilled to tackle such a big bell. The Linlithgow magistrates therefore decided that old St. Michael must be sent south by sea to a foundry in London. By May the recasting was complete and St. Michael was carefully transported north again aboard the *Samuel and Jean*, whose master, James Drumond, landed his unusul cargo safely at his home port of Borrow-stounness, as Bo'ness was then correctly called. From there St. Michael was carted over Flints and back home to the belfry. There came with it a bill for £55–3–6, but as the craftsmen at the London foundry had used the original metal, this was reduced by £27–13–1, leaving the magistrates less to pay and the church with a link with its past.

In those days the bells were very important in the life of the town, because the first service at St. Michael's was held at the early hour of eight o'clock, and the magistrates were determined that no-one should have any excuse for missing it. They gave orders therefore that the bells should be rung at 7.00 a.m., then again at 7.30, and then again for ten minutes before eight, with the bell-ringer being instructed to ring 'as lang as ane may gang between the West Port and the Kirk'. It is said that any latecomers were also chided along by Meg Duncan, an old woman who lived in one of the little houses at the foot of the Kirk Gate, and to this day her sharp tongue lives on, for the smallest of the three bells in St. Michael's steeple was nicknamed after her, and it is still rung after its big brother and sister have ceased tolling, to warn latecomers to hurry up the hill, just as its namesake did so many years before.

Another custom which is still kept up at St. Michael's is that unlike the bells at other churches which are only rung before the service, those at St. Michael's are also rung again towards the end, just after the minister has finished his sermon and before the final hymn. This dates back to the days when many of the families who attended St. Michael's travelled to church by carriage. While the families were at worship in the kirk, their coachmen took the horses down to the stables at one of the hostelries in the High Street, and the ringing of the bells warned them that it was time to go back and collect their masters and mistresses and the children for the journey home to Sunday lunch.

After today's Sunday service it is well worth lingering or returning on a weekday between ten and noon or 2 p.m. and 4 o'clock to explore the church and admire its many interesting features. St. Michael's is indeed a wonderful church to visit, especially with children, because it is a veritable Noah's Ark of a kirk and there is a complete menagerie of animals and birds and fish for them to find, from the gold fish at the foot of the baptismal bowl, which acts as a reminder of the original Christian symbol, to the old lead weathercock, which sat atop the original spire and can now be examined at ground level in the corner next to the war memorial at the east end of the south aisle. Round the corner and up the steps in the apse the scene is dominated by the most impressive of St. Michael's many stained-glass windows, and as it is dedicated to the memory of West Lothian's most famous zoologist, it is indeed appropriate that it depicts so many birds and beasts.

The zoologist was Professor Sir Charles Wyville Thomson, whose home 'Bonsyde', now the whitewashed Earl O' Moray Hotel, overlooks Linlithgow Loch from its site on the slopes of the Erngath Hills. After conducting several successful seabed surveys off the coast of Scotland, Sir Charles was appointed in 1872 to lead the scientific staff aboard the 2,306-ton steam corvette H.M.S *Challenger*, which was to explore the ocean beds of the world and whose findings aroused as much interest amongst our Victorian forebears as those of space explorers do during our own times. The *Challenger*, with its fully equipped laboratories, set sail from Sheerness in December 1872 and, before finally returning home to Spithead in May 1876, travelled a total of over 70,000 miles in the Atlantic, Antarctic and Pacific Oceans. Soundings were taken at over 350 places, and the resulting mass of scientific evidence resulted in a knighthood being conferred on Professor Thomson by Queen Victoria.

Sir Charles did not live long to enjoy his well-deserved

honour, because the strenuous work of the long expedition had damaged his health, and he died only six years later in 1882. It was then that his colleagues and students at Edinburgh University decided to honour his memory by erecting a massive stained-glass window in St. Michael's depicting the whole universe and very appropriately including underwater scenes. Many of the professor's students came to the service of dedication, and naturally they were particularly interested in how the artist had portrayed the ocean bed, whose secrets Sir Charles had done so much to reveal. They admired the sharks and the spouting whale, and then stopped in horror when they saw the lobster, because the artist had depicted it as red, and as every schoolboy knows, lobsters do not take on this vivid hue until they are boiled for the table. The tale of the lobster, however, had a happy ending, for just in time to save the artist's blushes from becoming as red as his shellfish, word came from a follow-up expedition to the *Challenger's*, in Australian waters, that an until then unknown species of lobster had been discovered and that it was, if not quite red, a very satisfactory shade of pink.

Below the window dedicated to Sir Charles, the beautifully carved choir stalls installed in 1956 are also alive with animals ranging from the cheekiest of little monkeys to a wee puddock, and not forgetting the church mouse. Birds too feature in St. Michael's, from the white dove on the canopy above the stalls, to the huge golden eagle which forms the lectern because its wings, it is claimed of all the birds were strong enough to carry both the Old and New Testaments of the Bible.

Still more finds can be added to the list in this ark-like kirk, if legendary beasts are included. Amongst them are the dragon, which St. Michael is depicted as slaying, and the white unicorn, which was Scotland's heraldic beast long before the lion was adopted. Nowadays in St. Michael's, the lion and the unicorn flank a huge Scottish coat of arms on the west wall of the kirk, and many visitors like to sit in the pew beneath, as they imagine that it must be the royal pew. The royal pew is in fact more discreetly situated on the other side of the pulpit in the chancel, and its coat of arms does not compete with the flamboyantly painted one in the west aisle, which actually marks where the Provost and Magistrates sit at the annual

The New Entrance at the top of the Kirk Gate leading into the Peel, the royal park which surrounds Linlithgow Palace, dates from the reign of King James V (1513-42). Courtesy of John Doherty.

'kirkin' o' the council'. Although this massive coat of arms does not denote the royal pew, it does, however, have royal connections. For the story behind it is that when in 1660 the Commonwealth ended with the restoration of King Charles II, the Linlithgow councillors sent a messenger to Edinburgh with instructions to return as quickly as possible with the largest and most impressive royal coat of arms that he could purchase in order to show that while the burgesses of the Royal and Ancient Burgh had lived happily and profitably with Cromwell's men for the past ten years, they were now definitely loyal to the crown! And to this day the big shield supported by its golden lion and its silver unicorn still has pride of place on the west wall of the church.

St. Michael's other royal connection is its famous Queen's Pulpit, whose intricately carved figures depict Queen Margaret, wife of Malcolm Canmore, Mary Queen of Scots and Queen

Victoria. A fourth niche remains to be filled, and it is hoped that one day it will be filled with an equally beautifully carved wooden statue of our present Queen. It was from this pulpit that one of St. Michael's best-known ministers, Dr. Ferguson, who wrote the history of the kirk, used to preach. Sadly his ministry was marred by the tragic accidental deaths of two of his daughters, one of whom died when her hair caught fire while she was drying it in front of the manse fire and the other when she fell through the ice while she was out skating with her boy friend on Linlithgow Loch. To remind him of the former, Dr. Ferguson had a special stained-glass window installed in the church, so that as he looked up at the end of each of his sermons, he always saw depicted in front of him the Boy Samuel worshipping in the temple and was reminded of his little daughter in all her childhood innocence.

The Boy Samuel window looks down on the Celtic side chapel, whose specially designed furnishings include a modern version of the ancient Celtic cross. Other crosses to be found around St. Michael's include the original consecration marks carved in the stonework all those years ago when Bishop Bernham first blessed it in 1242.

Old though St. Michael's is, the adjacent royal palace has an even longer history. Like Livingston Peel, Linlithgow Palace began life as a royal hunting lodge, where, when the sport was good, the king could spend the night instead of cutting short the chase to ride all the way back to Holyrood. Subsequently Linlithgow always maintained its original reputation as 'ane palace of pleasance' and remained the Scottish royal family's favourite holiday home for five hundred years.

But Linlithgow did know more warlike times, as for instance when it was seized by Edward I of England, who fortified it during his invasion of Scotland in 1301. Edward spent the whole of the winter of that year and the following one at Linlithgow, and evidence that the palace was still mainly built of wood comes from the records of his stay, because they show that he employed 107 carpenters and 80 ditchers, but no masons, in the construction of the extra fortifications with which he strengthened his northern headquarters.

After Edward's death, his son Edward II continued the

St. Michael's Church, Linlithgow, from the south. Its graveyard is well worth exploring for the details it provides about the former townsfolk who lie buried there. Courtesy of John Doherty.

campaign against the Scots, but lost Linlithgow, thanks to the guile of a local farmer. For months, farmer Binnie was forced by the English garrison at the palace to supply them with loads of hay for their horses. Week after week he made his regular delivery until the guards on the drawbridge grew so accustomed to his arrival that they did not even bother to challenge him, far less search his cart. Then on one delivery farmer Binnie, instead of driving into the palace courtyard, halted his horse in the middle of the drawbridge so that the cart was positioned right below the portcullis. Suddenly the jeers of the English guards about the bumbling old farmer being even slower than usual died in their throats when to their horror they saw the load of hay heave up. Hidden beneath were a dozen Scottish soldiers. As the twelve leapt from the cart, the panic-stricken English tried to raise the drawbridge, but the fully laden cart kept it firmly in place. One of the guards did manage to release the portcullis, but its descent only made matters worse for the English, because it jammed on top of the hay cart and defeated their efforts to pull the horses and their load into the inner courtyard and thus at least stop the other waiting Scots, who had appeared from their hiding places around the Palace, from rushing over the drawbridge.

Farmer Binnie's success was something of an embarrassment to Robert the Bruce. He did not have enough men to fortify the Palace, and so he was forced to order that it be destroyed, lest it fall again into the hands of the enemy. It was left to the Bruce's son, King David II, to set matters right at Linlithgow, and this he did by granting the lands around Linlithgow Loch to one John Cairns on condition that he 'built the manor house there for the King's coming'. This he did, and as the years passed Linlithgow became a more and more substantial palace. In 1339, for instance, forty-three shillings was paid for 'lead for the King's hoose', but this building was burnt by the English in 1424, and it was therefore not until the reign of James I that it began to take on the shape which we know today.

Parts of the reconstructed palace were obviously completed by the early 1430s because there are records of purchase of 'ells of broad cloth', 'lengths of arras' and 'paints for Matthew', the king's decorator, but James never saw his dream completed, for he died in 1437. Work was still proceeding over thirty years later, when in 1469 his grandson James III decided that Linlithgow would make a beautiful wedding gift for his bride, Margaret of Denmark, who in turn brought Orkney and Shetland as part of her dowry.

The gift of Linlithgow Palace as a wedding gift by James III set a precedent for succeeding Stewart monarchs, but apart from one occasion in 1474, when plague drove James and Margaret from Holyrood, they seldom stayed there for any length of time. James IV, on the other hand, needed no plague to drive him to Linlithgow, where he spent many of his happiest hours. In 1503, with his marriage to the little English princess Margaret Tudor about to take place, he employed the most skilful craftsmen in Scotland to make the palace as magnificent a gift as possible for his fourteen-year-old bride. This 'Wedding of the Thistle and the Rose' truly caught the imagination of the people of the time, and crowds turned out to welcome them on their first visit together to Linlithgow.

Although the marriage did not turn out to be the happy romance for which the Scottish people might have hoped, the all too short reign of James IV was otherwise a golden age for Scotland, the enthusiastic young King encouraging medicine, printing, alchemy and even aviation. In Edinburgh, James founded the Royal College of Surgeons, but he was not content simply to leave others to study medicine, and shocking his court officials even more when he gave the Edinburgh doctors permission to dissect the body of an executed criminal, he himself set up a surgery at Linlithgow Palace. Whether out of his usual generosity or whether out of the need to obtain patients on whom to experiment, James apparently gave money to those on whom he experimented, because the palace records contain several records of payments made to local people for taking part in bloodletting sessions. Another Linlithgow man was paid after the king pulled out several of his teeth, but the treasurer notes that this patient failed to keep his next appointment for further extractions!

Fortunately most of the experiments which the king conducted were not so painful, and those in magic often provided after-dinner entertainment for his nobles and their ladies at the famous feasts which James loved to give in the Palace's huge banqueting chamber, where he completed 'the glassinnying of all the wyndois' for the first time. Feasting and entertainment at Linlithgow reached their climax at holiday times such as Easter and Christmas, when the celebrations lasted for a whole month, from St. Nicholas Eve on December 5th right through to Epiphany or Twelfth Night on January 6th.

It is said that James was pleased to allow the introduction of English-style Christmas celebrations of the type found traditionally at the Tudor court in London in order to try to lessen the homesickness of his bride. Young Margaret must have felt most at home at the first of the Christmas festivities, when before they became involved in all the extra work of the many Christmas services, the choirboys from St. Michael's sang schule were invited across to the Palace to take part in what was described as the Saint Nicholas Frolic. At this the Queen presided over a feast which ended with the serving to each boy a slice from a huge Christmas pudding. Hidden in one slice was a bean, and the boy who was lucky enough to find it was presented with a special present by the Queen, a deed still remembered to this day whenever we speak of a bean feast.

Another event at the St. Nicholas Frolic was the choosing of one of the nobles as the Lord of Misrule or the Abbot of Unreason, and he was then in charge of arranging and compering all of the other celebrations during the month of Christmas feasting and revelry. As well as appearing himself as a magician, King James welcomed all other entertainers who turned up at the Palace, and as all were rewarded with his usual generosity, there was no shortage of wandering minstrels and strolling players for these royal command performances. While they were all a welcome addition to the fun created by the court jester, James was particularly pleased when unusual novelty acts appeared, and these included acrobats and tumblers, fire eaters and sword swallowers, illusionists and contortionists and fellow magicians.

The palace cooks also apparently had to indulge in trickery to keep the King and his nobles happy and content as feast followed feast every night throughout December and into January, because it is said that they created special novelty dishes such as the cockyntrice. As the name suggests the cockyntrice consisted of the front half of a proud young cockerel served with his fiery red cock comb still held high, but when it graced the royal table the cockyntrice appeared to be a mysterious combination of fowl and beast, because its rear end consisted of that of a young suckling pig carefully sewn onto the breast of the cock. The cockyntrice was cooked by stuffing and then spit roasting it before it was served gilded with egg yolks mixed with saffron and powdered ginger, so that it appeared as a golden legendary beast fit indeed for any royal feast.

The cavernous stone-flagged kitchens where the intriguing cockyntrice and all the other dishes for the royal feasts were prepared can still be visited in the north-east corner of the palace. There was no running water and all supplies had to be carried from the well far below in the lowest basement of the palace, but in many other ways the kitchens were surprisingly well equipped with what are now considered modern conveniences such as a refuse shute so that all waste could be disposed of straight into the moat below, and serving hatches so

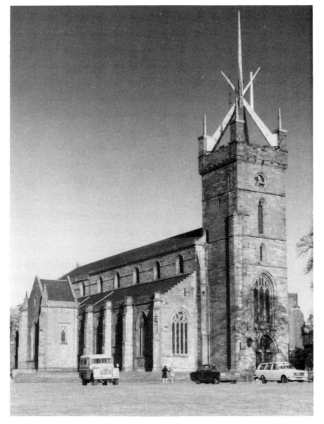

St. Michael's from the north. Atop the tower stands the controversial Crown of Thorns, commissioned when minister by the Very Rev. Dr. David Steele, former Moderator of the General Assembly of the Church of Scotland and father of the leader of the Liberal Party.

that the dishes could be served speedily to the guests in the adjoining banqueting hall, which could seat as many as three hundred people.

There were three means of cooking available to prepare the food for this huge number of diners. One was baking in an oven, and this is impressively large, with enough space, it has been discovered, to accommodate no less than thirty children, so it can be imagined just how many pies could be baked at a time. The routine with the oven was to build a fire in it overnight so that, on the same principle as a modern night storage heater, when the cooks began work in the morning the embers of the fire could be raked out, leaving the stones glowing hot and ready to bake the pies, which ranged from doocote pie, whose pastry was stuffed full of tender young pigeons or squabs as they were known, to rabbit pie, and from colley pie, whose contents consisted of the blackbirds of nursery rhyme fame to game pie, whose filling was supplied from the hunts which James and his followers so loved when resident at Linlithgow.

It is interesting to note that the contents for all of these pies could be obtained fresh all the year round, freshness being preferred to using beef or pork or mutton as all cows, pigs and sheep not required for breeding had to be slaughtered each autumn since there were no root vegetables or other forms of fodder to feed to them to keep them alive throughout the winter. This meant that at the start of the winter, beef, pork and mutton all had to be salted away, and evidence of this can be found in the opposite corner of the Palace kitchens at Linlithgow, where the giant salt cellar occupies a whole corner of the wall. Salting could be done in two different ways. Dry salting consisted of sprinkling salt between the layers of meat, while the other method of soaking in brine produced an only slightly less unpleasant result.

Most of the salted meat products were cooked by being boiled in big cauldrons placed over an open fire in the huge hearth, whose chimney towers above. The same fire also served to boil the broth in the kail pot which simmered away by night and day.

The third and most popular method of cooking in the Palace kitchen at Linlithgow was spit roasting, and early each morning the barons of beef, haunches of venison and sides of ox which were to be served at that evening's banquet were hoisted up through a trapdoor immediately below the spit. Once the joint was safely secured, the two little spit boys began their day-long task, endlessly cawing the handles at either end of the long iron rod, and basting the roast from time to time with its own gravy to ensure it did not become too dry. So unpleasant was this hot smoky job that the little spit boys plucked up courage to protest to the King that they as well as the roasts were being cooked and James agreed that the laddies could have the old archery targets from the bow butts below the palace to shelter and protect them from the flames. When the boys reported that the straw in the old targets was catching fire, the King suggested that they soak them with water, and when this caused more problems because of the smoke, James agreed that the spit boys should be paid an extra £6.33 pence a year so that they could afford to buy an extra suit of clothes to change into when their long day was done, because their working outfits smelt so much that no-one would go near them.

As well as the big spit on which the beef and venison were roasted, the boys also had to look after a whole range of smaller spits, from those used to cook the suckling pigs, through those used for 'barn yard fowlis', to tiny ones used for quail. Other fowl and game birds cooked for the feasts at Linlithgow are known to have included pheasant, partridge, black cock, grouse, wild duck, water hens, coot and swans from the loch. At Linlithgow the swans seem to have taken the place of the peacocks often mentioned at banquets at the English court because, like the peacocks, they were very carefully plucked and once roasted all the feathers were replaced so that when carried on high into the banqueting hall they looked as if they were swimming, just as they had so recently done on the loch below the palace windows.

Other items which the loch provided for the eighteen or twenty courses or removes presented to the King and his guests at each feast included freshly caught trout and perch, while eel were another welcome delicacy. The eels were specially bred and tended in a wooden eel ark, a contraption similar to those seen at most modern trout farms, which was moored out in the loch and where the tender young elvers could easily be caught when required, speared with the five-pronged barbed iron fork which can still be seen in the Palace museum.

Another unsavoury reminder of the feasts is the dark little room which opens off the south end of the banqueting chamber. This was the *vomitarium*, to which, as its name suggests, the nobles could retreat after ten or twelve removes to make themselves deliberately sick. This was done by choosing one of the little feathers thoughtfully provided and tickling the back of their throats. They could then return to enjoy the other half-dozen or so courses still to come.

This privilege was allowed only to the lords, and a second

way in which the ladies were discriminated against was that after the feast when the tables had all been cleared away and after the musicians in their gallery had played for dancing and the entertainers had performed, the women were expected to withdraw, leaving their menfolk to enjoy their drinks and their jokes, a practice still remembered in many homes by the use of the term 'drawing room'. At Linlithgow Palace withdrawing meant moving through to the big room on the opposite side of what is claimed to be the largest fireplace in Scotland, whose roaring log fire used to heat both this room and the banqueting hall by means of open arches which, although now built up, can still be seen.

On the nights of feasts it is said that whole tree trunks were burned in this huge fireplace, but on other evenings, when there were fewer guests, the banqueting hall was partitioned by screens in line with the famous Queen's View window, leaving only the top half of the room to be heated. The fire was lit only in the middle section of the fireplace, allowing the two outer sections to be used as ingleneuks. This must have been a most pleasant feature on cold winter nights, these cosy fireplace corners allowing guests to sit almost on top of the fire itself and after the meal relax over their games of cards, chess or backgammon. Smaller ingleneuks can be found in the fire-places of several of the other rooms in the Palace, including that in the royal bedchamber. One of the ingleneuks is even thoughtfully provided with a ledge at elbow level on which to rest a tankard of ale or perhaps a glass of hot mulled wine.

Linlithgow Palace was well provided with an enormous wine cellar, and several of the bottles which it once contained can be seen in the Palace museum, all unfortunately long since empty. Much of the wine drunk at the Palace was rich red claret, but records show that other fine wines were also imported from as far away as Cyprus. Very conveniently the cellar was situated directly below the royal suite of rooms, with a stair providing direct access from the King's private dining room. Be careful if you venture down, because in those days such a rich hoard had to be carefully protected, and the stair is still equipped with a trip step which was designed to trap anyone who had no right of entry and had not been warned about it!

Entry to the whole of the royal suite was naturally restricted, and few would ever have been admitted to the royal bed-chamber, which is the innermost room at the north-west corner. Today its bare stone walls and floor always make it seem cold and draughty, but it must be imagined as it once was with its walls covered in heavy tapestries, rich rugs on the floor surrounding the beautifully draped four-poster bed and fires blazing in all three of its fireplaces. These are situated in the main bedroom itself, in the Queen's Oratory, and in the little solarium.

The Queen's Oratory, with its roof bosses carved with white unicorns, was where early morning prayers were said. Later in the day the Queen returned there, and as well as its impressive oriel window it has several smaller lower windows which permitted the Queen and her retinue of ladies in waiting, while sitting embroidering or tambouring, to look out and enjoy the wonderful view over the loch, where the King and the lords might well be fishing or hunting on the far bank.

Immediately adjacent to the Queen's Oratory is the King's Oratory, which also had a small shrine for private prayer, then up the steps and across the main bedroom is the solarium with its large window for the sun to stream through, but with its own fireplace also to provide warmth on the days when the sun failed to shine.

In the opposite corner of the bedchamber a hatch gave access to a staircase which is said to have led down to a strongroom containing jewellery to go with each fresh outfit the King or Queen chose from the wardrobe in the little dressing room above. Today the most interesting feature of the royal dressing room is the garde robe, which contained the royal toilet. Like all of the other lavatories which can be found at several points around the Palace, it was built into the outer walls, but like all of the other conveniences it was dry, and it was said that it was this considerable inconvenience which was one of the main reasons why the Scottish royal family and their court moved regularly from one palace or castle to another, waiting a discreet length of time before they returned.

To return now to the main bedchamber, it is believed that it was here on a bitterly cold night in December 1542 that the most famous event in the whole history of Linlithgow Palace took place, the birth of that most ill-fated of queens, Mary

Queen of Scots. Immediately after the baby was born a
horseman was despatched to carry the news to Falkland Palace
in Fife, where Mary's father King James V lay dying after his
defeat by the English at the Battle of Solway Moss. For James
the news of the birth of a girl was the news he was dreading,
for he feared that the Scottish nobles would never accept rule
by a queen. 'It cam' wi' a lass and it'll gang wi' a lass' are said to
have been his dying words, meaning that the Stewarts had
inherited the crown through the marriage of Princess Marjory,
daughter of Robert the Bruce, to Walter her Lord High
Steward (as described later in the chapter on Bathgate), and
that they would lose it through the infant Mary.

James V died at Falkland without ever seeing the baby born
to him at Linlithgow, but during his lifetime he too was a
frequent visitor to the Palace and was responsible for its
completion. One of the most interesting episodes of his stays
there occurred in the next room of the royal suite, the Presence
Chamber. Unlike the bedchamber and its associated rooms, the
Presence Chamber was open to many of the king's subjects,
because it was there, as the name suggests, that they were
presented to him when they came to court. Just like going to
Buckingham Palace nowadays to receive an honour, coming to
the Presence Chamber at Linlithgow was an important and
exciting event for many of King James' loyal subjects, and the
room was made as beautiful as possible to add to the sense of
occasion, from the specially designed floor to show those who
were to be presented exactly where to stand, to its unique
rainbow window whose fourteen panes of coloured stained
glass cast an image of a double rainbow when the rays of the
morning sun shone through them, but for His Majesty these
daily receptions were a definite bore. One day he decided
therefore to swap places with his faithful servant Rab Gibb,
who down the ages has been variously described as the king's
jester and the royal stirrup man. To begin with, Rab joined in
the pretence, listening patiently and painstakingly to the many
requests for royal favours and grants of land, until, becoming
as fed up as his royal master usually did, he demanded, 'Awa
ye greedy loons and bring me here my ain true and trusty
frien' Rab Gibb, the only man at my court who serves me from
stark love and kindness'. According to tradition, James V was

so delighted with Rab's performance and his words that he rewarded him with the estate of Caribber on the banks of the River Avon on the road between Linlithgow and Armadale, where old Rab subsequently built his castle, and the incident became so well known throughout Scotland that the saying 'For stark love and kindness' was often engraved on the engagement and wedding rings sold at the Luckenbooths outside St. Giles in Edinburgh and on snuff boxes where it usually appeared under a symbol of clasped hands.

Another romantic tale connected with James V is of how he provided Linlithgow Palace with its crowning glory, the intricately carved three-tier fountain in the courtyard, which although it had one of the first piped water supplies in Scotland, is said on the nights of feasts to have flowed with red wine. The detailed carved figures on the fountain depict the famous Scottish Three Estates, the lords, the clergy, and the merchants, and it is intriguing to wonder whether it inspired Sir David Lindsay of the Mount, brother of the Preceptor of Torphichen, to write his famous *Satyre of the Thrie Estaites*, because it was first performed at Linlithgow Palace before King James and all of his court as the highlight of the Christmas celebrations at Epiphany 1540 in the same way as William Shakespeare wrote *Twelfth Night* on another similar occasion to entertain the English court. Lindsay's play was of course meant to do much more than entertain by alerting the King to the condition of Scotland and to the immorality of the Church in particular, but this it failed to do. The Reformation followed, and when the Lords of the Congregation descended on Linlithgow, they proceeded not only, as we saw earlier in this chapter, 'to cleanse' St. Michael's Church, but also stormed into the Palace where they smashed the statues above the original east entrance to the couryard before storming up to the royal chapel where, tragically, they destroyed all of the figures of the saints, leaving behind only the empty niches which we see today.

The royal chapel does however still contain many items of interest, from the carvings above the niches which survived the attentions of the Protestant wreckers and which depict castles and palaces, to those below which show little cherubs playing a whole variety of musical instruments. Also on the walls can be found several consecration crosses, while above the entrance door on the outside wall is a carving of a bishop's mitre and to its right the holy water stoup. As with all churches and chapels in medieval times, the palace chapel was built facing east so that worshippers could kneel in prayer facing towards the Holy Land, and it was at the east end that the high altar was situated against the wall separating it from the vestry, where the priests robed before the services.

Most intriguing feature of the chapel is, however, the very unusual window set high on the inside wall. There are various explanations of its purpose. It was definitely deliberately cut on a slant, so it may have been a leper squint similar to the one mentioned in the chapter on Torphichen Preceptory and the one to be seen in St. Michael's Church situated in the wall behind the font, but would there have been lepers actually within the Palace? It seems that this may have been the case, for Robert the Bruce believed that he suffered from this dread disease, and although it may not have been the same as the leprosy still sadly found in third world countries in Africa and Asia to this day, many Scots in the Middle Ages certainly feared that their skin troubles were related to it. The little room behind the window would indeed have provided space for several of these unfortunate sufferers, and from the way that the window is constructed they could definitely have seen all that was going on at the high altar, without themselves being seen, which would thus have satisfied the demands of the Church that they take part in worship without contaminating the other worshippers including the King and Queen.

An entirely different possibility is that this was a guard window, but to what purpose? The obvious suggestion is that it was intended to be manned by a bodyguard armed with a bow, to stand guard over the King when His Majesty was at his most vulnerable kneeling in prayer during the Mass. But would an assassin not have been stopped long before reaching the inner sanctum of the royal chapel?

This leads to the third suggestion, that it is indeed a guard window, but a guard window similar to the one in St. Mary's Church at Queensferry, which enabled the priests to keep guard over the supplies of communion wine.

James V certainly appears to have been less welcoming to

casual visitors to the Palace than his father James IV, because one of his first acts when he was old enough to rule for himself was to order the construction of a wall between the Palace and the town and the building of the Outer Entry, whose gateway can still be seen and admired. James also appears to have had a good conceit of himself, because he took the opportunity to have carved upon it the coats of arms of the four orders of chivalry to which he belonged. One shows the lion rampant with, below it, St. Andrew on the cross. This was the coat of arms of the Order of St. Andrew, which subsequently became known as the Order of the Thistle. Another shows the English Order of the Garter, with St. George slaying the dragon. Next comes the Order of the Holy Roman Empire, and its depiction of a sheep with a golden fleece is a reminder of the importance of the wool trade in medieval Europe. Finally, and appropriately next to St. Michael's Church, is depicted the Order of St. Michael, with its golden fleur de lys, whose order of chivalry was awarded to the Scottish king by France, with whom Linlithgow had so many links during the 'Auld Alliance'.

Both of King James V's wives came from France. The first, the Princess Madeleine, never saw Linlithgow Palace which, in keeping with the old tradition, her royal husband had given to her as a wedding gift, because she died after only two months in Scotland, all of which she spent at Holyrood where she was buried amongst scenes of great mourning and at which it is said the colour black was worn for the first time at a Scottish funeral, so intense was the grief of the citizens of the capital.

James V again turned to France for his second queen and this time married Mary of Lorraine, or Mary of Guise as she is usually known, who was to become mother of Mary Queen of Scots. When she reached Linlithgow she appears to have been truly thrilled with her palace wedding gift, because she is said to have ·announced that it was more 'princely than any of the chateaux in the whole of France'.

It was to France that Mary of Guise sent her baby daughter Mary after the death of James, to keep her safe from the threatened 'rough wooing' of the English, and it was there that the young Mary grew up, and was married and widowed before returning to Scotland and her battles with John Knox and the Protestant Lords. While Mary was growing up in

France, her mother, perhaps not unnaturally, surrounded herself with French friends, servants and soldiers, and it is said that many of the French-sounding place-names in the Linlithgow area came into being at this time. The palace stables, for instance, were always too small, and most of the horses had to be farmed out to graze, and to this day one of the estates is still known as Champfleurie, the Field of Flowers, while the spot to which Mary of Guise and her followers rode for their picnics is still known as Champany from 'La campagne', the countryside.

When Mary Queen of Scots did eventually return to Scotland, she paid four visits to Linlithgow. The first was in 1561, only three weeks after her arrival at Holyrood. In 1565 she and Darnley stayed while marching to Glasgow to put down the revolt of the Earl of Moray and the Protestant Lords. A year and a half later Mary spent her last night with Darnley at Linlithgow, when they stopped there on their way back to Edinburgh and his violent death the next night at Kirk O' Field. Mary's last visit to the palace came on 23rd April 1567, the night before she was abducted by Lord Bothwell.

Mary's son, James VI, came first to Linlithgow in 1579 when he was twelve. He stayed for only one night, but he got to know the Palace much better during his third visit in 1585, when he stayed for much longer because of the plague which had broken out in Edinburgh. Five years later in 1590, when James proposed to Princess Anne of Denmark, he maintained the tradition of offering Linlithgow as a wedding gift, and Danish court officials arrived 'to tak' sasine' of the Palace, and a banquet impressive even by Linlithgow standards was given on May 15th to make a suitable impression on the visitors.

Next year James duly brought his new bride to Linlithgow to show her her gift, and they paid routine visits over the next decade, but after 1603 and the Union of the Crowns with the departure of the king for the court in London, the Palace was sadly neglected. In 1607 the roof of the North Quarter fell in and the inner wall developed such a list that the Earl of Linlithgow wrote warning the King that it 'looked as if at any moment the inner wall shall fall and break your majestie's fountain'. For ten years, however, nothing was done – until 1617 when James made his one and only royal visit to Scotland following the Union. After so many years without its accustomed royal activity there was great excitement in Linlithgow about the return of the King. As he entered the High Port, dominie William Drummond suddenly appeared before him dressed as a lion and delivered a poem of welcome, which he had composed.

That night James and his court dined royally in the great hall of the Palace, or the Lyon Chamber as it was called, but why it was so called is not explained. One suggestion is that there was a huge tapestry depicting a golden lion rampant hanging on the north wall, but there is also a strong possibility that a real lion was once kept in a cage at the top of the old main stair leading into the hall, as was the fashion at the English court, where the royal collection of animals gifted by diplomats and housed at the Tower of London provided the origin of London Zoo. While there is no actual evidence of a lion ever having been kept at Linlithgow Palace, it is known that James IV did start a royal menagerie and that the pride of his collection was two Scottish wolves.

On his return visit to Linlithgow, James VI saw for himself the damage which the years of neglect had wrought and ordered that the whole of the north wing should be reconstructed. Stone was obtained from Kincavill Quarry on the road between Linlithgow and Winchburgh and the work was carried out at a cost of £4901–19–2. Along with carvings of the thistle and the rose to symbolise the Union of the Crowns, James's initials, using the Latin 'I' instead of 'J', were carved above many of the windows, but James did not live to see the fine new guest bedrooms which the new wing provided, served by three turnpike or newel stairways, because he died in March 1625 before returning to Scotland ever again.

He was succeeded by his son King Charles I, and again there was great excitement in Linlithgow when news arrived that he was to make his first royal visit in July 1633. The Scottish Privy Council sent out an order to Linlithgow Town Council to supply sufficient food for the King and his retinue, including twenty-four well-fed young oxen, and they also ordered that the local lieges be strictly forbidden 'to slay, sell, buy or eat any kind of partridges, black cocks, earth hennes, termigants, caperecailzies and muirefoullis', as all of these game birds would be required to ensure that there were enough dainty dishes to set before the king.

The visit of King Charles not only interfered with his subjects' diet, but with their household arrangements too. They were ordered to provide 'clean, handsome and neat lodgings for the King's attendants', and to make certain 'that the bedding should be clean and well smelled'. Both the insides and outsides of the houses had to be put in good order, for it is recorded in the town records that Nicol Townis, owner of a thatched tenement which was in a disgraceful condition, was ordered to slate the roof, while the old school near the Palace was also to be repaired.

At the Palace itself, a large number of masons, quarriers, wrights and labourers made last-minute repairs, including the cleaning of the stonework of the famous courtyard fountain. New matting was laid in all of the rooms to be used by the King, and the royal apartments were all freshly plastered and decorated. Among the local tradesmen involved in the preparations were the local baxters or bakers who were summoned to assist the palace cooks. Even the beggars who usually frequented Linlithgow's streets were affected by the royal visit, as they were ordered not to be seen on pain of a sound whipping while the King was in town. The beggars were apparently not the only blot on the landscape which the Provost and Magistrates wished to hide from the royal eyes, because they also decreed that no middens must be visible and that all filth must be removed from the streets. In addition the roads over which the King would travel had to be repaired, and Tam Dalyell of the Binns was delegated to supervise this work, with powers to force all of the local farm labourers to provide the necessary manpower. Many of the roads were little more than causeways of stones fit only for pack-horses, and these had to be widened to allow the royal carriages to use them. King Charles had several of these large cumbersome heavy coaches, but he also had a vast quantity of baggage, and as mentioned in the chapter on Livingston, he ordered his subjects throughout Linlithgowshire – as West Lothian was then known – to supply him with carts and sufficient horses to pull them. In all, over 600 horses were requisitioned, and at daybreak on July 1st 1633, the whole cavalcade set out from Holyrood to make the twenty-mile journey to the first halt on the royal progress at Linlithgow Palace.

As the royal carriage appeared beneath the arch of the High Port, the two town drummers, clad in new scarlet uniforms, beat out a tattoo, and as the crowds cheered, the royal retinue rounded the Cross Well and travelled east into the grounds of the Peel and on into the Palace itself. For one night all of Linlithgow's royal style returned as Charles lorded it over the feast at which roast ox was the highlight. Then next morning he departed for Stirling. Linlithgow's long-awaited royal visit was over, and Charles was to go down in history as the last monarch ever to sleep at the Palace.

Seventeen years later in 1650, following the execution of King Charles by the Roundhead government in 1649, Linlithgow Palace survived an occupation by Lord Protector Oliver Cromwell and his soldiers, but almost one hundred years later it was not so lucky when, during the Jacobite retreat in 1746, it was occupied by the government dragoons under General Hawley. On the night after the Battle of Falkirk, they grazed their horses beside the palace fountain which only a year before had run with wine to welcome Prince Charles Edward Stuart, and they lit fires to keep themselves warm as they camped in the courtyard. Next morning, either by accident or by intent, they failed to put out the fires, and within hours of their departure in pursuit of the Prince, the Palace was engulfed in a blaze which caused such extensive damage that it was never restored.

Even as a ruin, however, Linlithgow well lives up to Sir Walter Scott's description of it in *Marmion:*

'Of all the palaces so fair, built for the royal dwelling,
In Scotland, far beyond compare, Linlithgow is excelling.'

D

CHAPTER 4

Blackness, the Binns and Hopetoun

Visit Blackness Castle and you immediately discover how it got its name. To reach it on its rocky site on the shores of the Forth it is necessary to drive right along the long narrow promontory, 'ness', 'nez' or nose of black basalt whose seaward end it dominates.

What is not so clear is why Blackness was built as Scotland's only ship-shaped castle, poised with its graceful stone bows jutting out into the waves, as if ready to set sail like a medieval man o' war on the very next high tide. According to the Ancient Monuments experts of the Department of the Environment, Blackness acquired its strange shape simply because of its geographical situation, but according to local tradition, there is a much more romantic tale to tell. According to this version Blackness with its tall Main Mast Tower and its lofty Stern Tower, which just as aboard *The Great Michael* or any other Scottish warship housed the captain or governor's quarters, was deliberately built in the shape of a ship in order to fulfil a promise to the king.

The promise was made by Archibald Douglas to King James V after the latter had appointed him Lord High Admiral of the Scottish Fleet. Involved in the customary battles against the English King, James was anxious that his Scottish navy should be as active as possible and was appalled to learn that his new Lord High Admiral could not go to sea because he was always violently seasick. Enraged, the King threatened to dismiss Douglas, but Douglas wished to avoid this fate at any cost, not because of any masochistic love of the sea, but because of the rich harvest which he was enjoying selling positions in the Scottish navy. Some quick thinking was called for and the crafty Douglas promised King James that if he allowed him to retain office as Lord High Admiral, then he in turn would provide Scotland 'with a ship that the English could never sink': Blackness was the result.

Whether or not this story is true, it is certainly correct that

The Stern Tower added to the impression that Blackness Castle was like a stone galleon ready to sail out into the River Forth. The smooth green lawn was originally a treacherous salt sea march, which added greatly to the castle's defences.

Blackness not only looked like a stone battleship but made full use of the sea for its defences as the Forth made an ideal natural moat whose narrow water gate is still intact. Originally, however, Blackness was equally well defended from the landward side, because what is now smooth green lawn was once a saltwater marsh, the safe path across which was known only to the castle garrison.

Even if any enemy succeeded in crossing this treacherous marsh, Blackness still had its strongly fortified yett or main gate to defend it. With its skilfully constructed narrow entrance passages at right angles to each other, the yett in the days before the invention of cannon gave Blackness complete protection against the use of battering rams, while each sharp corner gave its defenders a position to fall back to in the unlikely event of the gate ever being forced.

A much more likely fate for Blackness, as with every Scottish castle, was that it might be besieged, but here again Blackness was well provided for with an inner courtyard to store food and a freshwater spring to provide a plentiful supply of water from the well. As such a suitable site for defence it is possible that Blackness has been fortified ever since Roman galleys berthed in the bay to supply the legionaries and the auxiliaries at work on the Antonine Wall, which began a short way up the river at Carriden, which means the fort on the hill.

During the peaceful Norman conquest of Scotland, the lands of Carriden came into the hands of a noble French family called the De Viponts, and it is possible that the castle was built by them to defend their estate. By the fourteenth century Blackness was in the hands of the Douglas family who by the reign of King James II were strong enough to menace the power of the Scottish throne. This threat as far as Blackness was concerned was ended in 1443 when the castle was seized from the Douglases by Chancellor Crichton, who was the king's governor of Stirling Castle.

This led to one of the most intriguing incidents in the history of the castle when Crichton drew up his will and left his prize not to his eldest son, but to the King. Young Crichton was furious and, determined not to be robbed of Blackness, imprisoned his father there and threatened to defy the King. James could not let this situation go unchallenged, and so in 1453 began the famous siege of Blackness, including the use of ships, so that the castle could not be provisioned by sea. But in the end Blackness proved too strong even for the King, and James was obliged to negotiate, Crichton only agreeing to surrender the castle in exchange for the 'lands of Strathurd'.

Even once Blackness was in royal hands, the fear remained that this powerful stronghold on the Forth might yet again be seized by the king's enemies, and so during the childhood of James III, to prevent any such possibility, it was decided that the castle should be demolished. This delighted the merchants of Blackness because they had for long been protesting about being forced to pay a kind of medieval danger money for the protection of their harbour and ships by the castle; they were now given permission to recoup some of this by utilising the stones from its battlements to build a new pier. Fortunately for

Blackness Castle derives its name from the long promontory of black basalt on the tip of which it sits, surrounded by the waters of the River Forth.

the castle, however, this right was rescinded before any damage was done.

Just how important Blackness was can be judged by the amount of manoeuvring there was for its possession during the reign of Mary Queen of Scots. Throughout her childhood in France the castle was garrisoned by French troops, who held it despite two attacks by Mary's enemies. On another occasion it was the French soldiers who went on the attack, when they sailed across the Forth 'and spoulzeit several of the Fife touns', before returning to Blackness with considerable booty.

Later in her reign, in 1573, Sir James Kirkcaldy brought over from France one year's income from Mary's French dowry to try to help the Queen's cause in Scotland, but could not deliver it to Edinburgh Castle as he originally intended because it was being besieged by the supporters of the young Prince James, and so he brought the money to Blackness, where he believed the governor was loyal. Unfortunately the governor saw the money as his opportunity to buy his pardon from the Regent Morton, and so without hesitation he changed sides and clapped Kirkcaldy in irons. Once the governor rode off with his prize, Kirkcaldy managed to persuade the soldiers to revert to their original support for Mary and to set him free, when he in turn imprisoned the governor's brother who had been left in command.

When Regent Morton heard this news, he decided to enlist the help of Kirkcaldy's wife to recapture the castle. Acting on Morton's instructions, she rode the eighteen miles from Edinburgh to Blackness where her delighted husband entertained her to a banquet in the Stern Tower, but despite the lateness of the hour she declined to spend the night and insisted that she must return to the city. It needed little persuasion to convince Kirkcaldy that he should accompany her on the first part of the journey and that he should take most of the castle garrison as an escort, but they did not ride far, because as they rode up the steep hill at Mannerstoun on the outskirts of Blackness, they were ambushed by Morton's men led by Captain Andrew Lambie.

As Kirkcaldy cursed his ill luck and his foolishness in being lured out of his castle stronghold, he was even more devastated to see his wife allowed to ride free and to realise that she had been party to the plot to capture him. Despite being imprisoned in Edinburgh Castle, Kirkcaldy managed to escape, and shortly afterwards Lady Kirkcaldy was found strangled, murdered in her own bedroom, a deed for which her husband was later executed.

For two hundred years Blackness was used as one of Scotland's state prisons. Many of its captives were religious prisoners, ranging from Cardinal Beaton to John Knox's son-in-law, the Rev. John Welsh. Welsh was one of the six leading Scottish clergymen imprisoned by King James VI for daring to claim that they had the right to meet in general assembly without his presence. Even after months shut up in Blackness they refused to acknowledge the King's prerogative, and their defiance enjoyed much popular support, Lady Culross assuring them that 'the darkness of Blackness was not the blackness of darkness'.

Religion in the Scotland of the sixteenth and seventeenth centuries was clearly a troublesome business. Gilbert Brown, Abbot of New Abbey, was lodged in the Main Mast Tower and accused of being a 'trafficking and seducing Papist'. Then in

1624 it was the turn of an Edinburgh Bailie, William Rigg, to be imprisoned for daring to challenge the teachings of the Episcopalian Church. His was not a lone voice, however, and soon a whole stream of Covenanting prisoners were to experience the dank horrors of the dungeons of Blackness, most graphically described by Adam Blackadder, son of the famous Covenanting leader, who wrote of a dungeon 'full of puddocks and toads'. This may well have been the most dreadful of the cells at Blackness, the Black Pit, which was situated right in the bows of the castle jutting out into the Forth and into which the river water flooded at every high tide, not to drown the prisoners, as some tales would have it, but to provide the only means of primitive sanitation.

One of the longest-serving prisoners in Blackness was Lord Ochiltree who was kept captive there for twenty years for having dared accuse the Duke of Hamilton of treason, his sentence only being cut short when Blackness was taken by Oliver Cromwell's soldiers when they invaded Scotland after the execution of King Charles I in 1649. It was during their occupation of the castle that one of the most dramatic incidents in its long history took place. Some munitions exploded, not only blasting a massive hole in the thick stone battlements, but according to local legend leading to the appearance of the Devil himself.

By a coincidence it was as an explosives store that the castle ended its active career, because although there is no truth in the popular belief that the Act of Union of 1707 guaranteed the garrisoning of Blackness, soldiers were based there until after the end of the First World War, and its comparatively remote situation made it ideal as a munitions base. The munitions could also be transported by sea, and the pier at which the ships carrying them berthed can still be seen. At one time a miniature railway carried the explosives from the berth into the castle, but today the pier, like the castle it served, lies in ruins.

Such is not the case with the neighbouring village pier, because it has recently been restored by the B.B.C., the Blackness Boat Club. While today the pier is used solely by the club's members for their pleasure craft, this was certainly not always the case, because Blackness in the sixteenth century was one of Scotland's busiest harbours, second in importance indeed only to Leith.

Blackness owed much of its business to the fact that it was the out port for Linlithgow and many of its imports were destined for Linlithgow Palace. These ranged from timber for the palace roof to fine arras cloth for its walls and from fine rich red claret to a fresh-caught sturgeon for its famous feasts.

To store both imports and exports while they awaited transport, the Guild of Linlithgow Merchants built a huge three-storey warehouse on the shore immediately behind the pier. It was called the Guildry, a name still borne by the hideous block of modern flats built on its site on the river side of Blackness Square when the historic old building was torn down by West Lothian County Council during the 1960s.

Such insensitive treatment of Blackness was not always the case, because in the Middle Ages, although Linlithgow was only three miles away, the Provost and Magistrates of that Royal and Ancient Burgh deemed Blackness so important that they decreed it should have its own official, the Baron Bailie. Today the post still exists and is faithfully renewed annually on the First Tuesday after the Second Thursday in June, when the lieges of Linlithgow loyally ride down to Blackness as part of their annual Riding of the Marches, despite the fact that local government re-organisation in 1975 hijacked the old port and placed it incongruously in Central Region.

As the Provost's party, the Dyers and all the others riding the bounds arrive in the square at Blackness, they are welcomed by the Baron Bailie, who duly dispenses the traditional Blackness Milk, which is a much more potent drink than that usually supplied by the local dairy herds, as it is liberally laced with whisky.

Then after delivering his annual report on the progress and welfare of the village, the Baron Bailie is re-appointed to rule for another year. Things were not always so peaceful, because in past centuries the Baron Bailie was kept very busy keeping the peace between the sailors who frequented the little port, and he had powers ranging from the imposition of fines right through to ordering floggings to deal with crimes which in their turn ranged from discharging ballast into the harbour to smuggling.

Smuggling was a particular problem because Blackness was a tobacco port and was at one time headquarters for the Mitchell family before they established themselves in Glasgow. For Blackness, tobacco was an export cargo rather than the import which might have been expected. This came about because of the British Navigation Laws, which insisted that all goods from Britain's colonies had to pass through this country no matter what their eventual destination.

Tobacco from Virginia and the West Indies was therefore imported through the Clyde by the Glasgow tobacco barons, carried right across Scotland in large panniers strapped to the backs of pack horses and re-exported through Blackness to the Netherlands where it was manufactured into excellent Dutch cigars. Unfortunately for Blackness its once prosperous trade suffered a whole series of blows. First, despite vigorous protests from Linlithgow, the custom house at Blackness was closed and its officers transferred to the newer and better harbour at Bo'ness three miles up river. Next the far distant American War of Independence meant that the former colonies need no longer heed the old British Navigation Laws and so could send their tobacco direct to the Continent, and then the completion of the Forth and Clyde Canal resulted in what little remained of the transshipment trade being switched to its eastern terminal eight miles upstream at Sealock — or Grangemouth as this upstart port soon became known. Finally the government excluded Blackness from the limited list of British ports to which it restricted tobacco trading in an effort to stop smuggling.

Mention of smuggling reminds us that local lore in Blackness still maintains there is a secret tunnel from the village all the way to the Binns, the home of the Dalyell family, which overlooks it from its hilltop vantage point. The Binns takes its somewhat unusual name from this setting, for it is derived from the Gaelic Bens and Beins meaning hills. According to local tradition it has been a place of occupation ever since Pictish times, which would of course tie in with the other tradition that these early inhabitants of Scotland always insisted on building their homes on solid rock, because the hilltop rock did indeed outcrop in the Binns kitchen before it was paved with flagstones.

The House of Binns takes its name from its hilltop site overlooking
the River Forth. 'Binns' is a corruption of the Gaelic 'Bien' meaning
hill. The house was given to the National Trust for Scotland by Mrs.
Eleanor Dalyell in 1944.

The real story of the House of Binns begins in 1612 when
the lands of Binns and Mannerstoun were sold by Sir William
Livingston, who had himself bought them only thirteen years
earlier from James, Lord Lindsey. This time the purchaser was
one Sir Thomas Dalyell, and it was the last time that the House
of Binns was ever bought or sold, because it is the Dalyell
family home to this day.

The original Tam Dalyell was the son-in-law of Edward
Bruce, Baron of Kinloss and Master of the Rolls, in which last
capacity Bruce accompanied King James VI to London following the Union of the Crowns in 1603. Fortunately for young
Dalyell, Bruce took him with him. Thus Dalyell became one of
'the Hungry Scots', as the English courtiers contemptuously, but
at the same time perhaps rather enviously, nicknamed the
newcomers from the court at Holyrood, because of their
obvious eagerness for power and position. For Dalyell the move
to Scotland Yard was a definite success, because he was
appointed Depute Master of the Rolls, and it was with his new-
found wealth that he purchased the Binns and was able to
finance the complete reconstruction of the house, which is
aptly described in the Second Statistical Account of Scotland as
'An irregular mass of building, garnished with turrets'.

It was this fine new house which his son and namesake, the famous or infamous General Tam, persecutor of the Covenanters, inherited. While 'Bluidy Dalyell' as he was nicknamed by his enemies is inevitably remembered for the relentless and allegedly often cruel ways in which he hunted down his fellow Scots who would not obey the King and use the Book of Common Prayer, it is clear to any visitor to the Binns that there was another side to this famous Scot besides that of the harsh though efficient soldier. For it was the same General Tam who was responsible for much of the beautiful decoration of the Binns which survives to this day and which, including ornate plaster ceilings, makes it one of Scotland's finest stately homes. At one time Dalyell even hoped for a royal visit from King Charles I, the monarch whom he served so loyally, when he made his only tour of his northern kingdom in 1633. Italian plasterers were summoned to the Binns to decorate what was to be the royal bedchamber, but unfortunately for Dalyell he carried out his task of ensuring that the road from Edinburgh was so improved for the royal retinue that the King was able to travel direct from Holyrood to Linlithgow Palace without the hoped-for overnight stay at the Binns. Although Charles never slept in it, however, the royal bedchamber is still there to be admired by modern visitors, including recently Anneka Rice in the popular Channel 4 television programme, 'Treasure Hunt'.

As well as being a man of excellent taste, General Tam was also a scholar, and at the Binns he amassed what was in its day one of the best libraries in Scotland which, as one contemporary noted with awe, 'required a ladder to reach all of the books'.

Outside too, General Tam devoted much time to improving his family's estate, including the establishment of a walled garden and the planting of copses of deciduous trees, whose offshoots still survive, not just to improve the look of his lands, but to provide shelter belts for the beasts and crops which he actively encouraged his tenant farmers to have.

But inevitably, despite these kindlier aspects of General Tam's character, it is the many relics connected with his more violent side that attract visitors to the Binns. Most famous are probably his huge leather riding boots in which, when wet, rainwater is said to have boiled and bubbled after a particularly hot pursuit of the Covenanters. His comb also survives, recalling his heartbreak combined with fury when he learned of the execution of King Charles in 1649 and his immediate vow neither to cut his hair nor his beard until the monarchy was restored. Dalyell was always a man of his word and this comb must indeed have had long locks to keep tidily under control during the eleven years of Cromwell's Commonwealth, which as a loyal royalist Dalyell spent in exile at the Russian court at St. Petersburg, as Leningrad was then known, until the restoration of King Charles II in 1660.

Largest of the relics connected with the General is the massive marble-topped table on which he is said to have played cards regularly with the Devil. At one of these nightly gambling sessions the Devil is alleged to have lost heavily and, being a notoriously bad sport, lost his temper and threw the table top right out of the house. It remained lost for over 250 years until early one misty summer morning at the beginning of this century some troopers of the General's famous old regiment, the Royal Scots Greys, which he founded at the Binns in 1681, were watering their horses at the pond at the foot of the long entrance drive. As it was an exceptionally dry summer, the water level was unusually low, and as their horses drank, to their surprise they saw a large object just below the surface. Intrigued, they succeeded in harnessing their horses to it and dragged it out to discover that it was the long-lost marble table-top. Since then it has occupied a place of honour in the Binns entrance hall, where despite official pronouncements by experts on antique furniture that it is definitely not of General Tam's age, it is still much admired by the house's many visitors as a memento of his dealings with the Devil.

Another story which is always told is of another blazing row which the two had which resulted in Auld Nick threatening to blow down the Binns. Dalyell decided to take no chances, and so he summoned his estate workers and ordered them hurriedly to build protective walls. As soon as they were complete the Devil returned and, looking them over, declared, 'Well now, I'll just have to huff and puff harder and blow down your house and your guid new walls'. 'Oh no you won't,' retorted Dalyell, 'For I'll build a turret at every corner to pin down my walls', and to this day there are still walls and at every corner turreted towers, which appear to serve no useful purpose!

Despite his alleged arguments with the Devil, the Covenanters were still convinced that it was Satan who made Dalyell impervious to their best-aimed bullets and that it was definitely no coincidence that his name began and ended with D and L and was pronounced in the way that it was. 'To each his own', declared the Covenanters and insisted that the Devil tutored his disciple at the Binns in the latest of torture refinements, whether it be roasting his prisoners alive in the big oven which can still be seen in the kitchen or crushing them with the dreaded boot, and it is true that Dalyell is always credited with introducing the terrible thumbscrews into Scotland.

With all these links with the supernatural, it is not surprising to learn that the ghost of General Tam still returns to haunt the Binns when, mounted on a grey charger of the type ridden by the troopers of his famous Scots Greys, he enters his estate by the Black Lodge on the road between Bo'ness and Queensferry, rides across the ruined bridge over the Errack Burn, gallops up the winding road to his old home and dismounts in the middle of the dining room, which is not as strange as it seems, for it is built on the site of what was originally the courtyard.

The General's choice of point of entry is also appropriate because, although changed many years ago, the Black Lodge was where the main entrance was in his day, and when it was still in use in Victorian times many coachmen insisted that their horses often tried to bolt at this spot because of some unseen presence.

Further east at the new main entrance at Merrilees, the same pond where the marble table-top was found is also said to be haunted by a kelpie or water fairy, but the oldest and most persistent of all the Binns ghosts is very appropriately one of the site's original inhabitants, the Picts, who appears in the shape of a small brown-clad figure gathering wood on the hillside near the Binns Tower.

Like everything else at the Binns, there are stories attached to the tower, which is a well-known landmark in the area and can easily be seen from the M9 motorway. According to one version there was always great rivalry between the Dalyells and their immediate neighbours the Hopes of Hopetoun House, whom the Dalyells always looked upon, despite their grander home, as upstarts who had begun life as butter merchants in Edinburgh's High Street. None the less the Dalyells liked to know what their neighbours were up to, hence the building of the tower so that they could spy on all that was going on. Another version is that the Dalyells and the Hopes had a friendly wager as to who could spend £20 in the most useless way and that the Binns Tower was built as a result.

Today, although the tower is not open to the public, it is included as a point of interest on the excellent nature trail which the National Trust for Scotland has laid through the attractive grounds, and it is the Trust's flag which flies from its turreted top as a reminder of the Trust's pride in the fact that the Binns was the first private house in Scotland entrusted to its care. This came about in 1944, when Lady Eleanor Dalyell presented her home to the Trust, while at the same time retaining the right of residence for her family, the right to appoint the steward for the estate and, most intriguingly of all, the right to the long-lost Binns treasure, should it ever be found.

One last tradition connected with the House of Binns is that just so long as there are apes on the rock of Gibraltar it will remain British, and so long as there are peacocks at the Binns it will happily remain the home of the Dalyells. Each spring the number of eggs hatched by the peahens in the shadow of the old grey walls of the Binns seems to increase, and the peacocks strut its lawns apparently completely undisturbed by the ever-increasing numbers of visitors, so it seems that the present Tam, the controversial Labour Member of Parliament for Linlithgow, his ever-popular wife Kathleen, daughter of retired Scottish Law Lord, Lord Wheatley of Scottish local government re-organisation fame, and their two children, can look forward to many more years in residence.

One feature of the Binns, which is shown to all visitors, is the doorway and the flight of stairs which leads down into what is believed to be one end of the tunnel which, as mentioned earlier, is said to link the house with Blackness, but no-one has investigated since one of the Dalyells' pet dogs went down during the 1930s and was never seen again.

Even without the tunnel link, however, it does not take long to get back down to the village, past the 'small holdings,' the neat little cottages each with its two or three acres of ground, which the government established during the 1920s to rehouse some of the many servicemen returning from the First World War. Down the hill on the bend at the entrance to Blackness itself is another reminder of the Great War in the shape of the little village church with its unusual steeple, which was built as a place of worship for the sailors of the Royal Naval ships moored out in the Forth. At first it was an Episcopalian church, but now it shares its minister with Carriden Parish Church in Bo'ness. The model sailing ship hanging from its ceiling is a last reminder of its seagoing origins.

For a time in Victorian days it seemed that Blackness might become one of the newly popular seaside resorts, and several holiday homes were built along the shore of its West Bay, mainly by Falkirk businessmen who looked upon it as a weekend getaway, but probably because of its limited sands it did not develop. During the 1920s and '30s Blackness was a popular choice of day visitors, especially from neighbouring Bo'ness, whose miners held their annual summer sports on the grass beside the East Bay. A footpath linked the town with the village, and many Bo'nessians walked along the shore to enjoy a pint at Blackness Inn. That inn was sadly destroyed by fire, but mine hosts Jim and Valery Slavin have succeeded in bringing a surprising amount of traditional atmosphere to its modern whitewashed replacement.

Hopes that Blackness would become a holiday village were again revived after the Second World War, when the hillside to the east was considered by Butlins, but in the end that organisation's Scottish holiday camp went to Heads of Ayr, and the coast between Blackness and Hopetoun was left entirely undeveloped.

Hopetoun, the home of the Marquess of Linlithgow, was begun in 1696 by architect Sir William Bruce of Kinross, and the west facade of the house still represents his work, but no sooner was it completed than the Hopes decided in 1721 to have their home completely redesigned as one of the new-style Georgian mansions and hired Scotland's most famous architect,

This aerial view of Hopetoun House, home of the Marquess of Linlithgow, clearly supprts its claim to be the most impressive stately home in Scotland. The west front is by Sir William Bruce, 1699-1701, and the east front by William Adam and his sons (1721 onward). Picture courtesy of Hopetoun House Preservation Trust.

William Adam, to do the job. He created Scotland's first Georgian stately home, whose interior was completed in similar style by his two sons, Robert and John. The full splendour of Hopetoun is best appreciated by approaching it from the east, entering the estate by the Queensferry gates on the shores of the Forth just past Fisheries Cottage on the road to Society. From this direction, seen across its smooth green lawns with their ha-ha or hidden ditch to keep out straying animals, the perfect symmetry of its main block and its two curving wings can be seen to full advantage. To the left stands the magnificent ballroom, and it comes as something of a surprise to discover that the equally impressive block which balances it at the end of the right-hand wing houses the stables. But in a way this is appropriate, because the ballroom was originally an indoor riding school, and the fact that so much space was originally devoted to horses is a reminder of just how important they were in past centuries, a theme of the Museum of the

Scottish Horse, which is now one of Hopetoun's permanent attractions. At Hopetoun there was a class structure even amongst the horses, with three standards of stables for riding horses, carriage horses and the work horses of the surrounding estate and its farms.

Life in the big house itself was equally 'upstairs, downstairs', with the public rooms and the bedrooms belonging to the family and their guests on the ground and first floors, and the kitchens and servants' rooms in the basement and attics.

A broad flight of stairs leads up to the main entrance, but a later look at one of the oil paintings inside the house, which intriguingly shows the plans for its conversion to Georgian style, shows that this is one feature of the house which for some reason was never actually completed, as the original idea was to have the stairs finish with sweeping curves to north and south.

The entrance hall at the top of the stairs with its portraits of past members of the Hope family is a link between the original late seventeenth-century house and the subsequent Georgian one, and just as outside some licence is used with the painting of imitation windows to create a perfect symmetry, here inside some of the doors are not what they at first sight appear. Here in the light and airy entrance hall with the real doors open is the best place to view the vistas which Adam aimed to create looking out along the drive to the east and in the other direction through the Garden Room and out across the pond to the west.

Although the Garden Room with its wood-panelled walls is quite large, it in turn seems quite intimate compared with the adjoining Parade Room with its vivid red and gold decor. It was here that King George IV held court at the reception which was a highlight of his Scottish tour in 1822. The visit was so carefully stage-managed by Sir Walter Scott that it was indeed appropriate that Sir Walter's knighthood was bestowed on that occasion shortly before the monarch embarked to sail back to London. All of the original furniture for the Parade Room is still there designed to sit against the walls, leaving the whole centre of the room clear for guests before or after dinner to perambulate or parade, thus giving this room its name.

The Yellow Drawing Room takes its name from the yellow

silk brocade which adorns its walls. It is one of the finest examples of the Adams' work as interior designers, and the ceiling with its covered cornice, its rococo spandrels and its gilded frieze decorated with animal masques is one of the most ornate in the country. Of particular interest is the fact that many of the furnishings are·the originals specially designed for Hopetoun House by Scottish carpenter James Cullen, whose work rivals that of the English master craftsman, Thomas Chippendale.

Hopetoun's Yellow Drawing Room is an art gallery in its own right, with most of the most famous works of art in the house decorating its walls. The canvasses include 'The Grand Canal, Venice' by Canaletto, Rubens's 'Adoration of the Shepherds', a large hunting scene which is thought to be by Titian, and several smaller but equally interesting works by the Dutch artists Teniers and Backhuysen.

As was the fashion of the time, other rooms at Hopetoun did not have set purposes, but as they are furnished at present the State Dining Room, the Library and the Royal Bedchamber are amongst the most impressive, while the little counting house with its iron door to protect the estate's cash and documents contains many interesting papers about what life was like for the Marquess, his family and servants in past centuries. Many of the Hopes did not spend all of their careers at Hopetoun, but served their country by becoming Governor-Generals and Viceroys in Australia and India, and these aspects of the family's history are well illustrated in the museum, one of whose most unusual exhibits is a stuffed emu. This bird was brought home from Australia and roamed the grounds for many years at Hopetoun before it eventually died.

Today Hopetoun does not boast anything quite as exotic as an emu, but the estate, which can be viewed in its entirety from the rooftop outlook post, does possess peacocks, tumbler pigeons and other ornamental birds as well as its famous herds of red and fallow deer and its flock of St. Kilda sheep, all of which can be seen by following the well laid-out nature trail.

Someone who undoubtedly would have fully approved of the interest which is taken in the birds, beasts and plants of Hopetoun is Dominie Dawson, who for no less than forty-three years was the estate's schoolmaster, for he was long before his time in introducing his young pupils to nature study and what would nowadays be called environmental studies. Dawson came to Hopetoun from his first school at Cupar in Fife and soon astonished the estate workers, because instead of teaching their children in the dark cramped schoolroom next to Abercorn Church, as his predecessors had laboriously done, he led them forth Pied Piper-like about the estate teaching as he went. All of the children were encouraged to gather items on these nature walks, and back in the classroom Mr. Dawson encouraged them to push aside the desks and benches to make room for displays of their finds. As Dominie Dawson's unusual methods became well known, regular visitors to Hopetoun House were persuaded to bring back exotic items which in turn were used by him for object lessons.

After school too Dawson was well ahead of his time, organising extra-curricular activities ranging from swimming in the Forth at the little beach at Society to fishing trips. Dawson's informal approach did not, however, mean that his scholars lacked discipline, for they knew full well that 'the maister' could wield the tawse as capably as his fishing rod. 'Be careful to check the smallest acts of disobedience and you will never be troubled with any great ones', he wrote, but while he was quite prepared to make his presence felt and strap his new pupils into shape, he eventually had his own unique method of abolishing corporal punishment, as is described by his niece Jean Butler. For in her biography of her uncle she wrote, 'One day in school an interesting and amusing ceremony took place. The faithful tawse which had proved such a useful ally during the first few months were declared to have served their purpose and outlived their usefulness and were solemnly cut in pieces, some of the girls carrying away the bits as trophies of a bygone age'.

Any doubts which parents might have had about their dominie's unusual approach to both lessons and discipline, so very different from the strict formal methods of neighbouring masters in Bo'ness, Queensferry and Linlithgow, were dispelled at the annual inspections when the parish minister at Abercorn and the whole of his kirk session turned up to examine the bairns and expressed themselves entirely satisfied with the results, however much the methods broke with tradition.

In 1874, however, Dominie Dawson's freedom to teach in his own way was suddenly threatened when the government decided to standardise Scottish education, and inflexible dictates about the curriculum and methods were issued by the Scotch Education Department in far-off London. Many of the old-style dominies decided to resign and accept the pensions which they were offered rather than try to adapt to the new regime, complete with its intimidating inspectors, but Dawson, despite complaining 'that it is now expected that children shall be regularly turned out by the gross like so many little human vessels duly warranted to contain a certain amount of knowledge', stuck to his post.

Despite complaining that he had been reduced 'to nothing more than a grant earning machine', Dawson still managed to bring his own flair to the methods insisted on by the new Department of Education and opened an hour early each morning to gain time for his own ideas, without endangering his pupils' chances in official tests. His determination paid off, because in the first official inspection he was granted 'the highest possible grant for discipline and organisation'. He was also rewarded by the building of the fine new grey Gothic school building at White Quarries on the main Bo'ness to Queensferry road, which still serves Hopetoun Estate and the surrounding area to this day. Soon after its completion in 1878, Dominie Dawson found himself with more pupils than ever before, because of the opening of a shale mine adjacent to the school, which brought an influx of miners' families. These rough tough youngsters were a new challenge for the now ageing schoolmaster, but he met it just as he did many others, including the education of a young Turkish boy who was a guest at Hopetoun House. Dawson taught on in the new school for twenty-one years until he finally laid down his chalk on September 11th 1899.

Abercorn, where Dominie Dawson taught for a lifetime, is one of the oldest parishes in the country, the monastery of Aebercurnig is mentioned several times by the Venerable Bede, and it was the residence of a bishop from as early as the seventh century. According to Bede, in 696, when Aegfrid,

King of the Northumbrians, whose kingdom included Lothian, was slain in battle with the Picts, Bishop Trumuini, who then held the see, considered Abercorn too close for comfort to the Pictish lands across the Forth in Fife and evacuated the monastery until more peaceful times should return.

At this time Abercorn also had a castle, a simple square stone-built peel tower standing on a green mound. In 1176 a dispute took place between the keeper of the castle, John Avendale, and Richard, second Bishop of Dunkeld, regarding the patronage of the parish as the monastery had died out by then. The claim of the Bishop triumphed. By 1160 the whole church, with its lands belonging to the Bishop of Dunkeld on the south shore of the Forth, including Abercorn, Cramond, Preston and Aberlady, were erected into a Burgh of Barony called the Barony of Aberlady.

Next century the estate of Abercorn passed by marriage into the hands of the Graemes and was held by the patriot John the Graeme, who as a supporter of Sir William Wallace fought and died at the Battle of Falkirk in 1298. The estate then became the property of the Black Douglases and suffered the fortunes of that great house as they challenged the Stewarts for the right to the Scottish throne. After repeated attacks it was besieged by King James II in 1455 and taken by storm on 8th April. The supporters of the Douglases were slaughtered and Abercorn Castle destroyed, never to be rebuilt.

The Stewarts gave Abercorn to Claud Hamilton, the first Viscount Paisley, third son of the Earl of Arran. During the reign of Mary Queen of Scots the Hamiltons remained loyal to the Queen, and their lands including Abercorn were consequently forfeited, but Abercorn was restored to them by Mary's son James VI when in 1606 he created the first Earl of Abercorn. From this family it then passed in turn to the Mures, the Lindsays and the Setons and was sold by Sir Walter Seton in 1678 to John Hope, father of the first Earl of Hopetoun.

Although the monastery at Abercorn died out, it continued as a parish church, parts of which have Norman characteristics, although most of it dates from after the Reformation and it was largely renovated in 1838, when it was floored for the first time, the walls lathed and an early form of central heating introduced. The minister at that time was the Rev. Lewis Irving and, writing in the Second Statistical Account of Scotland in 1843, he says that 'it forms a comfortable place of worship, nearly adequate to the wants of the community. There are no sittings let, the whole, with exception of the private seats of the heritors, being allotted to the parishioners. The church bell, of considerable size, and handsome workmanship, presented by a naval gentleman, was formerly the bell of a Danish ship of war and formed part of the spoil at the Battle of Copenhagen at which Lord Nelson is said to have turned his telescope to his blind eye and thus by refusing to withdraw turned what looked likely to be a defeat into one of the most important victories of the Napoleonic War. A communion roll, embracing all the members, has been kept since 1832 and regularly revised by the kirk-session, previous to the dispensation of the Lord's Supper, which takes place twice a year. The number on the roll is at present 390; the average number of communicants at each time is 350. The kirk-session consisting of the minister and seven elders, has, for seven years past, revived the custom, once maintained in the parish, of holding stated diets for prayer once a month. This practice proves a benefit in many respects.'

Abercorn today is a very peaceful spot and as well as the old church other features of interest include the burial vault of the Dalyells of the Binns, which was erected in 1623, and the graveyard, which contains many interesting tombstones, carved with the tools of the trades of those buried below as well as two very unusual hog-backed stones, both decorated with fish scales.

Just below Abercorn on the shores of the Forth is the strangely named hamlet of Society. Today it is a very popular summer picnic spot, but the little inn which existed at this point on the shore in Victorian times has long since disappeared. Amongst the inn's patrons were no doubt the crews of the little sailing ships which used to be beached in this sheltered cove to land cargoes of coal for the fires of Hopetoun House and to take on limestone from the Hopetoun Estate. Possibly it was the trade in coal which gave Society its name, because the sailors may well have said that they were delivering fuel for 'the society folk', meaning the Hope family.

While the Hopes had their coal delivered to what was

virtually their private harbour at Society, when the family acquired their first car the Marquess arranged with the grocer in the neighbouring village of the Newton to stock gallon cans of petrol for him, and the cans were brought all the way from Leith once a week by horse-drawn cart. As a result of the Hope family's early interest in motoring the grocer soon acquired one of the first petrol pumps in Britain, which was erected outside his whitewashed village store, so that today the adjoining filling station is proud to boast that it is the oldest in Scotland.

The Newton, of course, means The New Town and takes its name from the fact that it grew up very rapidly a hundred years ago to house the sudden influx of miners and their families, who came to the district to work in the newly sunk Whitequarries Shale Mine. The stone-built miners' rows, which still line the main street, were much superior to the brick-built miners' rows of Bo'ness, and the shale oil company was insistent that they should be described as cottages. While the rows or cottages have survived along with the homely little village inn, the Duddingston Arms, the church where they worshipped on the Sabbath in the neighbouring hamlet of Woodend fell into disuse and has been demolished.

From the Newton the road continues east along the crest of the hill, providing spectacular views out across the Forth to Scotland's only Royal Naval Dockyard on the opposite shore at Rosyth in Fife and straight ahead to Queensferry's two famous bridges. Shortly before the road dips down to Queensferry, on the right-hand side can be glimpsed Dundas Castle, the private residence of Sir Stewart Stewart-Clark and his family. The original castle, which is now a ruin, is believed to have dated from the eleventh century. Several additions are known to have been made to it around 1416 when it was turned into what was described at the time as a fortalice by warrant of Robert, Duke of Albany, and by a subsequent warrant issued by King James I in 1424. At this time its massive walls were raised to a height of seventy-five feet. The castle was the stronghold of the Dundas family, who traced their ancestry back to the reign of King David I, when one of their ancestors obtained a charter to these lands from the King. Twelve generations later, James de Dundas died without a male heir and was succeeded in 1450 by his brother Sir Archibald. His son and successor became a confidant of King James III and an ambassador to the English court. In 1488 James rewarded him by making him Earl of Forth, but sadly for Dundas, the King died before placing the royal seal on the warrant and it was deemed invalid.

From then the lands of Dundas passed through another twelve generations of the family until in 1792 the family line seemed doomed when Captain Dundas drowned at sea, when the East India Company's merchantman *Winterton*, of which he was in command, ran aground on the coast of Madagascar in the Indian Ocean. Happily, however, six months later in January 1793 his wife gave birth to a son, James. It was James who decided to replace the old castle of Dundas with a fine grey stone Victorian mansion, and the much larger accommodation which it offered was no doubt greatly appreciated, because his wife, Lady Mary Duncan, daughter of the naval commander who became a national hero by winning the Battle of Camperdown, bore him a family of eleven: six sons and five daughters!

CHAPTER 5

The Queen's Ferry and Dalmeny

Call it Queensferry or, like the locals, simply The Ferry, but never South Queensferry, because according to its inhabitants The Royal and Ancient Burgh of Queensferry should never be insulted by being prefixed by a direction. Queensferry takes its proud title from Queen Margaret, the Hungarian princess who was shipwrecked at this point on the shores of the Forth when a great gale blew her tiny sailing ship completely off course while she was attempting to sail home to her native land after a visit to the English royal court in the year 1069.

Margaret was accompanied by her brother, Edward Ethling, thus explaining the place name Port Edgar, where the marina is situated right below the span of the Forth Road Bridge, just to the west of the town, while the other local place-name, Echline on the hill above, where the modern primary school bears the name, is said to be a corruption of Ethling.

Once ashore, Margaret and Edward naturally enquired about the Scottish royal court, and on being told that it was at that time in Dunfermline they asked to be ferried across to the Fife shore, thus making the first crossing of what was soon to become known as the Queen's Ferry. Having landed at what is still known as Queen Margaret's Hope, they wasted no time in reaching the Scottish court, where it appears to have taken Margaret not a great deal longer to capture the heart of King Malcolm, because the following year he married her and made her his queen.

Once wed, Queen Margaret soon made her mark not only upon her husband Malcolm Canmore, but also apparently upon all of his nobles, whose manners she is said to have felt left much to be desired. Margaret is indeed credited with originating the rather strange custom of sewing buttons on the sleeves of gentlemen's jackets, a fashion which she is said to have instigated to prevent them wiping their noses and their mouths on their cuffs. Much more importantly, she also decreed that they should stop worshipping in the time-

The Forth Railway Bridge, completed in 1890, has a total length of 1½ miles, at its highest is 360 feet above high water mark and at its deepest 80 feet below the surface, and took 5000 labourers seven years to build using 81,000 tons of steel. Painting it is a non-stop operation which has given the language a phrase for a job which is never done: 'It's just like painting the Forth Bridge'.

honoured manner of the Irish Celtic church and instead adopt the practices of Rome, a move which later resulted in her sanctification and the creation of a shrine to her holy memory in Dunfermline.

Queen Margaret also wanted to win over the people of Scotland and so to convert them to the new ways, she established a free ferry across at Queensferry to take them to the shrines at Dunfermline and St. Andrews. At first the oarsmen were monks from Dunfermline Abbey, and this practice continued until the Reformation, with money for the upkeep of the ferry coming from the offerings collected in the church. Queen Margaret herself made many crossings at the ferry on her way to and from Edinburgh Castle, where her little stone chapel with its whitewashed interior still stands right on top of the rock, overlooking the city and the Forth.

Alexander I made his most famous crossing of the Forth in 1123, when he was caught in a fierce gale. Buffeted by the wind, the little ferry was swept down river, until just as the King was sure he would be drowned, it was driven ashore on the island of Inchcolm. There he was looked after by the island's only inhabitant, an old hermit, who gave him shelter in his small stone cell, which can still be found just to the west of the centre of the island. The hermit fed him on shell fish, until in the end the gale died down and the King was rescued. To show his gratitude Alexander gave orders for an abbey to be built on Inchcolm, which from then on was often known as the Iona of the East. The extensive ruins of the Augustinian monastery, which earned Inchcolm this title, are well worth a visit to explore the covered cloisters, the strangely shaped chapter house and the long, low, little church itself, and this can be easily done during the summer season either by ferry from Aberdour or, following in King Alexander's wake, aboard the *Maid of the Forth* sailing from the Hawes Pier at Queensferry.

Another king who was not as fortunate as Alexander I was his namesake Alexander III, who reached the pier at Queensferry late one dark and stormy night. The ferrymen were not at all keen to sail and pleaded with the King to rest the night in Queensferry and continue his journey next morning when the weather had calmed down, but Alexander was eager to get home to his young French wife who was waiting for him at Kinghorn and demanded that he be rowed across. Despite the wind and the waves the ferry made it to the other side and the King rode off along the Fife shore, but just beyond Burntisland in the dark and the wet his horse stumbled and he was thrown, falling to his death over the cliffs at Pettycur, only one mile from Kinghorn and his queen.

Alexander III's death plunged Scotland into many years of strife, but although more peaceful times had come by the reign of James VI, the weather was still as stormy as ever when, in 1617, he tried to cross at Queensferry. The occasion was James's only tour of Scotland after going south to London following the Union of the Crowns in 1603. The river was rough and unwelcoming when the royal party reached the shore at North Queensferry, but anxious to reach the comparative civilisation of Holyrood before nightfall, the King insisted on making the crossing. The ferry carrying James did reach the southern shore in safety, but one of the accompanying fleet of small boats was sunk and several of his courtiers were drowned. Immediately rumours sprang up that the boat had also been carrying the royal treasure chest, thus creating a Scottish version of how King John lost his silver on the Wash.

By this time, following the Reformation and the consequent disappearance of the priests from Dunfermline Abbey, the rights to operate the ferry had been divided into sixteen parts, each of which gave its owner the right to operate one vessel on the crossing. Just how busy the ferry became can be judged from the fact that the first turnpike road in Scotland was constructed to provide a good fast link from Queensferry to Edinburgh. To travel on the new turnpike which ran north-east from the city through the village of Mutton Hole, as Davidsons Mains was then known, it was necessary to pay tolls, so the payment of charges to cross the present Forth Road Bridge has a historic precedent.

While the road to Queensferry was improved, the ferry itself deteriorated and complaints reached their climax after the year 1784, when it was decided that the rights to operate the ferry should be put up for annual public auction, as a result of which the boatmen whose bids were successful were more interested in making as much as possible during the forthcoming year than in providing a decent service. Passengers complained that the piers, especially at the New Halls Inn, as the Hawes Inn was then correctly called, were in a ruinous condition and that there was no superintendent of either the piers or the boats. They also complained that the temptations of the nearby inn were often too much for the ferrymen, who apparently spent the fares which they earned in hard drinking bouts, with the result that they were often drunk when in charge of the ferries. But most annoying of all to travellers in a hurry was that there were frequent occasions when no boats were available at Queensferry, because all of the ferrymen lived in North Queensferry on the other side.

The outcome of all this discontent with the running of the ferry was that in the end an Act of Parliament was passed in 1809 to regulate the Queensferry Passage, and from then on it

A panoramic view of the two Bridges, the Cantilever Railway Bridge (1890) to the right and the Suspension Road Bridge (1964) to the left. This is the view from South Queensferry looking north to Fife.

was very well managed with not one, but two, superintendents. It was also laid down that the ferrymen would never be called up to serve in the Navy, and that soldiers in uniform as well as those on their way to enlist in the Army would always be offered free passage. This privilege was also extended to licensed beggars, while a tariff of fares was published for other passengers and also for their animals. For the hire of a small boat by day the charge was half a crown, but if a traveller arrived after dark, then the charge doubled to five shillings. Most importantly, the Act of Parliament laid down that ferries must always be available at all hours of the day and night and that no more than two-thirds of the boats must be at the same side at the same time.

The biggest change of all at the ferry took place in 1821, when for the first time a steamship was introduced on the crossing. Very appropriately it was called the *Queen Margaret*. Built at a cost of £2369, it cost £12.14 a week, including the crew's wages, to operate and was very much the wonder of the age, because not only did she cut the crossing time to only twenty minutes, but when the wind dropped, she could also tow the other sailing boats.

The new steam ferry and the good management ensured by

the parliamentary legislation ensured that the Queensferry Passage was one of the safest in the country, but a serious accident did occur early in Queen Victoria's reign, not aboard one of the ferries, but on the Hawes Pier, when in October 1838 a coach plunged into the water. Despite rescue attempts by boatmen and onlookers, a young lady and her servant, who were its only occupants, were both drowned before they were pulled free.

Four years later in 1842 a much happier event took place on 5th September, when Queen Victoria, accompanied by Prince Albert, made the crossing while on their way to Balmoral. By this time business at the ferry had increased to such an extent that the little *Queen Margaret* had been replaced by what a contemporary account describes as a 'very superior seaboat, the *William Adam,* length ninety-eight feet and breadth thirty-two, which leaves the south side every hour and north side every half hour from sunrise to sunset'. The same account goes on to describe the Queen's crossing as follows: 'The *William Adam* was honoured by conveying Queen Victoria across the firth on her royal progress to the north. The day was most beautiful; the sea covered by numerous steamers and boats, gaily adorned; indeed the whole scene was calculated to make a great impression, not speedily to be forgotten. It is understood that the Sovereign expressed the greatest satisfaction with all the arrangements made on board the steamer. Mr. Mason, the superintendent took the helm, while the attentive skipper, Charles Roxburgh, attended to the other duties.'

By coincidence it was another Mr. Mason, Mr. R.A. Mason, who over a century later on 4th September 1964, as superintendent of the ferry, made all the arrangements and accompanied our present queen when, after making the first official crossing of the new Forth Road Bridge, Her Majesty sailed back from North Queensferry to the Hawes Pier on the last crossing made by the modern electric paddle steamer *Queen Margaret.* Thus the ferry started by a queen crossing the Forth, ended with a queen making the same passage.

Now the once familiar smartly painted black and white ferries, *Queen Margaret, Robert The Bruce, Mary Queen of Scots* and *Sir William Wallace,* with their broad car decks, and all the smaller ferries which preceded them are only memories, but in a way it is surprising that they lasted so long, because since the start of the nineteenth century there had been many attempts to replace them with a fixed link of some type.

In 1818, for instance, Edinburgh engineer James Anderson produced detailed plans for an early forerunner of the present Forth Road Bridge. Anderson's idea was to span the river with a chain suspension bridge whose 1500-foot long main spans were to have been constructed of Swedish steel specially treated with linseed oil, which he maintained would keep it rust-free and thus do away with the need for constant painting. The twenty-five-foot wide main carriageway was to have been made of American oak covered with a surface of gravel mixed with sand and chalk, bound together with pitch and tar, and there were also to be footpaths for pedestrians on either side. While Anderson had done his planning well, he had chosen the wrong time to put forward his proposals, which he costed at £175,000, an enormous amount at the time. They were rejected as much too costly for the country to bear, 'as it was still impoverished following the long war against Napoleon'.

A road bridge was not the only alternative to the ferries to be proposed during the nineteenth century. Several Victorian engineers were convinced that a tunnel was the solution, but in the end it was the coming of the railways which got things moving and it was decided that a rail bridge must span the Forth, to open up the East Coast route. At first it was intended that the new bridge would be similar to that already spanning the Tay, but the disaster which befell that structure in 1879, when only two years old, forced the planners back to the drawing board. Instead of the original idea of a railway viaduct, they decided that the way to solve the problem of this long windswept crossing was the now world-famous cantilever Forth Railway Bridge.

For two years before work began on the bridge early in 1893, English civil engineer Sir Benjamin Baker, who gained his knighthood for his efforts, conducted painstaking experiments on wind pressure using sets of gauges installed on the shores of the river. These experiments convinced him that the pressure of 56 lbs per square foot specified for the design by the committee set up after the Tay Bridge was blown down was

The intrepid skill and daring of the 'spidermen' who spun the support cables of the new Forth suspension road bridge between the years 1958 and 1964 is truly captured in this view, taken 500 feet up by official bridge photographer, John Doherty. One of the four former car ferries is seen below. Courtesy of John Doherty.

'considerably in excess of anything likely to be realised' and that it was therefore safe to go ahead with the actual construction, which was entrusted to Sir William Arrol, who was also knighted for this his greatest work.

Building the bridge took seven years, during which 54,000 tons of Siemens-Martin open-hearth steel, the strongest steel in the world, were fabricated in workshops specially built at Queensferry and erected by a labour force of 5000, who

Crowds streamed over the new Forth Road Bridge on its opening day on Friday 4th September 1964. Her Majesty Queen Elizabeth, accompanied by the Duke of Edinburgh, performed the opening ceremony, and after crossing the bridge returned across the river on the final voyage of the ferry *Queen Margaret*. Courtesty of John Doherty.

completely swamped the little town's native population as well as those of neighbouring villages such as Dalmeny and Kirkliston, where many of the men were housed because it was easier to transport them to their work out on the bridge each day from these places, which were on a higher level than the Ferry itself. It was at this time that Kirkliston gained the nickname of 'cheese town' because huge quantities of cheese had to be imported into the village every week to feed the largely Irish labour force.

The spans were built out over the river as balanced cantilevers each reaching out from a main pier, the twelve-foot-wide circular struts being erected plate by plate using two-ton hydraulic cranes. As the bridge began to take shape like a giant Meccano set, it attracted thousands of sightseers every weekend, and when it was eventually completed there was great excitement as the Prince of Wales arrived to perform the opening ceremony. Officially he did so by driving home the final gold rivet, but the bridge had cost so much that the rivet was gold in colour only, a brass one having to suffice.

Someone who would have liked to see the whole bridge finished in gold was Edinburgh writer, Stewart Dick, who in his book *The Pageant of the Forth* declared that to finish it with 'the cheapest possible coat of red lead' was an insult and that it should be completely redecorated with a gilt finish: 'It is a strange thing, he wrote, 'that so wonderful a monument of engineering skill as the Forth Bridge should be so unsightly. Perhaps in the future some modern engineer will design a bridge that is beautiful as well as strong'.

Fortunately no-one else appears to have agreed with Mr. Dick, and the new Forth Bridge became one of the wonders of the Victorian age, with its constant painting passing into the language as an example of a task never done. A tradition also grew up that it brought good luck if passengers threw pennies out of the carriage windows and over the side of the bridge into the river below, a custom still kept up by some travellers, much to the delight of Queensferry schoolchildren, who regularly comb the shore to supplement their pocket money.

The Forth Bridge received worldwide publicity in the 1930s when Alfred Hitchcock, with an undoubted eye for spectacle. chose it as the setting for John Buchan's hero Richard Hannay's escape from the train in the first film version of *The Thirty Nine Steps*. As the train screeched to a halt in the middle of the bridge Hannay, played by Robert Donat, was seen clambering out onto the girders high above the Forth and the scene proved so effective that although it does not appear in the original novel, it was featured again in the second film version made during the 1950s, with the late Kenneth More in the hero's role.

The bridge's adventures changed from fiction to fact in

1939, when it became the scene of the first German bombing raid of the Second World War. German spotter planes were sighted high over the Forth early on the morning of Monday, 16th October and vanished as fast as they had appeared, but shortly after two o'clock that afternoon the City of Edinburgh Squadron, based at R.A.F. Turnhouse, was scrambled to intercept a whole flight of enemy bombers heading in over the North Sea. Within minutes City of Edinburgh Squadron's Spitfires were all in the air, ready for the coming action.

According to the following day's *Scotsman*, 'The first contact between the R.A.F. machines and the enemy raiders took place off May Island, at the entrance to the Firth of Forth at 2.35 pm, when two enemy aircraft were intercepted'. From then on a series of dogfights developed as the Spitfires tackled the German Heinkel HE IIIs and Dornier DO 17s. Two were brought down in the sea, off Crail and off Port Seton, but at least ten more of the bombers droned on dangerously up the Firth.

At Queensferry the air-raid siren wailed into life for the first time to warn of a real raid, but most of the town's inhabitants thought it was only another practice and stood staring skywards as the first of the planes duelled high above the Forth Bridge. While the local people were convinced that it was only a practice, the stationmaster and his staff at Dalmeny decided to take no chances and halted the Edinburgh to Fife passenger train. As a single bomber roared overhead and flew on high above the cantilevers of the bridge, they raced along the length of the train urging passengers to leave the compartments and take shelter in the station buildings, but few heeded them.

Then the air-raid siren at Queensferry police station in the High Street sounded the all clear. Slowly the train pulled out of Dalmeny Station and proceeded out onto the bridge just as the main body of German bombers appeared overhead. As the horrified passengers watched, the Germans released their bombs, but fortunately for those aboard the train their target appeared to be the cruisers *Southampton* and *Eden* and the destroyer *Mohawk* which were at anchor just downriver from the bridge, and not the bridge itself.

So harried were the Germans by the Spitfires that fortunately most of their bombs landed in the river, but one struck home, hitting the bows of the *Southampton,* thus making her the first naval vessel damaged in the war. The bomb did little actual harm to the *Southampton* herself but it sank the Admiral's barge and a small pinnace which were moored alongside, while flying shrapnel injured three of her crew. More sailors aboard the neighbouring *Eden* and twenty-five men on the deck of the *Mohawk* were also injured, bringing the total casualty list to thirty-five.

As the train continued across the bridge, however, its passengers were delighted to see several Spitfires in hot pursuit, and two more bombers were brought down, one over the Pentlands by the fighters and the other over the woods behind North Queensferry by anti-aircraft guns. As the train reached the Fife shore this bomber exploded in flames.

While the Germans on this occasion had not apparently been after the bridge itself, it was their target on many other occasions during the next five years as they appreciated full well its vital importance as a communications link, but they were always thwarted by the R.A.F. and by the giant grey barrage balloons which were erected to give it added protection. Desperate for a propaganda coup, the Germans therefore determined to fake a photograph showing that they had scored a direct hit on the famous bridge, and this they did very cunningly by publishing an out of focus picture of the bridge, printed upside down, so that Inchgarvie Island could be described as the explosion caused by the German bomb!

Despite the Germans the Forth Bridge survived the war, but by then the clamour was for a road bridge, as even with petrol rationing road traffic had increased so much that cars and lorries were having to wait up to two or three hours to make the crossing at peak times. During the 1930s several plans had been put forward, not only for a bridge, but yet again for a tunnel and for the first time for an imaginative barrage dam.

Under the slogan of 'Dam the Forth' the barrage was the brainchild of two well-known Bo'ness businessmen, architect Matthew Steele and owner of the Viewforth Hotel, John Jeffrey. The advantages they claimed for their dam were many and varied, but during the work-starved years of the 1930s one of the most persuasive was their contention that building a dam would provide far more jobs for the thousands of miners and other local men who were on the dole than the erection of a bridge. They pointed out that a bridge would be built of steel, which would be manufactured outside the area and that the steel would have to be erected by skilled men brought specially to Queensferry, probably from England. On the other hand, Mr. Jeffrey and Mr. Steele claimed that building a huge barrage dam, besides providing thousands of jobs for unskilled labourers, would create work for West Lothian miners as thousands of tons of whinstone would be required to form the barrage. They also pointed out that many more men could have been given work levelling the district's many old coal and shale bings to provide additional material for the dam, which they planned should span the river almost on the same site as that used for the road bridge.

Behind the dam the water level was to be controlled so that it would always be several feet above the natural highwater mark, and the Forth from Queensferry to Stirling would thus have been transformed into an enormous artificial lake. All the ugly black mudflats which mar the beauty of the river at low tide would have been covered and, as a hotelier, Mr. Jeffrey had visions of his manmade lake becoming a popular water playground for the whole of Central Scotland. As on the Swiss lakes and on the River Clyde, small steamers would have provided cruises, while fast motor launches would have provided regular waterbus services to the picturesque little villages on either side of the Forth, such as Culross and Dunmore, which would have become popular holiday spots whose mud-silted harbours would have been given a new lease of life by the raising of the water level.

During the 1930s, when the dam project was being discussed, seaplanes were much in the news, and as part of their campaign Mr. Jeffrey and Mr. Steele pointed out that the huge artificial lake behind their barrage would make an ideal landing place for these planes whose passengers would have been ferried ashore to a terminal at Blackness Bay. With talk of war filling the air, they were also careful to stress that their proposed dam would not damage Rosyth as a royal naval dockyard, as even the largest warship would have been able to sail through the locks which they planned to build in the centre of the barrage to raise vessels from the river level to that of the lake above.

Another advantage which Jeffrey and Steele claimed for their project was that the water dammed up behind the barrage could have been used to create hydro-electric power for all in the towns in the Forth Valley and that the millions of gallons of water would also have been available for industrial use, which would have been a big inducement to bring new factories to West Lothian, Stirlingshire, Clackmannanshire and West Fife. This use of the water would not have spoiled the amenity value of the lake, as purification plants would be built. The constant high water available in the lake to the west of the dam would also have been a great advantage for the docks at Bo'ness and Grangemouth as it would have meant that even the largest ships were able to enter or leave port without any costly delays waiting for the right tides. Deeper water, it was stressed, would also be of great benefit to the Grangemouth Dockyard Company as it would enable it to launch much larger ships.

Thus, at the same time as creating a fast dual carriageway road between West Lothian and Fife across the top of the barrage, the dam would endow the whole Forth Valley with many other advantages, but the coming of war in 1939 put a sudden end to the whole idea for which Jeffrey and Steele had campaigned so hard at meeting after meeting throughout the preceding decade.

When peace came in 1945 the idea was not revived, but recently there have of course been suggestions for barrages across the Solway, Morecambe Bay and even in the English Channel, with many of the arguments of the two Bo'nessians advanced in their favour, so possibly they were just before their time, and much more farsighted than their critics in the 1930s gave them credit for.

From 1945, however, the drive was on to build a road bridge, but it was not until 1964 that the dream was realised and the 'Highway in the Sky', as it was nicknamed at the time, became a reality. When it was opened amidst amazing crowd scenes which resulted in Scotland's largest-ever traffic jam, the Forth Road Bridge was the longest in Europe and the fourth longest in the world, although it has now been outdistanced by the

Humber Bridge and Portugal's Salazar Bridge across the Tagus at Lisbon. But the Forth Road Bridge is still a very impressive sight with its 3,300 foot-long slender central span slung from its two 512-foot-high main towers. On either side are spans measuring 1340 feet, each with a southern approach viaduct of 1437 feet and a northern viaduct of 842 feet, making a total length to this modern engineering marvel of just over one and a half miles.

The four-lane carriageway or road deck is suspended by steel wire rope hangers from the two main cables which stretch in one length of 7,000 feet from the northern to the southern anchorage and pass over the tops of the two main towers. These towers, the tops of which workmen can reach by express lifts, are made up of welded steel units fastened together with large high-strength alloy steel bolts. The cables consist of some 12,000 galvanised high tensile steel wires, a fifth of an inch in diameter, which were hung in position one at a time, bundled into strands, secured at the anchorages and finally compacted into a circular shape two feet in diameter. The road deck provides two roadways twenty-four feet wide as well as two cycle tracks nine feet wide and two footpaths six feet wide and at its lowest point is one hundred and fifty feet above high water mark on the river below. All of the traffic is monitored by closed circuit television cameras from the bridge headquarters at the southern end, where the toll plaza is also situated. Beneath it lies a giant electric blanket to prevent ice forming and do away with the risk of skidding.

Queensferry is to some extent inevitably overshadowed by its two famous bridges, but it is well worth descending from the viewpoint at the Road Bridge car park to explore the long High Street with its two level terraces, reminiscent of Chester's famous Rows. Oldest building is that of the Priory Church of St. Mary of Mount Carmel, with its unusual stone-flagged roof dating back to 1441, when James Dundas of nearby Dundas Castle gave a piece of his land, 'lying in the toun of the Ferry, for the church of St. Mary the Virgin and for the construction of certain buildings to be erected there in the form of a monastery.' He also gave money to build the church and monastery on condition that prayers be said for 'the souls of the grantor and his wife and ancestors and successors', and this wish is still faithfully honoured twice a year at the Patronal Festival of St. Mary on 16th July and again on 1st November, All Souls' Day.

The Priory became a house of the Carmelite Order, and in addition to their usual daily round of worship and their gardening, farming and teaching activities, the friars at Queensferry maintained a hostel for travellers delayed by bad weather; the rocks just to the north of the monastery show traces of cutting to form a landing stage. In 1560, at the time of the Reformation, the last Prior, Thomas Young, handed back the buildings and the land to the Laird of Dundas, and this action was later confirmed by a charter signed by Mary Queen of Scots on 8th April 1564.

During the seventeenth century the old church was used for worship by the townsfolk of the Ferry from 1610 until 1635, when they moved along the High Street to their own Parish Kirk, a plain stone building, which although no longer used for worship, is also worth visiting. After the move by the congregation, the chancel of St. Mary's continued to be used as a burial place by the Dundas family, and the remains of the church still contain several interesting Dundas memorials, including a carved coat-of-arms on the east wall and a tombstone slab, dated 1608, in what is now the Baptistry, where the font is also dedicated to the memory of several members of the Dundas family, as are several of the stained-glass windows, installed when St. Mary's was restored in 1889 mainly through the efforts of Bishop Dowden of Edinburgh for the use of members of the Episcopal Church in Scotland.

Sadly, by this time all of the domestic buildings of the monastery, its cloisters and the nave of the church had been demolished, their stones carried off no doubt over the years to be used as building materials for houses along the High Street, but architect John Kinross made an excellent job of preserving and utilising all that remained. This consists of the chancel with its impressive high-pitched vault, the rectangular tower and the south transept, which was originally a side chapel and which now houses the Baptistry, whose fine font with its panels of the four Evangelists and its carved angel cover were designed by the late Sir Robert Lorimer. Another interesting feature of the church is the little guard window, which looks down from the tower into the chancel and from which one of the friars could keep watch to make sure that no one dared steal the communion wine or — worse still — the sacred communion vessels from their little stone cupboard to the left of the altar. On the right-hand side of the sanctuary can be found the *piscina* or sink, where these communion cups were washed after use. The stone *sedilia* or clergy seats can also be seen built into the wall.

St. Mary's is beautifully furnished and obviously very lovingly cared for, and many of the modern items, which so well complement its ancient treasures, are also well worth looking at. These range from the chairs made specially by Gordon Russell Ltd., which are similar to those which the firm designed and produced for Coventry Cathedral, and the other furnishings designed by Ian Lindsay, consultant architect for the fabric, to the oil painting of the Scapular Vision. This work of art by Donald Gorrie, which hangs to the left of the chancel arch, depicts the most important incident in the history of the Carmelite Order, which occurred after the failure of the Crusades forced the Friars to leave their Church of the Blessed Virgin on Mount Carmel in the Holy Land and to wander throughout Europe, dedicating in each place where they settled another church to St. Mary of the Mount. During this difficult time in their history their Prior-General, St. Simon Stock, prayed for a sign that the Carmelite Order would survive, and on 16th July 1251 his prayers were answered, when the Holy Mother appeared to him in a vision and, touching his scapular or shoulder cape, promised her special protection. Although this incident took place in England, the painting in St. Mary's at Queensferry includes many local touches, including the tower of the church and St. Margaret landing from a ferry boat.

St. Mary's close connections with the river are also recalled by the crest and ensign on display beneath the tower, for these came from H.M.S. *Temeraire,* a naval training establishment whose young members always worshipped in the church until they moved to Dartmouth in 1960, on which occasion they presented these mementos. Outside in the centre of the garth or monastery gardens, in the centre of what were once the cloisters, lies an anchor, and it very fittingly symbolises the place which this unusual church has occupied throughout the centuries in the life of Queensferry. Outside too on the right-hand side of the most easterly of the windows on the south side is a Mass Dial, a special sundial, used for regulating the times of services, before the invention of clocks, and a reminder perhaps that it is time to move on further along the High Street.

To the east on the other side of the street stands Queensferry's oldest occupied dwelling, Plewlands House. A typically Scottish stone-built L-shaped mansion with its newel stair tucked neatly into the angle of the arms, it was originally an impressive home for one of the burgh's richer families, but when it was restored during the 1950s it was divided into several flats. While some overlook the High Street, others have windows facing the Loan, the steep lane which leads down the hill from the high ground behind the town and joins the High Street at this point. In the little square opposite can be found the strange carved stone which gives Ferry folk their nickname of the Bell Stane Birds. From the square other dark narrow lanes lead on down to Queensferry Harbour. One is called Covenanters' Lane, a reminder of how these hunted men used to hide in the cellars and attics of the harbourside homes until the tide and the wind were right to allow one of the sailing ships to slip out of the harbour and carry them to the safety of Protestant Holland, until the coast was clear for them to return to Scotland to continue their fight for freedom to worship as they wished.

These steep harbour lanes were also ideal hide-aways for Queensferry's famous smugglers, whose haunts included the shoreside inns such as the Stag's Head and the Queensferry Arms as well as their own headquarters, the Black Castle, which still stands on the other side of the High Street and from which local legend insists a secret underground tunnel led right down to the river, but it is so secret that no-one can find it now.

While the smugglers plied their trade by night, Queensferry harbour was also busy by day, especially when the shoals of small silver sprats swam up the Forth. 'They'll be up to pay the rent', declared the Ferry folk, because the little sprats always seemed to arrive with unfailing accuracy around 'term time', the 28th of November, when all rents had to be paid and the profits from the fishing were doubly welcome. Nowadays sprats, which are wee cousins of the herring, are usually thought only fit for fishmeal for animal feed, but in the eighteenth and nineteenth centuries there was a very big demand for these little fish for salting. Millions were crammed into barrels each winter season and shipped out to Germany and the Scandinavian countries where they were considered a great delicacy, and the profits provided a rich sea harvest for the fishermen and the fisher-lassies who gutted, salted and packed them in the barrels.

Not everyone, however, welcomed the annual arrival of the sprats, because the catches, as well as providing money to pay the rents, also provided sufficient extra siller to spend on drink, and parish minister Thomas Dimma recorded his grave concern in the Second Statistical Account of Scotland, in which he wrote, 'Though this fish trade is most beneficial to the country at large, it is not favourable to the morality of the town. Forty or fifty carters are frequently in attendance and the consumption of ardent spirits is greatly increased. The carters who are not generally of the most exemplary character, cast an influence around the fishing season, which is most injurious to sound morals. Accidents of a most frightful character have occurred almost every year from the immoderate use of spirits and though there have been deaths both by fire and water, the votaries of dissipation are neither improved nor diminished in number'.

As well as the coming of the carters, the minister's worries were added to by the arrival of large numbers of fishermen from other Forth ports who hurried to Queensferry to seize their share of the shoals of silver sprats. From Fisherrow, Cellardyke, Prestonpans and Buckhaven, Mr. Dimma estimated that as many as a hundred fishing boats jostled for position in Queensferry's congested harbour. To try to ease the chaos on the narrow stone quays, the tax on each barrel of sprats, or garvies as the Ferry folk often called them, was lowered from fourpence if cured on the harbourside to only two pence if they were carted up into the town itself for gutting and salting. But no matter where the sprats were processed, as soon as the day's fishing was over and the catch safely ashore, the crews of all the fishing boats joined the carters and the fishwives to crowd into Queensferry's 'one inn, eight ale houses and four shops with accommodation provided for drinking', which, according to the minister, were 'all most prejudicial to the morals of the people'.

Today Queensferry High Street is still well provided with drinking places, from the new Moorings at one end past the Forth Bridge Hotel and the dramatically placed Seals Craig, situated on its rocky site directly above the shore, to the historic Hawes Inn at the other, but today instead of fishermen and carters, it is tourists and bus tour drivers who crowd their bars and restaurants and those of the streamlined Queen's Moat House, whose windows look out over the whole of the town and the river beyond. No matter where they stay, most visitors want to see the Hawes Inn, because it was there, within its old whitewashed walls, that Robert Louis Stevenson set the famous scene which gave his novel *Kidnapped* its name. Just as his hero David Balfour rode out from Cramond with his scheming uncle Ebenezer of the House of Shaws, so too young Stevenson came out from Edinburgh to visit the Hawes, or the New Halls Inn as it was originally called, and up the stairs on the first floor, the room where he wrote and where he set the meeting between Ebenezer, David and the skipper of the barque on which David was later to be shipwrecked can still be visited, and from its window can be seen the Hawes Pier from which David was rowed out into the firth.

Today one ferry still plies regularly to and from the pier, but it is a private one carrying workers to and from Houndpoint Island, the manmade base just downstream from the Forth Bridges, from which North Sea oil processed at British Petroleum's refinery at Grangemouth and pumped underground to storage tanks at Dalmeny is eventually piped aboard giant tankers to export it to the spot oil market at Rotterdam. This deepwater tanker berth has an unusual link with the Middle East whose oil supplies its millions of gallons of Scottish oil now replace, because its name of Houndpoint comes from a strange ghost story connected with the Moslem Saracen Turks and the Wars of the Cross, or the Crusades.

Local tradition has it that Barnbougle Castle, on the shore opposite, belonged originally to a noble family called Mowbray, whose most famous member, Sir Roger, was a member of the

The Hawes, or New Halls Inn to give it its proper title, at South Queensferry was the setting for the kidnapping of hero David Balfour in Robert Louis Stevenson's famous novel. The Forth Railway Bridge provides a dramatic background.

Knights of St. John. To become a fully fledged member of the order, a Knight had to take part in a caravan, as a Crusade campaign was called, and Sir Roger waited eagerly for the call to travel to the Middle East. The only way to get there was by sea, and as Sir Roger made his way down the rocky promontory beneath Barnbougle Castle to reach the little sailing ship which waited to take him on his journey of adventure, his faithful hunting hound rushed after him. Just as the sailing ship cast off, it jumped aboard and Sir Roger did not have the heart to put the dog ashore, and so it accompanied him all the way to the Holy Land. In Palestine it stood alongside its master in many battles, and Sir Roger and his dog became a well-known sight, until in the end in one battle the knight was cut down and slain. What became of the dog is not recorded, but it is said that on dark winter nights, when winds whip up the

waves on the shore below Barnbougle and gales rage out in the
Forth, its mournful howls are heard as it hunts for its long-lost
master, and so the rocky promontory is called Hound Point.
Usually the hound hunts alone, but on occasion it is accompanied by a white-robed Arab warrior, and when he appears it
is said to augur ill for the family which owns Barnbougle,
because local legend insists that the Saracan Turk has come to
carry off another of its members and that, following his ghostly
visit, one always dies.

   Today the owners of Barnbougle are the Roseberys, but they
do not live in the old thick stone-walled castle on the shore, but
in the much more comfortable and elegant Dalmeny House in
the green parkland behind it. Dalmeny Estate, which stretches
all the way from Queensferry to Dalmeny, was acquired by the
Roseberys in 1662, and the present handsome grey stone
mansion was built for the fourth earl in 1814. It was the first
Gothic Revival house in Scotland, designed by architect William
Wilkins, and it took three years to complete. Dating from the
period of the Napoleonic Wars, it is appropriate that the house
has the best collection in the country of mementos associated
with the French Emperor as well as many interesting items
used by the Duke of Wellington, who ultimately defeated him
at Waterloo. Since Lord Rosebery sold his English home at
Mentmore in 1977, Dalmeny has also housed most of the
family's other famous treasures, and its rooms whose walls are
lined with tapestries and works of art are now open to the
public throughout the whole of the summer season.
   Dalmeny House reached the height of its fame after the
fourth earl who built it was succeeded by his grandson,
Archibald Philip Primrose, in 1868, because the new Lord
Rosebery married one of the world's richest heiresses, Hannah,
daughter of Baron Meyer de Rothschild, and gained further
nationwide publicity when he went on to become one of the
nineteenth century's most prominent Liberal politicians. Despite being excluded from the House of Commons because of
his earldom, in the Lords he earned a reputation as a social
reformer and distinguished public speaker. In 1880 Mr.
Gladstone, the Liberal party leader, came to stay at Dalmeny,
and for weeks it was constantly in the headlines as Rosebery

Dalmeny House, home of the Earl of Rosebery, designed in Tudor Gothic by William Wilkins, 1814-17.

masterminded his famous Midlothian Campaign, which completely revolutionised electioneering techniques, as it brought politics to the people, most of whom had recently been given the vote for the first time.

Gladstone was not Dalmeny's only famous visitor. Queen Victoria herself called at the house overlooking the Forth on one of her journeys to Balmoral, and when in March, 1894, Gladstone resigned as Prime Minister, it was to Rosebery that Her Majesty turned to appoint the new premier. For the next ten years Rosebery battled with the major political controversies of the age, including Home Rule for Ireland, about which he quarrelled violently with his Liberal colleague, Campbell Bannerman. Thus when the Conservatives fell in December 1905 and Bannerman was asked by the King to form a cabinet, Rosebery retired from active party politics and retreated to spend more time at Dalmeny, and his comfortably furnished den is a favourite with visitors. There he spent much of his time writing, including a biography of his old friend Lord Randolph Churchill, father of Sir Winston.

Apart from politics, Rosebery's other great interest was always racing, and his horses won the Derby on three occasions in 1894, 1895 and 1905. A statue of one of his favourites, Old

Tom, now stands opposite the front door of the house, looking out across the fairways and greens of Dalmeny's own private golf course. Another unusual feature of Dalmeny is the public ferry which the Roseberys provide across the River Almond at Cramond, and visitors are welcome throughout the whole year to walk along the whole of the coastal walk, provided they respect the estate and do not picnic. Each March visitors are welcome to enjoy the spring delights of the acres of snowdrops which carpet Mons Hill, and the money raised by these special Sunday openings is devoted to nursing charities.

On a spring Sunday morning it is also pleasant to join the estate workers and the villagers of Dalmeny at worship in their fine Norman church, with its Rosebery family loft. The church is dedicated to St. Cuthbert, the saint to whom Durham Cathedral is also dedicated, and it is interesting to discover from the many masons' marks carved deep in the stones of both churches that the same skilled master craftsmen who built the great cathedral also built this little church in West Lothian. With its little cottages around the tree-lined village green, Dalmeny does indeed look very English, an effect added to by the square tower of the church glimpsed above the tree tops. But the tower is the one feature of Dalmeny Church which is not original as it was entirely reconstructed in 1926 and has been criticised ever since for being out of proportion.

Dalmeny was founded around the middle of the twelfth century and is typical of churches of the period, not only in Scotland, but throughout Northern Europe, with a small apse or sanctuary at the east end, a square chancel, a nave for the people of the parish to occupy, and a western tower. In total it is only eighty-four feet long by twenty-five feet wide at its broadest part. Nowadays it is usually entered by the small west door at the foot of the tower, but originally the main entrance was by the south door, as again was typical of churches of this period, and there are signs that there was once a covered porch. Today the most impressive feature of this south door, and the most ornate feature of the whole of the exterior of the church, is its double curved arch, whose stones depict a veritable menagerie of animals, both real and imaginary. Those which have survived the weathering of wind, rain and frost include a lion, a whale, a pelican and a serpent, while the legendary beasts range from a phoenix to a dragon, and from a serra or sea monster to a griffin and a centaur. There are also several stones depicting people, including one of wild men fighting and one of a king, seated on a throne, in front of which a knight is paying homage. Yet another stone depicts the Lamb of God, but what the whole complicated series means, or whether it ever had a meaning at all or was simply an elaborate diversion carried out by the masons, or possibly their young apprentices, is not known. To complete this impressive doorway, the two semi-circles of carved stones are surmounted by an arcade of interlacing arches, similar to, but more elaborate than, the one above the north doorway of Dunfermline Abbey, where the same masons are believed also to have worked.

Inside the apse and chancel the most interesting features are the roofs, which are vaulted, the ribs being supported by carved corbels at the eaves. These eight corbels are really rather grotesque, depicting the heads of both men and animals. Separating the apse from the chancel and the chancel from the nave are two roughly carved stone arches, each bearing a zig-zag or chevron design. The roof of the nave is today a raftered one, erected in 1766 when a great deal of restoration work was carried out. Originally it was concealed by a plaster ceiling, but this was removed when the most recent restoration of the church took place during the 1920s, as it was considered that the raftered roof is probably more like that built in the twelfth century.

Even more important than the removal of the plaster ceiling was the decision to remove the plasterwork which covered the stone walls. When the walls, which were originally bare, were plastered and decorated is uncertain, but locally it is believed that this was done during the Commonwealth period when Oliver Cromwell ruled from 1649 to 1659. During the restoration of 1926, only one piece of plasterwork was left, as it bears some kind of inscription, unfortunately too indistinct to decipher. What remains is protected by a tapestry depicting St. Cuthbert, St. Bridget and St. Adamnan, to whom it is known altars in the church were dedicated in pre-Reformation times.

The windows at Dalmeny are typical of those found in many English village Norman churches, with semi-circular heads.

The only stained glass in the church is in the little windows in the apse and was a gift after the Second World War from the Polish army officers who had been based in the area for several years as they fought to free their country from the German invaders; a reminder of this is the Polish eagle in the centre window, which depicts the Madonna and Child. On the north side the window shows St. Teresa, while that opposite it on the south side shows St. Margaret.

While the Poles were billeted at Dalmeny and at Linlithgow, where the little shrine to the Madonna which they built can also still be seen in the grounds of Laetare International Youth Hostel, Queensferry played host to the officers of the Free Norwegian Navy. Amongst them was Prince Olaf, and each Christmas a little Norwegian fir tree was smuggled across the North Sea as a reminder that his homeland had not forgotten him, a custom still kept up every year by Scandinavia's best-known shipping line, Fred Olsen Lines, which every December provides free transport to bring the Norwegian tree which is the centrepiece of London's festive decorations in Trafalgar Square.

In Queensferry the Norwegian officers had their headquarters at the Burgh Chambers on the front overlooking the Forth and there too a Christmas tree is still always lit, its lights reflected in the dark waters of the river. It is in August each year, however, that the old Burgh Chambers really come into their own as the setting for the traditional Ferry Fair. Celebrations begin at dawn on the Friday before Fair Saturday with the dressing of the Burry Man. The Burry Man is one of the most intriguing characters in the whole of Scotland's folk anthology, and he always attracts a great amount of attention as he parades the streets of the old burgh throughout Fair Friday. Some people maintain that the Burry Man takes his name from the Royal and Ancient Burgh, which is his home, but it seems much more likely that his title comes from the sticky green burrs of the burdock plant, with which he is covered from head to toe.

Gathering the burrs from the hedgerows around Queensferry, and from the sides of the plateau-like shale ash bings around the neighbouring villages of Dalmeny, Newton and

Winchburgh, takes all of the week before the Fair. Then at daybreak on Fair Friday, the Burry Man's supporters begin the task of putting on his bizarre costume. Wearing thick woollen long johns, knitted gloves and a balaclava helmet, the Burry Man stands with arms outstretched while the little hairy burrs are stuck all over him. When at last the final burr is stuck in position, the Burry Man, with a headdress of flowers and two colourfully decorated flower-covered staffs in his hands, is ready to walk the streets of the Ferry. As he makes his way along the long narrow High Street and up the steep brae past the old distillery and bottling plant, the Burry Man has the right to claim a kiss from every pretty girl he encounters, while all the other inhabitants and visitors are expected to contribute generously to the collection cans carried by his helpers.

The Burry Man's walkabout continues until dusk, thus keeping up one of Scotland's oldest folk traditions, but what exactly was its origin? One local legend says that the Burry Man was originally a shipwrecked sailor. Washed up on the shore at Queensferry without a scrap of clothing, he is said to have covered himself in the burrs to cover his embarrassment before venturing into the High Street to seek help.

A much more likely explanation is that the Burry Man started off as a fertility symbol, thus explaining his appearance at the beginning of the harvest season, the floral headdress and the bunches of flowers in his hands and, of course, all those kisses he receives during his annual perambulation.

Next morning Queensferry's celebrations continue with the Fair itself. Nowadays the main attraction is the crowning of the town's schoolgirl queen, chosen in turn from each of the town's primary schools, Queensferry Primary, Echline Primary and St. Margaret's, but older traditions are still maintained too. These include the Burgh Race around the boundaries of the town, and the High Street Race, recalling old 'Killiecrankie', the former town officer in his scarlet uniform and his Glengarry bonnet, bearing the traditional prize of a pair of boots. Another highlight is the fun as the local boys take it in turn to try to climb to the top of the greasy pole in the Burgess Park, an event which traces its origins to those days now long past when sailors used to scale the rigging and masts of the tall ships which used to crowd the Ferry's little harbour on the Forth.

CHAPTER 6

Bathgate: Slaves, Shale and Chloroform

Bathgate boasts a castle on its coat of arms, but it is the only trace to be found of it, because the site it once occupied is now occupied by the former British Leyland truck and tractor plant. Most important event in the history of Bathgate's former castle came when Robert the Bruce gifted it to his daughter Marjory. Princess Marjory married Walter her Lord High Steward, thus founding the royal house of Stewart. Later other Scottish kings and queens and especially James IV and his young English bride Margaret Tudor are known to have come to Bathgate to hunt over Bathgate Moss, where the golf course now lies to the south of the town, but its royal connections, unlike those of its northern neighbour Linlithgow, appear to have done nothing to encourage its growth, and throughout the Middle Ages Torphichen was of much greater importance and is to be found marked on early maps on which Bathgate is missing.

During the seventeenth century Bathgate was involved in Covenanting activities and one local man, James Davie, was shot by the government dragoons as he tried to escape, but on the whole the rural calm continued until after the industrial revolution in the middle of the following century greatly increased the demand for coal and made the rich seams below the area worth mining for the first time. At the same time improved roads made it easier to get the Bathgate coal to market, and so the town began to prosper.

In addition Bathgate also became a centre of the weaving industry thanks to the coming to the district of several Huguenot families who were refugees from religious persecution in their native France and who brought their skills with them. Best known were the Jarves, whose name is still recalled by the well-known Bathgate placename, Jarvey Street. The Jarveys married into local farming families, including the Simpsons of Slackend, just outside Torphichen, who gave Bathgate its most famous son, Sir James Young Simpson of chloroform fame.

Simpson's family owned a bakery in Main Street, and local families to whom he delivered morning rolls nicknamed him 'The Box o' Brains', because they knew that they always got the right change from young Jamie. Amongst the homes at which he called every day with his big wickerwork basket was the big house, Balbardie House, home of the Marjoribanks family, where the town's first Provost, Alexander Marjoribanks, gave him a second nickname of 'The Young Philosopher'. The nickname Simpson himself liked best, however, was that given to him by his one-legged schoolmaster. 'Timmerleg' Henderson who dubbed him simply 'The Wise Wean'.

It came as no surprise therefore to any of Simpson's customers, classmates or relatives, when at the age of only fourteen in 1826 he won for himself a place at Edinburgh University. When he reached the city, however, he found life entirely different from that which he had enjoyed in his West Lothian home town: 'I felt very, very young and very solitary, very poor and almost friendless,' he wrote forty years later in his memoirs. Fortunately another of Dominie Henderson's lads o' pairts, John Reid, who was later to become professor of anatomy, had made it to university a year or two earlier, and he provided Simpson with accommodation in his lodgings in Adam Street.

Reid could also claim to have provided him with the necessary inspiration to reach university, because Simpson often recalled how impressed he had been when he saw Reid return to Bathgate on his first Meal Monday holiday from his studies, 'no longer the rough schoolboy, who had left us only two months before, but suddenly changed into a sharpish college student, wearing an actual long-tailed coat and sporting a small cane'. It was Reid, too, who encouraged him to listen and learn from the discussions of the older students and who, as a special treat, took him to hear evening lectures by Dr. Knox and other leading medical men of the time.

Others, too, were beginning to notice young Simpson, and Professor Pillans persuaded him to enter for the Stuart Bursary. To his delight, Simpson won and from the prize of £10 he rushed out to buy 'a tippet for Mary', his only sister, who had looked after him since the death of their mother. It was not just the present which the carter delivered to Mary in

Bathgate Academy was built with a classical Greek frontage. It is from the steps in front of the old school that the annual oration is delivered by a former pupil on the eve of the town's John Newlands Day procession.

Bathgate, but a regular bundle of stockings to be darned, a fact which Simpson proudly recalled in 1861 when – rich, famous and successful – he came back to his home town to present a silver thimble to be competed for annually by the girls of Bathgate Academy, a school which owed its origin to another of Bathgate's famous sons, John Newlands.

Newlands grew up in Bathgate in the middle of the eighteenth century. After leaving school, he was apprenticed to a joiner and became a skilled craftsman, but while still a young man he decided to emigrate and seek his fortune in the West Indies. He settled in Jamaica and with the small amount of money which he had taken with him from Bathgate managed to buy some land and the slaves needed to work it. Newlands prospered and extended his estates to such an extent that by the time he died in 1799 he had become one of the island's richest plantation owners. After emigrating, Newlands never returned to Scotland, but apparently he never forgot his home town, because in his will he left most of his fortune 'to erect a free school in the parish of Bathgate'.

Unfortunately for Bathgate, Newland's relatives contested the will in a court battle which lasted almost fifteen years. In the end, in 1814, they largely won, and despite the determined and prolonged efforts of Alexander Marjoribanks to ensure that Newland's wealth came to the town, the court ruled that only one fifth of Newlands' estate should be devoted to erecting and equipping the school, which he desired in his will 'for the bairns of Bathgate'. Regretfully Marjoribanks and his fellow trustees decided that the £14,500 which the town received was insufficient to build the school, but they invested the money and seventeen years later in 1831 had amassed enough interest for construction to begin 'on an open site to the south of the town'.

Very appropriately, considering all of the work which Marjoribanks had done for nothing during the long legal wrangle, the road which it overlooked on its hillside site was named Marjoribanks Street, and two years later in 1833 the new school was ready to admit its first pupils. The opening of the Academy created a great deal of interest and excitement in Bathgate, because whereas until then all schooling in the town had been conducted in single rooms in various houses, the new school was housed in an impressive grey stone neo-classical building, complete with a stately pillared Greek portico, topped by clock tower. So concerned were the new school's trustees that this huge building, which they had created, with its flights of stairs and its rooftop balustrades, might prove too much of a temptation for its first pupils, who until then had always been under the immediate eye of the dominie, to run wild that they decided that special rules and punishments were necessary. In addition to the tingling terrors of the traditional tawse, they therefore decreed that a system of fines be established and that any boy or girl who dared push or jostle a classmate should be fined one penny, while any pupil who was so adventurous as to climb out onto the roof would be liable to a fine of two pence.

It was scarcely surprising that the Academy trustees were concerned about discipline, because when the school opened they appointed only four teachers, including the Rector, to teach more than four hundred pupils. Ten years later, writing in the Second Statistical Account of Scotland, Bathgate's parish minister, the Rev. Samuel Martin, recorded that the Rector and his three assistants, who were expected to teach Latin, Greek, English, French, Geography, Mathematics, Arithmetic, Handwriting and Drawing, had recently been joined by the school's first lady member of staff, who was responsible for teaching the girls sewing. Shortly afterwards, however, she was dismissed, not because the girls' stitches were not up to standard, but as an economy move.

The teachers who continued on the staff had to work hard for their money, as the trustess insisted not only on classes from nine to four Monday to Friday but also on Saturdays. In the end James Fairbairn, the Rector, appealed to the trustees that Saturdays should be regarded as holidays. After much argument the trustees agreed to allow the pupils and staff to have every second Saturday free from lessons, but only on condition that Easter and Christmas holidays were cancelled, to make up for the lost time. Fortunately for the teachers and the children Rector Fairbairn succeeded in getting the trustees to think again, and not only was it agreed that the holidays should be restored but also that the school should be closed every Saturday. But the teachers had to agree to stay late at school on Friday evenings to enable parents to come and discuss their sons' and daughters' progress.

Usually queries were about the work and behaviour of individual pupils, but on at least two occassions the Rector had to face a deputation of parents complaining about one of his masters. The first time the irate parents complained that the master in question had dared to read a newspaper when he should have been teaching their bairns. The second time it was even worse, because the fathers and mothers all alleged that the same teacher had actually fallen asleep at his desk in front of the whole class. This may not have said much for the master as a teacher, but it must have said a lot about him as a disciplinarian, for there were at the time no fewer than 140 boys and girls in his class, so his ability to keep them all quiet enough to enable him to doze off must indeed have been considerable.

No doubt as a result of some of these complaints the school was eventually re-organised in 1869. Older members of staff were asked to retire and the new teachers and those who remained, instead of teaching their subjects to pupils of all age groups, taught general subjects to a class of pupils who were all of similar ages as in a modern primary school. In

Bathgate Academy's well-known janitor Billy Spokes. A former army man, he ruled his playground if not with a rod of iron then certainly with a short bamboo swagger cane, which he was not afraid to use if any boys deserved it.

1874 primary education became compulsory in Bathgate, as in other parts of Scotland, but it was still only the wisest weans who got to go on to the Academy, and so it remained into the present century, with the dreaded 'Qualifying Examination' each spring deciding who were the brightest bairns, not only from Bathgate itself, but from all the surrounding towns and villages such as Armadale, Whitburn, Stoneyburn, Blackburn and Livingston, and who would benefit most from the classical education which it offered and who should wear its black blazer with its red and black badge and tie.

So it remained until August 1967, when West Lothian Education Committee decreed that education in the Bathgate area, no matter how good it already was, must be made to conform to their comprehensive ideals and that to accomplish this the Academy must be merged with the, in its own way, equally excellent Lindsay Technical High School. In order to accommodate the new monster comprehensive the Academy was forced to leave its historic home and its traditions in Marjoribanks Street and move into an undistinguished concrete block whose facade at the time was aptly described as resembling nothing more than 'a giant communal urinal', on the outskirts of the town at Boghall. Depsite the education committee, however, on one evening each year, on the Friday night before Newlands Day, Bathgate 'Bairns' still stubbornly return to the playground of the old Academy, for it is on its broad steps that one of the town's most distinguished sons is still invited to give the annual Newlands Oration.

Originally Bathgate remembered its benefactor on his birthday in April, but for many years now Newlands Day has been celebrated on the first Saturday in June. Each year the traditional procession with pupils from either the Academy or St. Mary's Academy representing Princess Marjory and Walter her Lord High Steward winds its way through the streets, but one custom, which in the main has disappeared, is that of decorating the streets with triumphal arches of clipped green box wood, gathered during the preceding days from Kirkton, Balbardie and all the other big estates around the town. As in Bo'ness, where the arches are still a spectacular feature of that town's annual Fair Festival, the Bathgate arches were mainly the handiwork of the local miners, but all of the workers from the North British Steel Foundry, Renton and Fishers and the other heavy industries which had grown up joined in the annual celebrations which allowed them to escape for one brief day from their usual more humdrum workaday existence.

Bathgate's biggest boost came thanks to a chance letter written by a Glasgow gasworks manager, Hugh Bartholomew. For Mr. Bartholomew sent his letter to James Young, and as a result Young earned for himself the nickname of 'Paraffin' and Bathgate gained the claim to fame of being the site of the world's first oil refinery.

Young was born in Glasgow in the Drygate, a narrow street next to the Cathedral, where his father had a joiner's and undertaker's business. As soon as Young was old enough to leave school he was apprenticed to his father, but in the evenings continued his education at the Andersonian Institute, from which Strathclyde University was later to develop. Amongst his classmates at the night school was a lad who walked there and back every evening all the way from his home at Blantyre. His name was David Livingstone, the future African explorer and missionary, and the two became lifelong friends.

During his course at the Andersonian, Young's hard work, enthusiasm and obvious talent for scientific research came to the notice of Glasgow University professor, Thomas Graham, who offered to make him his assistant. Young accepted, and so he left the family cabinetmaking business and began lecturing to the students. Even in those days there was a brain drain from Scotland to England, and Young was tempted south by an offer to become assistant to the Professor of Chemistry at University College, London. Again, however, just as today industry offered greater rewards than the world of education, and to advance his career still further, Young resigned and accepted the post of scientific adviser at Tennant's Chemical Works in Manchester, which was one of the first posts of its kind.

While working there he kept in regular touch not only with Livingstone, but with many more of his friends from his Glasgow night-school days, and from one of them, Lyon Playfair, he received a letter of particular interest. Playfair gave a description of an unusual underground spring which he had discovered while carrying out an inspection underground in a coal pit near Alfreton in Derbyshire and from which flowed, not water, but about three hundred gallons a day of a thin, treacly liquid which he described as 'burning with a brilliant illuminating power'. Playfair then went on to ask, 'Does this possibly come within the province of your works? If it does, I will send a gallon for examination. Perhaps you could make a capital thing out of this new industry'.

Young immediately wrote back expressing interest, and as soon as the sample gallon reached his Manchester laboratory he realised its possibilites, because his test proved that the treacly liquid was high-quality mineral oil for which there was great demand from industry to replace the poorer-quality whale oil used at that time. To his credit Young reported his discovery to his employers, but they were not as farsighted as he was and rejected this new line of development because they did not believe it offered sufficient growth potential for their already large and prosperous chemical works.

On the other hand Young was convinced that there would be a steadily growing market for good-quality oil not only from industry as the number of machines increased, but also from householders to light their homes in place of candles. Table lamps were already available, but many housewives would not have them in their homes: because the oil in them was of such unreliable quality the lamps often exploded and caused fires. James Young bravely decided to back his hunch and resigned his secure post at Tennant's to open his own small factory to process the oil from Alfreton, but just as he was about to go into production the underground spring dried up. Young's search of the Alfreton coal pit and the workings of surrounding collieries for another underground oil spring met with no success, but he reckoned that as the original find had occurred in a coal seam, then surely oil must be obtainable from the coal itself. His experiments proved him right and that by careful heating oil could indeed be obtained from coal, but the amount varied enormously depending on the sample of coal which was used.

It was obviously necessary to obtain the right coal, and here again Young made use of his Glasgow night-school friends who now lived all over the country, but with whom he still corresponded thanks to the new reliable penny post which had recently been started in 1840. Young asked all of them to send him a small sample of coal from their area. Amongst those who responded to his request was Hugh Bartholomew, who in a note said that he obtained the coal for his gasworks from a pit in West Lothian at a place called Boghead at Torbanehill between Bathgate and Armadale, and that the miners called it 'parrot or cannel coal', because when it was burned, it spluttered, making a noise like a chattering parrot, while at the same time giving a clear light as bright as any candle. Many of the miners, explained Bartholomew, burned this coal in little pans beside their kitchen range and depended upon it to light their little miners' rows. When Young experimented, he discovered all of Bartholomew's claims to be more than true and that the sample when heated oozed with oil.

Young wasted no time in moving north to Bathgate, where he obtained a site at Whiteside on the road to Whitburn, and in 1848 he opened the world's first oil refinery, complete with retorts to heat the coal and tanks in which to store the resultant oil. From there he not only supplied orders from all over Britain, but soon developed an export trade sending barrels of oil by ship across the Atlantic to the United States, years before that country discovered its own natural oil resources. It was at this point that Young showed he was a good businessman as well as a skilled scientist, because he took out a patent for the extraction of oil from coal, and it was so well drawn up that it withstood every attempt by later rivals to find a loophole and ensured that Young won every lawsuit which he brought in both Britain and America to defend his monopoly of his process.

The first lawsuit in which Young found himself involved, however, originated locally in Bathgate. It was brought by a Mr. Gillespie from whom Young had leased the Bathgate coalfield and who was furious that Young was not selling coal in the traditional way, but was instead making much larger profits from selling oil. There had been no mention of oil production when Young set up the deal and, furious that he had failed to realise the potential of the riches which lay buried beneath his estate, Gillespie demanded angrily that he should share in the greatly increased profits. The case began at the Court of Session in Edinburgh's Parliament Square in July 1853, and for over a week the Law Lords listened to scientists giving evidence for both parties. The crux of the case rested on the claim from Mr. Gillespie's lawyers that Young had breached his lease by mining not the coal to which it entitled him, but a substance which they described as 'bituminous earth'. So complicated was the case that it was August before their Lordships gave their decision in favour of Young. Bitterly disappointed and faced with heavy costs, Gillespie refused to give in and lodged an appeal. It was never heard, however, because at this point Young again showed his business acumen by offering a compromise of a small increase in price for every ton of coal which he mined, and Gillespie accepted.

While Young could well afford the increase, as the Bathgate oil bonanza was booming in these years before any American competition, the thought that Gillespie might come back in the future and try to demand even more encouraged him to seek alternative sources of supply. The decision proved a very fortunate one for Young, because while none of the other coalfields at Bo'ness, or in Lanarkshire, Ayrshire or Fife provided any coal with anything like the high oil content of the Torbanehill Mineral, as the original Boghead coal became known in the textbooks of the industry, Young instead found that immediately to the east of the carboniferous measures of the Bathgate coalfield lay another until then entirely unexploited mineral called shale. Young experimented in secret at his Bathgate Chemical Works and to his delight discovered that shale was indeed oil-bearing and although not quite as rich in oil as the Torbanehill Mineral was better than any of the other coal samples. Better still, this dark brown slate-like rock had until then been regarded as valueless, so by moving swiftly he was able to buy up the mineral rights to vast reserves at minimal cost.

The next ten years from 1853 to 1863 proved to be the golden decade of the young Scottish oil industry, for as yet there were no foreign rivals and Young's patent very effectively prevented any other companies from trying to open in Britain. With this complete monopoly and the price of oil rising steeply to three shillings and six pence a gallon (17½p), Young could easily have exploited the market, but he insisted on quality and safety and, before marketing paraffin oil for lamps, he spent two years experimenting to eliminate the explosions which had previously given oil lighting such a bad name. As well as using only pure oil to produce paraffin, he found that part of the solution lay in designing wicks. When at last Young released his patent paraffin lamps onto the market, they proved so reliable that his name was always linked with this product, and the nickname 'Paraffin' Young stuck with him for the rest of his life.

In 1864, Young's patent expired and immediately, in view of

his obvious success, many opposition companies opened oil works, all in West and Midlothian, until by 1871 there were over fifty producing a total of 25,000,000 gallons of crude each year. Formerly quiet rural villages such as East, Mid and West Calder, Broxburn and Pumpherston suddenly found themselves in the grip of oil fever and transformed into industrial towns, while whole new villages such as Addiewell, Seafield, Livingston Station, Deans, Niddrie Roman Camp, Winchburgh, Three Mile Town and Newton near Queensferry grew up around the new shale mines and oil works, which spread with an accompanying rash of pink shale bings (or tips) in a north-easterly band right across Mid and West Lothian to Dalmeny, where the shale seam dipped under the Forth to re-emerge across the river in a small pocket in Fife.

Labourers, including many from Ireland, flooded into the area to become miners in the new industry to an extent which they never did to the coal pits with their much more inward-looking communities. There were many almost Wild West touches to the West Lothian shale oil boom such as gunpowder, manufactured at Camilty Powder Mill near Harburn, where the well-known golf course is today, being delivered around the area by cart, not to the shale mines themselves, where it would be used for blasting, but to the newly established local co-operative stores which sold it in blue paper bags direct to the miners, who were responsible for buying their own supplies. Also, just as in the American West, in West Lothian ponies were suddenly in great demand because they were used to provide all of the motive power underground and to pull the heavy laden hutches full of shale to the surface.

All this activity, however, seemed doomed to stop as swiftly as it had started because by the beginning of the 1870s America's oil rush was under way, and soon imported crude oil from Texas was selling in Scotland for less than the local product. Again it was Young's ingenuity which came to the rescue, because he was ready to launch a whole series of bestselling byproducts from the same raw materials. Chance had already led Young to market candles when, after investigating why machine oil turned cloudy in cold weather, he discovered that it was quite simple to produce large blocks of white wax. Most profitable of all the byproducts was sulphate of ammonia, which he sold in large quantities to farms as fertiliser. In his fight to develop more and more byproducts to subsidise the price of the actual oil so that he could undercut American imports, no products, however small, were neglected. They ranged from petroleum jelly for use in ointments to a wax for beekeepers to a special oil for use in the giant lamps needed to illuminate the lighthouses around the coasts in the days before the introduction of electric generators, right down to mothballs. Still more profits were earned by supplying shale derivatives to many other Scottish industries including Dundee's jute mills, where formerly whale oil had always been used, and Kirkcaldy's linoleum factories, while other shale byproducts were used in the manufacture of rubber and paints.

As a result of all his enterprise Young's Paraffin Light and Mineral Oil Company continued to thrive despite American competition, and at his refineries Young was ahead of the Americans in being the first to introduce steam heating, continuous distillation, refrigeration units and thermostatic control. He was also the first to introduce the terms 'cracking' and 'scrubbing' towers, words which are still part of the oil jargon of the present-day industry.

While Young maintained and expanded his Bathgate Chemical Works, he also developed new sites and his refinery at Addiewell had an especially well-publicised official opening when he persuaded his old friend David Livingstone to perform the ceremony. Afterwards Livingstone, who was home on leave between African trips, rode back with Young to his home, Limefield House, which still stands on the edge of Livingston New Town, where it has been converted to serve as a retirement home. During his stay Livingstone entertained Young by building a model of an African kraal complete with thatched rondavels. All trace of it has long since disappeared, but the huge sycamore which Livingstone planted over a century ago can still be seen.

Even as Young was still expanding his refineries and their associated industries, his smaller rivals were proving less successful and either closed or merged with his enterprises until eventually in 1914, at the outbreak of the First World War, from a peak of ninety companies the number had dropped to only seven operating seven oil refineries at Brox-

burn, Pumpherston, Oakbank, Tarbrax, Philipstoun and Dalmeny, where by coincidence the tanks in which the North Sea
oil processed at Grangemouth is stored before being exported
through the Houndpoint Oil Terminal are hidden in the heart
of one of the original shale-oil bings.

During the War the seven Scottish oil producers all co-
operated to supply the Royal Navy with fuel, and their
considerable contribution to the war effort was recognised
when peace returned by a government offer to all of them to
merge and become part of the government-controlled Anglo-
Persian Oil Company. This they all accepted, and in 1919,
under the name of Scottish Oils they established their headquarters at Middleton Hall on the south side of the main road
from Broxburn to Uphall. There they established the excellent
sport and social facilities which were typical of this company's
caring attitude to its employees, and the excellent miners'
institutes which it established can still be seen at Winchburgh
and the other shale-mining villages in the area.

From the outset, however, the new company was faced with
difficulties because the best shale had been worked out and the
yield and crude oil per ton of shale dropped from forty gallons
in the 1860s to only twenty-two gallons in the 1920s, despite
more modern methods of extraction. The industry's 8000
workers were greatly relieved therefore when in his 1928
budget Mr. Winston Churchill, who was then the Chancellor of
the Exchequer, announced that the Scottish shale oil industry
would be exempt from the four pence (1½p) duty per gallon
which he intended levying on all 'imported motor spirit'.

No matter how welcome this relief was at the time, what the
Scottish oil industry really needed was positive discrimination
in its favour, but this it never managed to persuade successive
London-based governments to grant. All the time imported oil
was clearly gaining on the home product, and in 1924 Scottish
Oils itself hedged its bets by opening a new oil refinery on the
shores of the Forth at Grangemouth to process crude oil
imported by tanker from the Persian Gulf. With this competition directly on its doorsteep during the depression of the late
1920s and the 1930s, the shale oil side of the business suffered
badly, but still fought back determinedly by switching much of
its production to diesel fuel and new detergents including the

F

famous 'By-Prox', which helped it to remain financially solvent.

Like the First World War, the Second World War provided a respite for the hard-pressed industry, because while all work at Grangemouth ceased, the West Lothian shale miners and the refinery workers just over the county boundary at Pumpherston worked on without interruption and contributed greatly to the war effort. From 1945 onwards, however, imported crude was again available at much lower prices than shale oil could be produced, and it was clear that unless the government came to its aid the days of the Scottish shale oil industry were numbered. Throughout the 1950s while one by one the old shale mines closed, the Grangemouth refinery was vastly expanded with associated developments on both sides of Bo'ness Road. Ironically, many of the new buildings were constructed with SOL bricks, manufactured from waste shale at Pumpherston.

The final chapter in the hundred-year history of the Scottish shale oil industry was written in 1962, when apart from the workers at the Pumpherston Refinery, the rest of its 4000 men were dismissed. Pumpherston alone continued as it still does today, using oil imported by rail from Wales, and somewhat ironically, one of its main products is the detergent used to disperse oil spillages from the North Sea oilfields.

During the early 1960s a method was also found to utilise the red oxide blaize from the shale bings, the one byproduct for which Paraffin Young had never managed to find an outlet, and so the giant pink plateau-like shale bings, which were such a distinctive feature of the West Lothian landscape for over a century, have during the last twenty years gradually disappeared. A few of the largest ones still remain and now there is talk of preserving the one which lies to the south-east of Winchburgh as a tourist attraction, complete with aerial railway to take visitors to its flat top from which magnificent views of the two Forth Bridges can be obtained. In conjunction with British Petroleum, successors to Scottish Oils at Grangemouth refinery, the tourist board has set up a Shale Trail, starting with a video film and display at the refinery itself and continuing via Young's original refinery at Bathgate's Whiteside to Limefield, Pumpherston and finally to Winchburgh and its still massive bing.

But do the proposed tourist attractions at Winchburgh,

The clock tower of Bathgate High Church looms over the town's former Corn Exchange in Jarvey Street.

including the suggestion to open one of the low line of redbrick miners' rows to the public and the new shale oil museum at Livingston, need to spell the end of this once-flourishing industry? When the last miner came up to the surface at the end of the very last shift in 1962, it was estimated that over 30,000,000 tons of shale still remained to be mined, and many of the former miners who now stand as pensioners on the street corners of Winchburgh and the other mining towns are convinced that it could still be won, not by a new generation of miners but by using a method first suggested as long ago as the 1950s, when the shale industry was still alive. This method would avoid all need for mining by burning the shale below ground and piping the resultant oil to the surface. When this was proposed there were no metal pipes which could withstand the intense heat, but since then thirty years of space research have resulted in big advances in metallurgy, as can be seen locally in the highly sophisticated metal products produced by Cameron Iron Works at Livingston for markets ranging from the aircraft industry to North Sea Oil.

Another new development in the field of shale has taken place in the American market, in California, where controlled underground burning has been carried out, not to obtain oil but to produce a honeycombed lightweight stone, ideal for building in an earthquake-prone area, but which could no doubt also be used in Britain, thus creating a new dimension for this old Scottish industry.

Just how busy a place the Victorian shale oil boom made Bathgate is hard to imagine today, but with the limited travel facilities of those days making the cities of Edinburgh and Glasgow too distant for regular visits, Bathgate, as well as being the educational centre for the whole of the south side of West Lothian, with pupils even travelling in by train from as far away as Fauldhouse, was also the shopping and social centre for the whole area. Social life revolved around the Royal Hotel, whose long frontage filled the whole of the west side of the Steel Yard as George Place was then called, not because of Bathgate's links with the steel industry, but because at one time the town, like all others in Scotland, had its own set of measures and the steel yard rod was embedded there. Behind the main red sandstone building of the Royal there was a courtyard surrounded by the hotel's stables and coach houses. A short lane led out of the busy stable yard into Engine Street as George Street was then called, but no matter what the name, the shop directly opposite where the entrance to the yard used to be is still the saddlery business belonging to the Brownlee family, who supplied the hotel's horses and carriages with harness and tracery. Why George Street was called Engine Street, until the name was changed in 1937 to mark the coronation of King George VI, as was the case with the change from the Steel Yard to George Place, is not certain, but it is suggested that there was originally a steam engine situated where Engine Street Lane is still to be found and that it was

used to pump floodwater out of the underground coal workings which in recent years have caused so much damage by
subsidence to buildings in nearby High Hopetoun Street,
where even the new library has suffered from extensive
cracking.

Across High Hopetoun Street, named after the landowning
Hopetoun Estates, in Jarvey Street, stands the town's old Corn
Exchange, which like the Royal was the scene of many of the
town's annual social events such as Masonic dances, as Bathgate
has never had a town hall. Thus, after the day's business of
buying and selling was finished, the floor of the Corn Exchange was cleared to accommodate meetings, dinners and
dances. It was therefore appropriate that it eventually became
the local dance hall, and currently it is a disco. Directly opposite
is the Co-operative function suite, which is situated above a
whole line of Co-operative shops, now like Co-op stores in
many Scottish towns looking sadly neglected, but once crowded
and busy with members buying the little 'checks', the multi-
coloured coinage of the Co-op, which ensured that they shared
in the dividend at the end of every quarter. As at one time
Bathgate Co-operative Society paid a dividend of as much as
five shillings (25p) in the pound, this was indeed a powerful
incentive for local housewives. If they could not come to the
shops in Jarvey Street, horse-drawn Co-op carts and vans
ensured that milk, meat and bread were faithfully and regularly delivered every day to their homes.

Bathgate, like Bo'ness, Broxburn, West Calder and many
other West Lothian towns, was a place where the Co-op was not
so much a place to shop as a way of life. Wedding receptions
were held every Saturday afternoon in the Co-op function
suite, the pram for the first baby was bought from the Co-op
hardware department, and so on right through to funerals
conducted of course by the Co-op Undertakers.

Only on Sundays was the Co-op closed, for then the High
Church on the opposite side of Jarvey Street held sway.
Bathgate's original High Church, which occupied the same site
as the present building, was opened in 1739, when it replaced
the old kirk the ruins of which can be visited in Edinburgh
Road opposite the Gothic gates to Kirkton Park. It was a typical
Scottish eighteenth-century church, with the small belfry at the

The people of Bathgate raised the money to send this new ambulance to the front during the First World War. It is interesting to note the name 'Linlithgowshire' below the windscreen — the earlier name for West Lothian.

west end the sole exterior adornment. Its two-storeyed stone walls were harled to protect the sandstone from weathering, and it was roofed with grey slates. It served its Bathgate congregation for almost a century and a half until growth in the size of the town and its population made a larger parish church a necessity, and so it was demolished in 1883 to make way for the present much more elaborate Victorian church whose tall clock tower is a familiar landmark. Built in Norman style, it cost £8000 to erect and its bell, which when first hung was valued at £250, was gifted by former Bathgate Provost, John Waddell. The church's fine pipe organ was installed in 1899.

One feature of the original High Church which still survives in the present one is a strangely shaped wooden bench. This is a reminder of the power which the church once held and of old-time church discipline, because this is the famous 'cutty stool' or seat of repentance. From the Reformation to the early nineteenth century, the elders of the High Church kirk session assembled every week to discipline their fellow members of the congregation. Any who had been absent without what the session considered acceptable excuse from the previous Sunday morning service or who had been so rash as to speak during the minister's sermon or, worse still, had fallen asleep during it, were duly punished by being made to sit in full view directly below the pulpit on this seat of repentance. What made Bathgate's 'cutty stool' unusual was its double seat, designed to ensure that couples who had committed the worst sin of fornication shared publicly in their punishment together. The Bathgate kirk session also regularly disciplined any children of the parish who were referred to it for misbehaving, but instead of sitting on either of the seats, they were made to bend over the middle section so that their bottoms were suitably raised for the beadle to administer a suitable short sharp shock with the birch rod.

As in other towns, the congregation of the High Church split at various times because of the rows which have plagued Scottish church history, and other churches therefore grew up to serve these breakaway congregations. Most prominent is St. David's in George Street. Like the High Church, its present building replaced an earlier church on the same site. The foundation stone of the present St. David's was laid in 1905 by Lord Rosebery, and it was officially opened in 1906, when the programme described it as being of thirteenth-century Gothic design. Stone from the original church was used to build the imposing steeple, which like that of the High Church dominates the town. It is of plain design from the base to the belfry, where it opens out to the top of the vane.

It is interesting to note that the first minister of St. David's was the Rev. Samuel Martin, who wrote the description of Bathgate in the Second Statistical Account, quoted from earlier in this chapter, but who at the Disruption of the Church of Scotland the following year in 1843 left his charge to lead a large section of his congregation to form a new free church. St. David's rejoined the Church of Scotland at the union of 1929.

Another breakaway congregation which rejoined the Church of Scotland at the same time in 1929 was that of St. John's in Mid Street. The present church dates from 1894, and its congregation at that time was a combination of the Burgher and Anti-Burgher and Auld and New Licht breakaway factions

The last of the Bathgate weavers, Nisbet Easton, posed for the photographer beside his hearth. Weaving was said to have been brought to Bathgate from France by Protestant Huguenot refugees, and Jarvey Street is also said to have got its name from a French weaver, called Jarve.

caused by the controversies which split the church in 1799. In 1828 this congregation built a small church in Livery Street, but its numbers grew so rapidly that they outgrew it by 1856, when they sold the building to Bathgate's Roman Catholic population who were also increasing rapidly at this time because of the influx of shale miners from Ireland. The Catholic congregation prospered and grew until by 1908 they were large and rich enough to demolish the old church and start building a fine new one seating 800. The foundation stone was laid by the Most Reverend James A. Smith, then

Archbishop of the Diocese of St. Andrews and Edinburgh, and the church with its ornate high altar made of rich old Sienna marble was opened next year. With its unusual twin steeples, it is considered one of the finest Roman Catholic places of worship in Scotland, and its congregation has produced many well-known members of the Scottish hierarchy, including Bishop James Monaghan in Edinburgh and Bishop Vincent Logan of Dunkeld.

As Bathgate expanded during the 1950s a new parish church was built to serve the population of the large Boghall housing scheme to the east of the town, and at the beginning of the 1970s the equally modern St. Columba's Roman Catholic church was also opened in this part of the town.

The late 1960s and the early 1970s saw a huge expansion of council and Scottish Special Housing Association houses and flats to the south of Bathgate, at what had until then been the village of Blackburn, to serve the influx of workers at the new and much vaunted British Leyland Truck and Tractor Plant, which was supposed to, but failed to, regenerate industry in the area by attracting ancillary works to the town.

In Victorian times Blackburn's main industry was cotton spinning and there was a water-powered mill on the banks of the River Almond, which employed 120 men, women and children. The mill belonged to the Cameron family, and when it closed, rather than be out of work the women employees walked morning and night to another of the company's mills on the outskirts of Edinburgh. For the men fortunately other jobs were by this time available thanks to the growth of coal and shale mining in the area, while a local quarry produced stone which was said to be especially suitable for the floors of ovens.

Today, with the closure of the British Leyland Works in the spring of 1986, the population of Blackburn has plummeted, and many houses built only during the mid-sixties are being bulldozed, but at the same time there is also better news for the area with the re-opening of Bathgate Railway Station and the re-introduction of a thirty-minute service to Edinburgh, which should encourage more commuters to consider living in the district.

CHAPTER 7

The Bathgate Hills

With their narrow twisting roads, hairpin bends, deep dark forests of green conifers, lochs and rocks, the Bathgate Hills are like a miniature Trossachs, without the crowds of tourists. For although sandwiched between the M8 and M9 motorways, within very easy reach of both Edinburgh and Glasgow, this hilly heartland of West Lothian has happily remained almost undiscovered.

Shaped roughly like a triangle with Bathgate and Uphall at its southern base and Linlithgow as its northern apex, the Bathgate Hills can be easily entered from any of these towns by simply climbing up the braes behind them, not that it is necessary to climb too far, because their highest point, Cairnpapple, rises to a height of just over 1000 feet. It was Cairnpapple's official height of only 1012 feet which in the days before regionalisation gave West Lothian one of its claims to fame as the Scottish county with the lowest highest point, but despite its somewhat lowly height its position right in the middle of Central Scotland means that on a good clear day it is possible from its grassy summit to see right across from the East Coast to the West and to pick out the Bass Rock and Berwick Law beside the blue waters of the Forth, while Goat Fell can be glimpsed on Arran.

It was on this vantage point that what must have been some of West Lothian's earliest inhabitants established their head-quarters all of 4000 years ago, and their site on Cairnpapple makes an interesting visit. Today these people of such distant times are always known as the Beaker Men, because when their graves were excavated by Professor Stuart Pigott in 1947 drinking cups made of pottery were discovered beside each skeleton. These early men who lived on Cairnpapple appear to have had a belief in a life hereafter, and their clay cups were to enable them to enjoy a refreshing drink as soon as they re-awoke. Unlike the traces of hill forts which can be examined at nearby Bowden Hill and Cockleroi, all the evidence at Cairnpapple seems to point to its having been an important religious site for the Beaker Men. Whether they chose this place to worship their gods for some spiritual reason, such as being as close as they could reach to the sun, or whether they picked it for some much more mundane reason such as escaping from damp and dense forest, which would have made occupation of a low-lying site both difficult and unpleasant, or possibly for a combination of the two, is a decision lost in the mists of time, but archaeologists are convinced from finds which they have made that it was sufficiently important to attract other tribesmen from as far away as Wales. Again whether they came all that way to discuss tribal business, to take part in some special act of worship or to attend a burial, it is impossible to guess, but because of the remains which have been found, it is about burials at Cairnpapple that we know most. Many appear to have taken the form of cremations, with the ashes buried in urns around the site, but most interesting are the stone kist burials, and it is a dramatic experience to climb down into the centre of the cairn to examine these stone coffins of 4000 years ago.

To see Cairnpapple's most dramatic stone, however, it is probably necessary to come down from the hill itself into the village of Torphichen, which it overlooks, because it is believed that the famous sanctuary stone in the graveyard of Torphichen Kirk was probably originally the sacrificial stone from the Beaker Men's settlement. For although there is a Christian cross carved on the side of this small squat stone, there is also a strange cup-like cavity cut into its flat top, into which the blood of a sacrificial animal could well have drained, and it is suggested that when the Knights of St. John wanted a suitably important stone to mark the centre of their sanctuary lands at Torphichen, they converted it for their own purpose.

Rights of sanctuary at Torphichen date back to the reign of David I, when the King gave all the lands around the village to the Knights of St. John, who established their Scottish headquarters there around the year 1165. Rights of sanctuary were common inside Scottish churches, as witness the horror when Bruce burst into the church at Dumfries and murdered the Red Comyn, but what made sanctuary at Torphichen different was that it extended to one mile to the north, south, east and

A view of the 18th-century Torphichen Kirk to the left, with the medieval Preceptory of the Knights of St. John to the right.

west of the village. With the distance calculated from the old stone in the churchyard, these bounds were marked by tall standing stones and the idea was that any fugitive who could reach them was guaranteed safe shelter by the Knights until a fair trial could be arranged. In the strife-torn days of medieval Scotland, when the general rule was Jedart Justice, appropriately named after the turbulent old Border town and similar to the lynch law of the Wild West which meant that those wronged simply took the law into their own hands, this extension of sanctuary was a great advance, and the Knights kept a lookout from the watch tower of their headquarters from dawn until dusk to make sure that it was enforced.

What must be stressed however is that coming under the protection of the Knights did not mean that wrongdoers escaped their just desserts, but simply that they received a fair trial. If the matter was a simple local dispute the trial was held at Torphichen, but for more serious offences the Knights provided an armed escort to take the accused to the sheriff in Linlithgow, while in the case of major crimes the fugitive was escorted to the High Court in Edinburgh. Such was the case with the Laird of Tulliallan, whose estate lay across the River Forth in what used to be Scotland's smallest county with the longest name, Clackmannanshire. The Laird was in dispute with the Abbot of Culross over the rent of some lands, when unfortunately they met one day while out riding near Rosyth Castle. A fierce argument developed and when angry words gave way to blows, the Abbot was knocked from his horse and killed. The Laird and his servants immediately rode off and that night came seeking sanctuary at Torphichen. There, despite the fact that their crime involved the murder of a fellow churchman, the Knights lived up to their reputation and provided them with safe shelter, but as soon as it could be arranged they were taken for trial in Edinburgh. The verdict was an interesting one, because while the Laird and his servants were all found guilty of murder, only the Laird was executed, because the sheriff ordered the servants to be pardoned, ruling that they had acted as all good servants should in simply obeying their master's orders.

To guarantee sanctuary of this kind, it was necessary for the Knights of St. John to possess a building as their headquarters which could be defended against possibly enraged pursuers and glimpsed from the road leading into Torphichen from Bathgate. The Preceptory as it was called, after the Christian Precepts by which the Knights promised always to live, does indeed look like a stone square Border peel tower. But its chief purpose was to serve as a church, because the Knights of St. John were primarily a religious order of monks, able to defend themselves because of their involvement with the Crusades, whose many wounded also obliged them to develop their skills as doctors.

All three aspects of the work of the Knights, who claim to be members of the oldest order of chivalry in the world, tracing their descent right from their patron saint John the Baptist, can be found at Torphichen, even although the ruins of the Preceptory are all that remain of their once fine monastery. As befits the Knights' military reputation, the Preceptory is one of Scotland's few fortified ecclesiastical buildings, and defensive features still to be seen include the watch tower, with its narrow arrow slit windows, its tiny guard window looking into the church, and its tight twisting newel or spiral staircase which leads up to castellated battlements. Originally, however, the Preceptory had even more impressive fortifications in the form of a defensive outer wall which completely encircled the site and which was in turn surrounded by a water-filled moat, both of which have disappeared. The existence of the moat was recalled, however, a few years ago when council workmen were building houses opposite the preceptory, for their bulldozer suddenly sank through the foundations and began to disappear into a deep water-filled hole, a reminder of the fact that, like Winchester Cathedral, the Preceptory is actually built on hundreds of piles of oak. When the Preceptory was taken into the care of the Ministry of Works, now the Department of the Environment Ancient Monuments Division, in the 1920s, a piece of one of the oak piles was carefully removed and found to be practically fossilised.

The religious aspect of the Knights' life at Torphichen is well represented both by the choir and transepts which stand intact within the Preceptory and by the foundations of the other monastic buildings which can be traced round it. Both transepts have high vaulted stone ceilings and windows with fine stone tracery, but the most interesting features are probably the carved archway which originally led from the choir into the long pillared nave, where the village church now stands, and the small lancet window which is believed to be older than the main part of the building and which may come from a tiny chapel built on this site by St. Ninian, long before the coming of the Knights. Today the walls of the Preceptory are bare stone, but traces can be seen of how they were at one time lime washed and decorated, and behind the entrance door can be found the carving of a little donkey which is believed to be a mason's mark, by which one of these skilled but illiterate craftsmen indicated to the Knights how much work he had done and expected to be paid for.

Outside too the stones of the foundations tell a story, showing clearly the position of the cloisters and the central garth, the grassy central square where the Knights could relax by playing bowls and other games. On one side of the square lay the kitchen and adjoining it the frater or refectory, where the Knights ate their communal meals. Many of the more interesting stones from the ruins of the monastery have been saved and are on display in one of the three rooms on the first floor of the Preceptory, which also house a pictorial display about the life and work of the Knights when they went on a caravan, as it was called, or a crusade to the Holy Land.

Included in the display is a photograph of the famous eye hospital which the Knights of St. John still maintain in Jerusalem, but whether they ran one of Scotland's earliest hospitals at Torphichen is a matter of considerable controversy. 'To help their lords, the sick' was the most important vow taken by every Knight, including those at Torphichen, but apart from a passing reference in the Second Statistical Account of Scotland published in 1844 to the Knights' herb garden, which might suggest that these plants were grown to produce ointments and medicines, there is no actual written evidence of medical care being dispensed on a regular basis at Torphichen.

What is lacking in written evidence, however, is compensated for by the weight of local tradition, which goes so far as to pinpoint the exact site of the hospital wards, as on the east side of the monastery square in a building known as the Tenement, a block three storeys high which must have made a big impression on the villagers of Torphichen who must have been more accustomed to their own low thatched cottages. The Tenement has long since disappeared, but the marks of its night stair which led down from its dormitories for the Knights and possibly its wards for its patients can still be seen on the inside wall of the north transept leading straight down into the church, thus avoiding any need to go out into the cold.

If there was a hospital at Torphichen, then it was down this stone stairway that patients able to get up would have made their way down into the church to take part in services, which were the focal point of the Preceptory's day. Up this steep stair also the Sacrist would have taken the sacraments to the bedridden, but that still leaves Torphichen's most intriguing patients, the lepers, to be accounted for. That they were definitely treated by the Knights, local people insist is confirmed in stone by Torphichen's famous leper squint, a tiny slanting window in the south transept through which patients suffering from this terrible disease could peer and see all that was going on at the high altar, without their own horribly disfigured faces being seen and distracting other members of the congregation or possibly even bringing them into contact with the disease. The trouble with this evidence in stone is that modern experts on church architecture suggest that the oddly shaped 'Leper Squint', which overlooks the spot where the bodies of dead Knights were laid in state for twenty-four hours before burial, is not a leper squint at all. According to them this window and the Preceptory's other unusual window which looks down from the stair of the tower into the church and which has equally traditionally been known as the guard window, are both part of a complicated communications system to do with church procedure, which by the use of gestures, like the tick-tack utilised by bookies' runners at race courses, ensured that the Preceptor or Grand Master, who alone had his own private apartments, arrived at the altar at exactly the right moment in the service.

On the other hand it is known that the Knights did treat lepers at their St. Magdalene's Hospital in Linlithgow, where the former distillery of the same name still stands, and that Liberton on the southern outskirts of Edinburgh was the 'town' beyond the city walls to which lepers were driven, so it seems feasible that if there was a hospital at Torphichen, then it might well have numbered lepers amongst its patients. Whether Scotland's lepers, including Robert the Bruce, really suffered from leprosy or from some milder skin disease such as scrofula is yet another matter of controversy among Scottish historians.

But there is no controversy that Torphichen Preceptory definitely treated one royal patient. He was King Edward I of England, the Hammer of the Scots, and he was brought to Torphichen after the Battle of Falkirk in 1298. Edward had not been injured in the battle, in which he had his revenge on Sir William Wallace for the latter's victory at the Battle of Stirling Bridge twelve years before, but the night before the fray he had suffered two broken ribs when his restless battle charger had trodden on him while he lay in camp near Polmont. While he received treatment from the Knights for this painful injury, tradition has it that Edward urged his men to leave him and go out to capture the fugitive Wallace who, again according to local tradition, was at that very moment hiding only a mile away down on the banks of the

River Avon in what is still known as Wallace's Cave.

Torphichen's prouder connection with Wallace is that he too came to the Preceptory before the Battle of Falkirk, not to be treated by the Knights, who with their English bias fled to Linlithgow Palace, which was in the hands of Edward's forces, but to hold what was to turn out to be his last Scottish parliament. Among the business which he transacted at Torphichen was the granting of some lands at Dundee, and it is on this charter that one of the few examples of Wallace's signature survives.

Apart from the coming of the Wallace, Torphichen had many other contacts with the political events of the Middle Ages, through the activities of the Grand Masters of the Knights, who were often important figures in the government of Scotland. Most famous was Sir William Knollis in the late fifteenth century, while the sixteenth-century Sir Walter Lindsay was mentioned in *Ane Satyre of the Thrie Estaites* written by his relative Sir David Lindsay of the Mount and first performed at Linlithgow Palace in 1540. 'The Thrie Estaites' was a play intended to warn the nobles and churchmen of the day to mend their ways, and judging from the stories of feasting and gambling at the Preceptory itself, which date from as early as the reign of King James IV, over thirty years earlier, the Knights of Saint John were amongst those who should have taken heed. That they and the other Scottish clergy did not, led to the Reformation and the demise of the Knights, for their Grand Master at the time, James Sandilands, surrendered all of their lands in Scotland to Mary Queen of Scots. At the same time, however, he managed to ensure that he received back the lands of the headquarters at Torphichen as a secular grant for himself. Unfortunately for Torphichen, Sandilands died without a direct heir and his estate passed to a branch of his family who already had their own home at Calder Hall near Mid-Calder, where John Knox had celebrated one of the first Protestant communions. They saw no reason to leave their home to move to Torphichen, and so the Preceptory was left empty and the neglected building was soon plundered and its stones removed to provide materials for other buildings in the village including Cathlaw House.

Meanwhile worship in the new Protestant manner continued

in the Norman nave of the Knights' former church, which was walled off from the choir and transepts, but it was soon interrupted by the troubles of Covenanting times, when many of the Torphichen congregation, rather than worship in the Episcopalian manner decreed by king and government, preferred to desert their church and attend open-air conventicles up in the Bathgate Hills. There was of course the constant danger of being caught attending these illegal acts of worship by the government's redcoated dragoons, and so at each service lookouts were posted and, using the cry of the curlew or the call of the peeweep, they warned worshippers if any of the hated troops came into sight. Even the big communal communion cup was prefabricated to facilitate a swift getaway, and the bowl unscrewed and disappeared under one cloak, while the stem slid down a bodice and the base was quickly disposed of under a jacket. It is said that these frequent escapes so infuriated the government's general in Scotland, Tam Dalyell of the Binns, that he sent to the Netherlands for a stock of grey cloth and kitted his men out with grey uniforms so that they would not be so conspicuous, thus becoming the first commander in the army to realise the importance of camouflage and leading to his regiment becoming known as the Scots Greys.

A hundred years later strife again split the Torphichen congregation, when they quarrelled over the right of church patronage and many of them decided to secede from the church. Again they took to the hills and this time held their services in a field at Craigmailen Farm, where a carved cross still marks the preaching stone which served as a rough and ready pulpit. The name Craigmailen was never forgotten, and to this day it still occurs in the titles of two churches in neighbouring Linlithgow and Bo'ness which are still places of worship of United Free congregations.

In Victorian times the Torphichen congregation was divided yet again by the disruption of the Church of Scotland in 1843. Again many of the villagers decided to leave, but this time, instead of taking to the hills they built Scotland's first stone-built Free Church on a site at the top of the High Brae. The two congregations stayed apart for almost a century until in 1930 Torphichen's much respected former parish minister, the Rev. Hugh P. R. MacKay, at last managed to heal the breach

In this turn-of-the-century view the riders of the Linlithgow and Stirlingshire Hunt meet in Torphichen's oddly shaped Square before setting off for the Bathgate Hills.

and it was agreed that all of the villagers would once again worship together, and that St. John's, as the little Free Church was known, should become the church hall, a role which it still plays to this day, although recently its little belfry has been removed as part of a modernisation programme.

A similar very typically Scottish belfry is the only exterior decoration on the parish church, which stands on the site of the Knights' church, where the combined congregations now worship each Sunday. It was built between 1750 and 1756 as a gift to the village from its local laird, Henry Gillon of Wallhouse. While this was indeed a generous gesture to Torphichen, it is a pity that it was decided to demolish the fine Norman nave of the Knights' old church to make way for the new one, rather than find a new site. This may have seemed the obvious easy solution at the time, but sadly it robbed the Preceptory and Torphichen of its finest medieval building.

The kirk which Gillon had built in its place is typical of Scottish eighteenth-century church architecture, complete with a separate laird's loft, entry to which can only be gained by its own stair which leads straight in from the churchyard, thus making it unnecessary for the laird and his family to pass through the rest of the congregation. Having given all of the money to build the new church, Mr. Gillon looked forward

171

very much to taking his place in the laird's loft and shortly before it was completed even gave an extra £12 on top of the £300 which he had already provided, so that it could be equipped with a fireplace. Gillon, however, was in for a great disappointment because as soon as the new church was completed Lord Torphichen, who lived miles away in Midcalder and who very seldom ever visited the village, announced that he was claiming the right to occupy the laird's loft. Gillon was understandably furious and the case went to the Court of Session in Edinburgh, but after seven costly years of legal arguments the court found in favour of his lordship and Torphichen's benefactor Henry Gillon was never able to enjoy the comfort of the laird's loft or its fireplace, having to settle instead for the front row of the neighbouring gallery. At least he made certain of a comfortable seat, and large chairs instead of a pew are still a feature of the balcony to this day.

Unusual seating arrangements are indeed an especially interesting feature of Torphichen Kirk. As at most Scottish churches, Torphichen kirk session required seat rents to be paid, and as a sign to the population at large that the quarterly dues had been paid, these pews had doors which, once the occupants were seated, could be securely snecked behind them. Those who could not afford to pay had to sit on open pews, without doors, at the very front of the church and beneath the minister's eagle eye, where there was no chance to doze off even during the longest sermon, and these seats were soon known as the paupers' pews. The pews with doors including those with double the number of seats presumably for very large families, and one pew whose family appears to have grown to such an unexpected extent that it literally drove them round the bend, still remain, but the open-ended paupers' pews were all removed several years ago to make way, rather ironically, for the finest of all the seats in the church of today, the beautiful stalls of the Knights of St. John, who travel out to Torphichen from their modern headquarters in St. John Street just off Edinburgh's Royal Mile to occupy them once each year on the occasion of their St. John's Day service each June, when they renew their connection with the place where their Scottish history began. Sometimes instead of worshipping in the eighteenth-century church, the Knights in their distinctive

This interior view of the Knights of St. John's Preceptory at Tor-phichen was taken during a special exhibition mounted by the Order which helped form the basis for the permanent display which can now be viewed in the tower.

black robes embroidered with their famous eight-pointed white cross, whose four bars are symbolic of the four Christian virtues and whose eight points are a reminder of the eight Christian beatitudes, hold their service in the Preceptory and with their swords, banners and other regalia seem really to bring history to life. The Order of St. John is however emphatically not a museum piece, but since its revival in Scotland in 1947 has become more and more actively involved in a number of worthy causes from the running of homes for retired people to the provision of the mountain rescue service on Royal Deeside. In Torphichen, as in many other parts of Scotland, the Priory of St John is well supported by its followers in the St. John Association, and with so many links between the community and the order it is not surprising that many of the fitments in the church bear the badge of the Knights with the eight-pointed Maltese cross featuring on the font and the communion table.

On Communion Sundays the pews at Torphichen are covered with crisp white linen cloths, but another unusual feature of these pews is no longer regularly utilised, for the backs of several of them fold to convert them into broad communion tables.

While the pews at Torphichen are decidedly different, so too is the minister's pulpit for it is equipped with a high sounding board and on the back wall two coat pegs. The reason for these, it is said, is that in the past services at Torphichen were so long that the minister did not come for the whole of them, leaving the prayers, the Bible readings and the other preliminaries to his elders and arriving just in time for his sermon. The problem was that sometimes he left it just a little late in leaving Glebe House and on his arrival had to rush straight into church and up into the pulpit, so that the coat pegs were needed for him to hang up his riding cloak. Another sign of the minister's weekly ride to the kirk is the small stone at the gate of the churchyard where he is said to have quickly tethered his horse, but church historians insist that this stone is actually the base of a free-standing cross dedicated to St. Ninian, who is still remembered in the church by the beautifully embroidered pulpit fall, which bears his cross. Perhaps the Victorian ministers at Torphichen simply put the remains of Ninian's old stone cross to a convenient new use.

Opposite the cross or tethering stone is a small stone-built, slate-roofed building, and according to tradition this was specially erected to thwart the dreaded body snatchers, who rode out from Edinburgh to snatch newly buried bodies to supply to the anatomy professors and students at Edinburgh University. After every burial therefore it was the custom in Torphichen for the relatives of the bereaved to sit up all night in the little gatehouse until the body was thought to be of no further interest to the body snatchers. To avoid this unpleasant duty many families employed the old men of the village to do it for them, and their pay was always a bottle of whisky each, so perhaps this kept up their spirits during the long night watches.

Many of the gravestones in Torphichen churchyard are of particular interest, including that of village dominie Andrew Elder, who according to the inscription on his stone served the bairns of the village for no less than forty years. They must have appreciated his teaching, because the inscription, which sadly is fast disappearing because of weathering, adds that the stone was erected by his former scholars. Inside the church, incidentally, the dominie's pew can still be seen to the left of the pulpit. It is smaller than any of the other pews, so obviously the 'maister' was not expected to have a large family, a sign possibly that even in past centuries schoolteachers were far from the best paid members of the community. Still, at least in the case of old Andrew Elder his former pupils remembered him by erecting the stone by which he continues to be remembered over a century later.

Most famous of all the Torphichen gravestones are the Adam and Eve stones at the far end of the churchyard. In their own way they are perhaps a comment on the development of our society, for on the earlier of the two Adam and Eve are shown entirely naked, but on the later stone they are discreetly clad in sarks.

Near the west door of the church is a much more modern stone, but one that attracts the attention of many visitors, because it belongs to the Aitken family from whom was descended Lord Beaverbrook of war cabinet and *Daily Express* fame. He visited the family grave on several occasions, and on his last visit shortly before his death gave a generous donation towards the restoration of the two hundred year-old belfry from which the little bell calls worshippers to the service every Sunday morning at eleven.

The Aitken family farmed at Hilderstan up in the Bathgate Hills behind Torphichen, and it was there that one of the most exciting finds ever in these hills was made quite by accident. For as elderly miner Sandy Maund walked along the hillside just above the Hilderstan Burn one Sunday afternoon he stumbled over a large red stone, which as it bounced down the slope suddenly burst open revealing that it was laced through by dozens of tiny silver threads the like of which, despite his job, he had never seen before. Curious, he scraped away the earth from round it and dug out another stone, which when he smashed it open also sparkled. Old Sandy carried both stones home and did nothing about them until the following Saturday night when he walked down into Linlithgow and, while drinking in one of the inns, brought them out and passed them round his friends. His finds aroused so much interest that he was persuaded to go to Leadhills in the Southern Uplands of Lanarkshire, where it was known that Sir Bevis Bulmer was then prospecting for silver.

As soon as Sir Bevis saw the stones, he realised that a new source of silver had been discovered, and it appeared to be richer than anything he himself had ever found. Tests in the assay furnace confirmed this, and he encouraged the owner of the lands at Hilderstan, Sir Thomas Hamilton of Binnie and Monkland, who was the king's advocate in Scotland, to obtain a lease from James VI to work all the minerals in the Bathgate Hills, without mentioning the strong hope that silver would be found. What reward Sandy Maund received for leading Sir Bevis Bulmer and Hamilton to this rich find is sadly not recorded.

Work was started early in 1607 on the sinking of a shaft, and the first silver ore brought to the surface was so rich that the new mine was called 'God's Blessing'. The mine was the wonder of the age, and soon many visitors were riding out from Edinburgh to see it. Among them was Stephen Atkinson who was greatly interested in native precious metals and who a few years later wrote *A Historie of the Gold Mines of Scotland*. Unlike the majority of the other visitors, as someone with a special interest Atkinson was allowed to go down 'God's Blessing', and when he returned to the surface took away with him a lump of the silver ore. This he sent at once to his uncle in London, who quickly showed it to his friend the Earl of Salisbury who rushed to show it to King James.

James, who had taken up residence in the southern capital some four years earlier, following the Union of the Crowns, had extremely extravagant tastes even for a king, and by this time he was finding it difficult to obtain sufficient money from the English parliament to meet his needs. Lord Salisbury's description of the abundant riches available from the Scottish silver mine appears to have made James, with his ideas about the divine right of kings, consider 'God's Blessing' a heaven-sent miracle, and despite protests from the Scottish Privy Council he decided to take over this new-found horn of plenty. Sir Thomas Hamilton made no protest, for the king paid him £5000 as compensation, which was no small sum in the seventeenth century, and in any case it appears highly probable that already he knew that the wealth of the Hilderstan silver seam had been greatly exaggerated.

The King appointed Sir Bevis Bulmer to be both mine manager and surveyor in charge of discovering new sources of silver. Under him he had around sixty workers, many of whom had been brought all the way from the tin mines of Cornwall as the local Scottish coal miners were not considered skilful enough.

Even the Cornishmen failed to increase production, and so the King gave orders for miners to be brought from the silver mines of Saxony. The Germans, who were accompanied by an interpreter, travelled by sea to Berwick on Tweed from where they journeyed north by road. They were followed by other groups of miners from Holland, Wales and England, a 'foreign' influx which did not please the local country people, who complained bitterly about the frequent brawls among the silver mine workers, especially when they made their way down into Linlithgow to spend their wages in the Red Lion and other inns. Extra justices of the peace had to be appointed to try to keep law and order and also to try to prevent thefts from the mine.

Among the German miners' first tasks was the sinking of two new shafts, which were afterwards known as the Germans' East and the Germans' West. The mining camp appears to have been a hive of industry at this time as work went on around the clock on a shift system.

Conditions underground were very bad, as some of the workings were only one foot high, just high enough for a man to wriggle into. The low narrow tunnels were so cramped that the miners could not wield normal picks, but instead had to have special small-scale tools made for them. Some were imported from the Continent, and one of these tiny picks with a miniature hammer head and a shaft only one foot long is recorded as having been unearthed during exploration of the old workings at the end of the last century, but has since disappeared.

There was also plenty to keep the surface workers busy, as besides hauling the heavy loads of ore up the steep shafts, they also had to pump out the water to keep the workings reasonably dry. Their other tasks included felling trees and preparing

them as pit props to use in the tunnelling, and they also built
and thatched the offices and outbuildings at the mine.

The ore could not be cleaned or smelted at the mine head as
there was not sufficient water, and this work was carried out
four miles away on the shores of Linlithgow Loch, where a
small smelting house was erected, as well as at a spot on the
shores of the nearby River Avon, a tributary of the Forth,
which is still known as Silver Mill.

As output, despite the sinking of the new shafts, still failed to
come up to the King's expectations, he decided to stop smelting
the ore in Scotland as he thought that it was either not being
done efficiently or that the silver was being stolen. He ordered
therefore that all of the ore was to be transported to the
recently opened new harbour at Barrowstounness, or Bo'ness
as it is now known, on the Forth, where it was loaded into small
sailing vessels usually used to carry coal and brought south to
London. This proved a big mistake, for the transport of the ore
to the Thames proved costly, and the expense of obtaining the
pure silver by smelting it in the capital was increased still
further by the high cost of the coal required to fuel the
furnaces, as it also had to be brought south by sea. Silver even
appears to have been lost because of the inexperience of the
King's English smelters.

During the first year after King James took over the silver
mines over 200 tons of silver was sent south, but after 1609 the
ore became more difficult to obtain, and the deeper the miners
went, the poorer the quality became. The best of the silver had
obviously been mined by Sir Thomas Hamilton during the year
that he owned 'God's Blessing', and the other shafts which the
King had had sunk were never going to prove the blessing
which he had confidently anticipated. He decided therefore to
sell his royalty to work the remaining silver to a private
company.

This he did in March 1613 when he let the mines to a
consortium made up by Sir William Alexander of Menstrie,
Edinburgh goldsmith Thomas Foulis, and a foreign entrepre-
neur Paulo Pinto, who came to Scotland from Portugal. The
rent was to be one tenth of all the silver produced, and the
King also reserved the right to reclaim all the Hilderstan shafts
by paying Sir William, Foulis and Pinto the sum of £100,000
Scots as compensation for any work which they had done. The

new owners were however no more successful than the King, and after persevering for several years in the hope of striking a rich new seam, they finally abandoned all seven shafts which had been sunk since 1607.

It was not until over two hundred and fifty years later that a fresh attempt to find the elusive silver was made by Mr. Henry Aitken, who was a fully trained mining engineer and colliery owner near Falkirk in Stirlingshire. The details of his explorations were recorded by one of Scotland's earliest geologists, Henry Cadell, of House of Grange near Linlithgow.

Mr. Cadell states that Aitken first secured mineral leases of the lands in the Bathgate Hills from the Earl of Hopetoun, from Mr. Andrew Gillon of Wallhouse near Torphichen and from other proprietors and in 1870 began mining not silver but nickel which was in great demand and which sold at £4.13s per hundredweight. Nickel is a highly poisonous ore, and its discovery may possibly explain the frequent reports by seventeenth-century visitors to Hilderstan that both the children of the mine workers and the animals who stayed near the mine shafts always seemed sickly. Mr. Cadell in fact records that during mining operations in 1873, several hens were found dead near the entrance to the shaft, where they had been scratching around among the piles of nickel ore.

Encouraged by the discovery of the nickel, Aitken sank a new shaft to a depth of over 200 feet, but he found neither nickel nor silver. He had hoped to found a new company to develop the Hilderstan mines, and a prospectus had been prepared, but this setback and high costs forced him to give up the idea.

He went on to run successful coal and iron ore mines, but always the hope of finding silver haunted him, and over twenty years later he returned to the hills at Hilderstan to make one final attempt to find silver. This time he pinned his hopes on once more opening up the very first of all the shafts, 'God's Blessing'. Stones and rubble blocked the shaft by then, but this was all removed, and the mine was restored to working order. Careful exploration, however, revealed that the early miners had done their work well and that no silver remained. For two more years Aitken continued to search for silver, but in 1898, after spending several thousand pounds, he reluctantly abandoned the quest.

Thus, out of all the men who joined in the Bathgate Hills

treasure hunt, only the first owner, Sir Thomas Hamilton, really struck it rich. By the time he died in 1637 he had become Earl of Haddington and had amassed one of the largest fortunes any Scot had ever possessed.

Another link which the Bathgate Hills area had with early industrial development came through the birth of Henry Bell at Torphichen Mill, whose gable wall still stands as the focal point of a riverside wall along the shores of the River Avon. After his early education at Torphichen school and later at a school in Falkirk, Bell became apprenticed to his father at the mill but soon found he had no love for the miller's life. Instead he persuaded his father to allow him to walk the seven miles to Bo'ness where he began a second apprenticeship, this time at the shipbuilding yard of Shaw and Hart. During the two years that he worked at the Bo'ness yard, which built wooden-hulled sailing ships of about 300 tons, Bell may well in his spare time have strolled through the town's Kinneil Woods and seen the little workshop where James Watt had recently conducted his experiments on steam power. Whether it was this encounter or whether it was his own frustrations as a child at having so many of his little model boats swept away by the current down the fast-flowing River Avon, Bell became interested in the possibilities of harnessing steam power for navigation, thus making ships independent of the vagaries of tide, wind and weather. Bell wrote to Watt, but the reply he received could not have been more discouraging. 'How many noblemen and great engineers have puzzled their brains and spent thousands of pounds and none of them nor yourself have been able to bring the power of steam navigation to a successful issue!' declared Watt, but Bell refused to be put off.

By this time Bell had left Shaw and Hart's yard at Bo'ness and after a short spell as a millwright in London had become interested in working as an architect. He returned to Glasgow where he succeeded in getting the job of building the huge flour mill at Partick. About this time he married the daughter of the owner of the Baths Hotel at Helensburgh and found that one of the jobs expected of him as the young son-in-law of the family was every day to carry gallon upon gallon of sea water up from the Clyde to fill the therapeutic baths which gave the hotel its name and which attracted its guests. Rather than continue this irksome daily chore, Bell utilised his knowledge of steam power to pump the water up from the river, and this success revived his whole interest in designing a steamship. Enthusiastically he wrote to the Admiralty in London enclosing plans for a steam man o'war, and received a reply from no less a person than Lord Nelson, but shortly afterwards Nelson was killed at the Battle of Trafalgar, and no-one else amongst their Lordships realised the potential of Bell's plans.

In 1811 Bell decided to finance his own steamship, and he placed an order with John Wood, shipbuilder, at Port Glasgow. One year later the little thirty-ton *Comet* was launched. She proved a great success and is generally accepted as the world's first practical seagoing steamship. Although the *Comet* was built on the Clyde, Bell apparently never forgot the training he had received at Shaw and Hart's in Bo'ness, because when the new-fangled vessel, with her tall black funnel and her twin paddle wheels set amidships, required her first annual overhaul, he sailed her through the Forth and Clyde Canal to Grangemouth and on down the Forth to the yard where he had served his apprenticeship. As the *Comet* came steaming into the yard beside the harbour, it is said that the many Bo'nessians who had gathered on the shore to welcome this strange newcomer thought that the smoke belching from her funnel meant that she was on fire and would explode at any moment, so they ran well clear of the quayside.

By the time the *Comet* had been overhauled, the Bo'nessians appear to have acquired much more confidence in her, because it is recorded that several local gentlemen paid the princely sum of 7/6 (37½p) to become the very first steamer passengers on the Forth, when they sailed aboard her downriver to Leith. The *Comet* created such an impact that later the same year several local businessmen backed another Mr. Bell, who was no relation of the *Comet's* inventor, to purchase the newly built steamer *Stirling*, which had just been launched at Greenock, and to operate a steam service on the Forth during the year 1814. The *Stirling* proved so popular that for the 1815 summer season Mr. Bell had built the first two steamers ever constructed on the Forth, and both the *Lady of the Lake* and the *Morning Star* were launched on the same day at Kincardine.

While this Mr. Bell founded the first steamer company on the Forth, Henry Bell of *Comet* fame continued his career in the

West of Scotland, but he apparently had fond memories of the village where he was born, because in 1830 he revisited it and announced that he was seeking a site for a house in which to retire. He died, however, before this ambition was realised and was buried in Row churchyard, near Helensburgh, where his statue sits looking out over the Clyde. Although he did not live long enough to enjoy retirement there, Torphichen has never forgotten its famous son, and the Bell medals, donated by his descendants, are still competed for annually by the pupils at the village school, while there are plaques dedicated to his memory in both the school and the church.

For a village in which the church played such an important part in its life, it is surprising to find that Torphichen was also a very superstitious place, with the Witchcraig above the village a reminder to this day of its fear of the supernatural. Sir James Young Simpson's daughter, Eve, writing about her ancestors the Simpsons of Slackend, in 1896, states that if either cat or hare crossed her great-grandfather's path while he was on his way to market in Bathgate or Linlithgow, he immediately turned for home, because he was convinced that their appearance meant that he had no hope of getting a good price for his beasts at the auction that day. This is an interesting reminder that while today black cats are considered lucky, at one time in Scotland all cats were thought to be witches' familiars and therefore unlucky, while the crazy antics of the mad March hares were thought to prove that they were possessed by the Devil.

Eve Simpson goes on to relate further examples of the Simpson family's superstitions, including the fact that great-grandfather Simpson was always particularly careful in the spring at ploughing time to round off his furrows, because he was convinced that if a furrow was left open-ended, this would be an invitation to the evil Lord of the Soil or Spirit of Murrain to creep into his land. Despite all his precautions, however, on one occasion his herd of cattle was affected by a strange malady. One by one the cows became ill, and despite all of the old man's efforts, several of the beasts died. It was then that farmer Simpson decided the only way to rid his fields of the Spirit of Murrain was to make a sacrifice to it. One of the few remaining fit beasts was therefore selected, a deep pit was dug, the cow was led in and was then buried alive.

Another day old Simpson arrived home to find that a beggar woman turned away empty-handed from Slackend Farm by a serving maid had cursed the house and all who lived or worked there. Straight away he grabbed a kitchen knife and set off in pursuit of her. In the end he found her sitting on the doorstep beneath the lamp of the coffee house in Torphichen Square and, grabbing hold of her, slashed a cross on her forehead, as he believed this was the only sure way to remove the curse.

Sir James Young Simpson himself told another story of his superstitious forebears when in 1861 he spoke about his great uncle Thomas, who farmed the neighbouring lands of Gormyre, and had dealings with the Devil. According to Simpson, Thomas was so concerned that the Devil might gain control of his lands that he tried to humour him by giving him a little croft of his own. A stone dyke was carefully built around a triangle of land on the hillside above Torphichen, and this enclosed area was always left uncultivated so that it was available for the Devil to use as he pleased. Thomas Simpson, however, was so superstitious that he would never ever refer to it as the Devil's field, insisting that it should always be called the 'Guid Man's Croft' or the 'Guid Man's Acre'. Superstitious though he was, however, Thomas Simpson seems to have believed that he could have the last laugh on Auld Nick, because the acre which he walled off for him at Gormyre was the roughest and the stoniest in the whole area!

CHAPTER 8

The Dale and the Moors

Unlike many other West Lothian placenames, Armadale, or The Dale as it is more familiarly known to most of its inhabitants, is of comparatively recent origin. This area to the south-west of the Bathgate Hills was originally known as Barbauchlaw, a corruption of Boar Baughlee, which like the place name Balbardie in neighbouring Bathgate, is a reminder that the Scottish kings riding out from Linlithgow Palace used to enjoy hunting the wild pigs in these parts, for not only did the fierce boar offer good sport, but they also tasted delicious when served at palace banquets.

The name Armadale was first introduced in 1790 when the lands were purchased by Sir William Honeyman, who already owned large estates in Sutherland from where he borrowed the name. Sir William made his West Lothian purchase as a weekend escape from his law practice in Edinburgh, the completion of the new Edinburgh to Glasgow highway or the 'Great Road' as it was known, having recently opened up the Armadale area and made it comparatively accessible to the city. When Sir William, or Lord Armadale as he became, purchased his new home in West Lothian, it lay in attractively undisturbed farming country, but of course the new road, as well as enabling his Lordship to travel to and from the city, also helped turn Armadale into one of the new towns of the Industrial Revolution.

For a start it placed Armadale on a regular stagecoach route for the first time, and an inn was soon established where passengers could enjoy a quick meal and a welcome refreshment while the horses were changed at this the halfway stage on the twelve-hour journey between Edinburgh and Glasgow. The coaches also had to stop at Armadale because a toll house was established on the new highway at this point where it crossed the old road used by drovers and their cattle on the way south from the market trysts at Falkirk and Larbert and by the salters carrying their salt south from Bo'ness to inland

The tower of the Goth public house is Armadale's best-known landmark.

towns such as Lanark. The toll house at Armadale Cross was described at the time as being 'a small one-roomed hut with a lookout window in each wall', and just in case either cattle or coaches should try to slip by without paying, 'the Cross was heavily gated and barred'.

Later, at the beginning of the 1830s, Armadale was the scene of a daring highway robbery. This involved a stagecoach named the 'Prince George' which was owned by a Bathgate man called George Gilchrist. On a cold winter morning it set out on its usual run from Glasgow to Edinburgh with only one passenger besides Jock McMillan the driver. The lone passenger paid only to travel outside but asked that his one piece of luggage, a large tin box, be stored in the foreboot below the driver's seat and secured to the wooden floor boards with chains and a padlock. Near Airdrie the 'Prince George' was hailed by two men who looked like labourers. They paid to travel outside and clambered up on top.

Driving sleet turned to snow as the 'Prince George' travelled on past Forest Field Loch, midway between Airdrie and Armadale, where it was halted again by another two passengers. The newcomers were a tall gentleman and a young lady who wore a fur wrap, a thick veil and thick snow boots, obviously to protect her from the wicked winter weather. The gentleman already had tickets, which he waved up at Jock, as he helped his companion aboard, so there was no delay in setting off again towards Armadale. As they travelled on, Jock's attention was attracted to the fact that the two workmen seated behind him had produced a long length of greasy chain which they now both appeared to be busy cleaning. The continual clanging as they hauled the chain up and down through rags which they produced would have irritated Jock on any other day but on that day the wind was already making such a noise that he did not protest as he also knew that they would be getting off before too long as they had only paid to travel to Bathgate.

By then they were almost at Armadale Cross, and when he stopped at the toll, the two inside passengers dismounted and before departing gave Jock a tip of a silver half crown. At the next stop at the Royal Hotel in the Steel Yard in Bathgate, the two labourers with the chain got off so that when the 'Prince George' clattered out of the inn yard at the Royal and set off up Engine Street, as George Street was then called, Jock the driver was once more alone with the man whose tin trunk was stored in the boot. From Engine Street the coach climbed up High Hopetoun Street and on up the steep hill past Drumcross and on along the crest of the hills to Bangour. From there it was downhill to Dechmont, then along the flat past Houston House and into Uphall, where it pulled up in the forecourt of the Oatridge Inn.

As the ostler and the inn boy ran forward to change the horses yet again, the Glasgow passenger climbed stiffly down from the roof, frozen, but happy that his journey had apparently been completed uneventfully. For this as far as he was concerned was the end of the road, because waiting at the inn door was his opposite number from Edinburgh. After a brief chat the Glaswegian turned to Jock and assured him that there was no need to unload his trunk, because if Jock would just show it to his friend, then the friend would ensure its safe delivery once the coach arrived in Edinburgh. As Jock was anxious for a wee refreshment in the inn before journeying on to the city, he wasted no time in opening the boot. Then he stood back in shocked horror. For the shabby, battered old tin trunk was burst open and all that remained of its contents was a corner ripped off a £1 bank note.

Immediately the passenger from Glasgow and his colleague from Edinburgh revealed that they were plain clothes agents for the Commercial Bank and that the trunk had contained £6000 in notes, and gold and silver coins, a very large sum in the early nineteenth century. It did not take Jock the driver and James Smith the Glasgow bank agent long to work out what had happened. While the two workmen on top of the coach had made as much noise as possible with their chain, the two passengers inside the coach had been busy ripping out the wooden boards separating the passenger compartment from the foreboot. They had then smashed the lock of the tin box and quickly hidden the bags of gold and silver coins under the lady's fur cape, while her companion hid the bank notes in his pockets and under his coat before they left the coach at Armadale, £6000 richer than when they got on.

Investigations focused on the owner of the 'Prince George', Bathgate businessman George Gilchrist, because he alone knew in advance that the Commercial Bank intended moving this sum of money and on which day. He was deeply in debt and desperately in need of money, but he denied all knowledge of the highway robbery until his former friend but by then rival Bathgate stagecoach owner, James Morrison, went to the police and made a statement saying that when he and Gilchrist were out drinking, Gilchrist had often discussed carrying out just such a raid. Gilchrist was arrested and shortly afterwards his lady friend was also taken into custody, but 'she' turned out to be a rather effeminate looking young man called George Davidson. Davidson's arrest caused a great sensation, because he turned out to be clerk to the Sheriff-substitute of Glasgow, John McGregor. Both of the men who had posed as workmen on top of the coach were also caught, but were later released because of lack of evidence to positively connect them with the robbery which went on below them inside the coach.

Three months later Gilchrist and Davidson appeared for trial at Glasgow High Court, where the prosecution demanded the death penalty as the only suitable punishment for highway robbery. In court it was proved that it was Gilchrist himself

One bicycle makes up all of the traffic in this view of Armadale's East Main Street taken around the turn of the century. Courtesy of West Lothian District Library.

who, heavily disguised, had played the part of the gentleman and that Davidson had agreed to be his accomplice, because he had foolishly forged a money bond in the name of the Sheriff-substitute and desperately needed cash to repay it. In the end both men were found guilty and Gilchrist was hanged in public on 3rd August, 1831, but young Davidson succeeded in escaping the noose.

While he awaited execution in the condemned cell in Glasgow's Tolbooth, his mother managed to persuade the authorities to permit her, along with her husband, who was a church elder, to arrange a special service of supplication. Both the turnkeys at the Tolbooth were invited to be present and to take part in the service, and as they knelt to pray, they were overcome, bound and gagged, while their keys were grabbed from them. Davidson's chains were unpadlocked and he was rushed through the city to the Broomielaw, where he was put aboard a ship which was on the point of casting off, bound for Australia. There were many accusations that the Glasgow court officials had had a hand in engineering Davidson's escape, because of his former work in the Sheriff's office, but nothing was ever proved and Davidson was never re-captured. From Australia he made his way across the Pacific to the United States where he worked his way across the country to New York, where he lived as a recluse, always scared to leave his renting rooms in case the secret of his highway robbery on the road near Armadale should ever become known. Davidson never returned to Scotland, dying in exile in New York in 1904.

In addition to stagecoach passengers, the new Great Highway brought many more strangers to Armadale than had ever been seen in the district before. Amongst them every summer were the Irish farm labourers, who each year came over to Scotland in the hope of getting work at the harvest. To the townsfolk of Armadale these strangers, who either spoke Gaelic or whose southern Irish accents were so thick that their English sounded like a foreign language, were men to be regarded with the deepest suspicion. As well as their little bundles of belongings slung over their shoulders on sticks, the Irishmen also carried sharp reaping hooks to cut the corn, but as far as the people of Armadale were concerned these instruments were clearly weapons and were evidence of these invaders' desire for a fight.

Each year on the approach of the first of the Irish workers, daughters and valuables were all locked away and the youths of the Dale looked upon it as their duty to beat up as many Irishmen as possible before they got through the village. Having suffered this treatment on their way east at the start of the harvest season, when it came time for them to return home it was not surprising that the Irish contingent all arranged to meet in Bathgate, before proceeding west through Armadale.

This tactic, however, almost provoked the worst-ever clash with the Irish in Armadale in 1858, when an Armadale man on an errand to Bathgate overhead the Irishmen boasting of what they would do to anyone in the Dale who hindered their progress west. He rushed back to the village and gave such a vivid description of these threats to his friends and neighbours that the whole of Armadale was soon in a ferment. All of the women and children were made to hide in a barn while their menfolk set about defending their homes. Guns were loaded and those who did not possess a gun armed themselves with picks and axes. According to one report of the incident, 'Scouts were sent out to watch the approach of the enemy and after a while they returned in feverish haste with ominous information that a large body of Irishmen was advancing on Armadale, with bared hooks'.

The defenders lined up along both sides of Main Street, ready for the charge, but the Irishmen stopped before reaching the first of the houses. After eyeing each other up for some time, the impasse was at last broken by one of the local men stepping forward and informing the Irish workers that they could pass in peace, but that 'the first to strike a blow would fall a dead man'. Thus 'The Irish Invasion', as it was always called from then on when old men gathered to blether at the Cross, passed off without incident. In future years there were no other fights, the Armadale people being content simply to tease the Irishmen about their accent and give them wrong directions, or even on one occasion persuade them to cut a whole field of corn, which was not yet ripe, as a joke against a local farmer.

While the Irish incident ended without violence, during the previous year there was a much uglier incident near the town which resulted in the last public execution in West Lothian. A young Armadale man was making his way home from Bathgate shortly after midnight one Saturday night when he came upon a cluster of people at Boghead Bridge. When he approached he saw to his horror the body of a man spread out on the road and was informed by one of the crowd that it was that of Maxwell from Durhamtown, as the modern Whiteside was then called, and that if he did not want to meet a similar fate, he had better run home and keep his mouth tight shut. Immediately he got to the Dale, however, the Armadale youth knocked up the village policeman, P.C. Thomas White who, armed only with his baton, went straight out to Boghead, where three Durhamtown residents, John McLean, his wife and their lodger, were all arrested before they could leave the scene and locked up for the remainder of the night in Armadale's only cell. Early on the Sunday morning Constable White summoned help from the Bathgate constabulary and the three prisoners were transferred to the jail behind the Burgh Halls at Linlithgow. On the next day, Monday, all three made a brief court appearance before the Sheriff, were charged with murder and were remanded in custody. Subsequently at their trial McLean's wife and lodger were released for the lack of evidence, but McLean himself was found guilty and was hanged on the gallows at what is believed to have been the last public execution in Linlithgow. That was in 1857.

It is easy to imagine the excitement this news must have created when it was discussed at Armadale Toll, which was the main place of gossip for Nisbet Easton, or The Dasher as he was more usually called, and his cronies. Apart from the stories spread by The Dasher and his friends, most news arrived in Armadale borne by the letter carrier, who wore a scarlet jacket and who always carried a horn slung over his shoulder, with which to warn families who lived off the main road of his imminent approach. His route ran from Bathgate to Armadale, where he delivered his letters at 10 a.m. before continuing on out to Blackbridge. Then on his return journey he stopped in Armadale at 3 p.m. to collect letters waiting for posting. Armadale got its own first sub-post office in 1855, when it was opened by Mrs. Forsyth, the wife of the local blacksmith. She resigned in 1860 and was replaced by William Forrester, who had just opened the village's first stationer's shop and who incorporated the post office as part of his business.

At this time the people of Armadale demanded that in addition to the morning post they should also have evening delivery such as the inhabitants of Bathgate already enjoyed. This request proved too much for the old letter carrier, who resigned in favour of his nephew, John Easton, who became the most famous postman the Dale has ever known. 'John the Post', as he became known, walked the same route from Bathgate to Armadale and Blackbridge every day for twenty-five years and it was said that he knew exactly how many steps he took to complete his daily double round trip. It was also claimed that his pace was so regular and his gait so even that he never varied by a minute on the twenty miles which he covered. Over the years 'John the Post' got to know the handwriting on the letters which he delivered so well that he could tell the recipients who they were from before they opened them. John saved many of his customers the trouble of writing letters, because he could always be relied upon to deliver messages by word of mouth, and as the families in many of the households at which he called could not read, this service was much appreciated. In addition 'John the Post' also delivered other kinds of 'messages', such as boots to be mended by old Tam Graham the snab in Blackridge.

Throughout his twenty-five years 'John the Post' maintained his same reliable as clockwork service, but one day shortly before he retired he failed to arrive at Armadale on his morning rounds. It did not take long for word to spread around the Dale that the Post was lost in the snow, and a search party set out along the road to Bathgate. At first they could see no sign of John, then suddenly as they reached the site of where Barbauchlaw House had stood, one of the women spotted something red lying in the snow. It was 'John the Post's' red uniform jacket, and within minutes the rescuers dug him out of the deep drift into which he had stumbled and fallen beside the unfenced stream between the fields of Hopetoun and Hardhill. Although frozen by the cold, old John was still alive and was helped to the first house in Armadale. There he enjoyed a bowl of soup by the fire, but then insisted that he was fully recovered and insisted on going back out into the blizzard to finish his rounds.

In 1870, Armadale got its first post box when John Mac-Donald, a former miner, who had been forced to leave the pits because of ill health and who had taken over the sub-post office in that year from Mr. Forrester, made a slit in the wall of his home. Next year in 1871 the telegraph was introduced into Armadale at a cost of one shilling for twenty words, and one local man who received one of the first cables is reputed to have declared that he would have known it was from his brother, even if there had been no name on it, because he had immediately recognised the handwriting. Mr. MacDonald, who also ran Armadale's newsagent's, stationer's and bookshop and acted as the village registrar, continued as sub-postmaster until 1879. When he resigned he was succeeded by village draper Duncan McDougal, but three years later he went bankrupt and the post office was transferred back to the newsagent's, which by then was run by Mr. Beveridge. Finally in 1900 Armadale got its first Crown Post Office with a staff of seven consisting of Postmaster and counter assistant, three postmen and two telegram delivery boys. There were three deliveries every day apart from Sunday, two in the morning and one in the late afternoon at 5 p.m., and five collections, the last one at 8 p.m., letters and parcels being received and despatched by rail.

The railway first reached Armadale in 1855, when the Bathgate to Monkland branch line was completed. It was intended mainly to carry coal and ironstone to the Monkland Iron Company's Works. In 1858 the first passenger station was opened, complete with waiting room, ticket office and station master's office. Three years later the line was connected to the west by linking it with the Airdrie to Glasgow line, and in that same year the first through trains provided a service from Armadale to Edinburgh and from Armadale to Glasgow via Slamannan and Airdrie. The new service was provided by trains of the North British Railway Company and led to withdrawal of the last of the stagecoaches.

The loss of the passengers from the stagecoaches did not have as much effect on Armadale's inns and pubs as was feared because by this time the Dale had grown from the original rural village into a busy little industrial town whose coal miners, iron workers and brick makers all appear to have had a fair drouth, if the number of drinking places compared with the size of the community is anything to judge by. Armadale's first licensed premises was the toll at the Cross, and this appears to have been quite a common feature of toll houses throughout Scotland, the big difference at Armadale being that the toll also doubled as a dairy, so that anyone who was seen wandering home slightly under the influence was said to have been for the milk again.

Armadale's first actual inn was opened in 1797, when Mr. George Sean obtained a feu at the Cross and, under the title of the Armadale Public House Society, erected a modest building described as being 'one and a half storeyed' and consisting of several sitting rooms and two attic bedrooms. There were stables at the back, and as well as providing fresh horses for the stagecoaches which stopped there, it also offered horses for hire. To pay for the building of the inn, Mr.Swann borrowed money from a Mr. Reid in Bathgate, and part of the agreement was that if Mr. Swan ever wanted to sell, then first option must go to Mr. Reid, and this happened in 1808. Mr Reid, however, did not wish to move from Bathgate to Armadale to run his newly acquired business, and so he appointed John Harvie, who had until then been a stonemason, to manage it for him. Harvie was the brother of Thomas Harvie of Mill Farm and the father of the girl who is still remembered in Armadale's famous local song, 'Sweet Jessie O' the Dale'.

By 1862 there were no fewer than fifteen licensed premises in the town including the Crown Hotel, Thomas Bishop's pub in South Street, James Beveridge's Buckshead Inn, Mary Campbell's Railway Tavern, which later became the Masonic Arms, Ann Young's Star Inn on the north-east side of the Cross and James Verrier's inn on the opposite side of the street.

The amount of drinking and drunkenness in Armadale continued to increase throughout Victorian times, much to the concern of the Dale's more respectable townsfolk, until at the turn of the century, led by Provost Smith, they decided they must do something to tackle the problem. As their example they decided to copy the Swedish seaport of Gothenburg whose city fathers had had some success in curbing the drinking amongst its sailors by opening drinking places run by a co-operative society whose members not only shared in any profits, but also much more importantly, imposed their own rules to limit how much was drunk, rather than encouraging as much consumption as possible as other publicans were guilty of doing.

In 1901 a public meeting was held in Armadale and it was agreed under the terms of the Industrial and Provident Societies Act of 1893 to found the Armadale Public House Society with 'Auld Maikum', Mr. Malcolm Mallace, as its President, Mr. William Lowe as its Treasurer, and David Love and David Kerr on its committee of management. Shares were sold at a cost of five shillings each, but at first the new venture seemed doomed to failure as the shares did not raise enough to rent premises, far less buy any stock. The members of the committee, however, refused to abandon the idea and sought a meeting with local coal master James Wood, who after listening carefully to their proposals, promised to give them backing of £1000. With this support the Public House Society wasted no time in renting an empty shop in West Main Street, and under Mr. William Aikman as its manager, Armadale's famous Gothenburg opened its doors for the first time. In accordance with its rules the premises were functional and kept immaculately clean, but offered no temptations to patrons to linger. Cheaper prices than any of the other local hostelries, however, ensured its popularity, and at the end of its first year of operations the Goth as it soon became known was able to declare a profit large enough not only to pay its shareholders a 5% dividend on their investments, but to enable Mr. Mallace and his committee to buy the premises and erect the purpose-built Gothenburg whose clock tower is still the best-known landmark in the town. Although the original rules of strict regulation of the amount of drinking which was tolerated and the maintenance of high standards of cleanliness were maintained, those about keeping the premises strictly functional were relaxed and the newly built premises were the finest in the town, complete with a stylish horse-shoe bar.

The opening of the Goth's permanent premises proved a great success, and every year from then on, as well as paying a dividend to its shareholders the Armadale Public House Society was able to use part of its profits to benefit the town in many different ways, from paying the wages to employ a district nurse, Miss MacAffee, and providing an ambulance to providing funds for the local band and bowling green to sponsoring an annual flower show.

So successful was Armadale's Goth that for once its near neighbour Whitburn forgot its feelings of rivalry, and a similar venture was started there. According to the then parish minister, the Rev. Graham Mitchell, writing in the Second Statistical Account of Scotland in 1843, Whitburn was originally Whiteburn, in contrast to the village of Blackburn, which was situated at the eastern end of the same parish. The burn referred to is the River Almond, which forms much of West Lothian's southern boundary and all of its eastern boundary before finally flowing into the Forth at Cramond. The Breich Burn also flows through the parish and gives its name to the little village of Breich which lies on the main road from Edinburgh to Kilmarnock.

Whitburn too lay on a main road which provided the southern route between Edinburgh and Glasgow and, like Armadale, it grew up around a crossroads with a toll. As at Armadale too, there were coal seams in the area, but again as

In this nostalgic view, gilded gallopers await their young riders at the shows which were always a feature of Whitburn gala day. Courtesy of Margaret Stevenson.

with its neighbour, the difficulty of transporting heavy loads of coal from these inland coal fields delayed development until the middle of the eighteenth century, when the increased demand caused by the Industrial Revolution and the gradual improvement in the roads made mining worthwhile. From then until the disastrous miners' strike of 1985 Whitburn and coal seemed synonymous, but during the year-long dispute the underground workings at the town's famous Polkemmet Colliery flooded, and now, despite continued protests from the miners, their union the N.U.M. and Labour-controlled West Lothian District Council, the decision of the National Coal Board to close the pit seems final. Until the strike Polkemmet was kept busy supplying the special type of coal needed to fuel the coking furnaces of Lanarkshire's Ravenscraig Steel Works, but with the future of that plant also in doubt and cheaper foreign supplies of similar specialist coal available in the mean-time, there is obviously little incentive to make the N.C.B. change its mind and spent millions of pounds to try to pump out the flood water. So Whitburn's miners seem doomed to continue to swell the ranks of the unemployed in this industrially already very depressed area of West Lothian.

With the closure of Polkemmet all coal mining in West Lothian has ceased, a strange contrast indeed to the prosperous coalmining industry which existed in the county when the Whitburn colliery was developed during the First World War. The timing of its opening obviously had an influence on the nickname which the miners gave Polkemmet when they dubbed it the Dardanelles, some say because its opening coincided with that disastrous campaign, others because of the number of lives lost in the sinking of its shafts and the digging of its underground roads and coalfaces.

Officially, however, Polkemmet took its name from Whitburn's most important local estate. Originally this belonged to the Shaw family until it was purchased during the sixteenth century by the Baillie family who came to live there from their previous lands in Lanarkshire. Polkemmet remained in the hands of the Baillies for four hundred years, and they always took a very paternalistic interest in Whitburn and the surrounding district, Lady Baillie in Victorian times being one of the benefactors of Bathgate Academy, which Whitburn children continued to attend until 1969, when the former West Lothian Country Council decided to give the town its own comprehensive secondary school in a mistaken effort to create more local identity and make the place more attractive to incoming firms, which sadly never came.

Like Whitburn itself, most of its surrounding villages, which are situated on the bleak, windswept moorlands so familiar to drivers on the M8 motorway, are equally depressed. From their names of Greenrigg, Longridge and Fauldhouse, these places all obviously owe their origin to the farmers and shepherds who worked these inhospitable lands in past centuries. During the late eighteenth and nineteenth centuries there was also the quarrying of whinstone for the building of Edinburgh and the mining of ironstone for the iron works of nearby Lanarkshire, but today there seems little hope for either farming or industrial development in these parts.

Largest of the villages in this south-west corner, Fauldhouse, is first mentioned in records written in 1523 where it is spelt

Fawlhous, meaning the house on the unploughed land. It is mentioned again in 1540, when it is spelt Falhous. Originally it was included in the parish of Livingston, but in 1730 it was transferred to Whitburn. By this date coal was already being dug on a small scale, and by the time the Wilsontown Iron Company began mining operations in 1790, the population had risen to over 1330. In 1835 a bed of slatey ironstone was discovered and developed by the Shotts Iron Company and Messrs. Holdsworth of Coltness. Both companies sank a number of small pits and installed steam pumping engines both for pumping and for raising the ironstone. Once on the surface, the loads of ironstone were loaded onto railway wagons and carried a short distance away where the ironstone was dumped in piles and covered with earth or ashes to keep out the air while it was calcimed by burning. This process caused huge clouds of evil-smelling sulphurous smoke to billow up, making the scene, according to a contemporary report, 'Like a living Hell on earth'. This impression was enhanced by the fact that the sulphur killed all the vegetation in the surrounding area, as well as polluting the waters of both the Almond and Breich rivers to such an extent that no fish could survive in them. When the burning process was completed, 1000 tons of ironstone were reduced to 60 tons, and once the mainline Glasgow to Edinburgh railway came to Fauldhouse during the 1860s, much of the raw iron was transported south to the West Midlands of England.

British Industrial Sands worked the Levenseat Quarry and provided an elementary school for the children of their workmen. There was also a parish school at Crofthead. In 1873 six boys who left school and started work had to be re-admitted because of the Mines Act. Thirty years later in 1903 the Fauldhouse School Board opened a secondary school on the site of the parish school at Crofthead. This eventually became known as the Fauldhouse Junior Secondary and now, since the closing of the secondary department and the transfer of its pupils to Whitburn Academy, it has reverted to its origial name as Crofthead Primary under the headmastership of its well known dominie, Hamish Miller. Today two other schools, Falla Hill Primary and St. John the Baptist Roman Catholic Primary, also serve this small and somewhat remote community which is still regularly cut off by any severe winter snow.

The isolated situation of Fauldhouse has resulted in its always being a place with many colourful characters, such as Scrubbin' Jock who got his name from making scrubbing brushes from the heather on the surrounding moors and selling them round the doors of homes in other West Lothian towns, and Willie Woodcock, who used to call at all the houses in the area offering to either entertain the inhabitants by dancing for them or to pray for them in return for a cup of milk.

Today Fauldhouse still has its own distinct characteristics such as its interests in brass bands, and in sport, ranging from junior football to athletics and greyhound and pigeon racing. The village also has its own community centre which is equipped with a swimming pool.

From Fauldhouse narrow hill roads run across the moors, east to Stoneyburn, another former coalmining village, and west over the regional boundary into Strathclyde and the parish of Shotts, where the River Almond has its source at the foot of the Hirst Hill. To the north the scene is equally desolate, with the countryside pitted with the remains of long-exhausted collieries such as Benhar. All these waste workings give a lunar look to the landscape, and this impression is added to by soaring space-age masts of the B.B.C.'s Kirk o' Shotts and the I.T.A.'s Blackhill television transmitters, both of which are situated just over the boundary with Strathclyde, but which dominate this south-west corner of West Lothian.

Between the two tall towers, whose tops are often lost in the swirling clouds which cling to these high moors, the M8 motorway slashes its way across the invisible regional boundary. To the north lies the village of Blackridge, whose very name seems to sum up so much of this district. Traditionally it was part of the parish of Torphichen.

Today Torphichen has many more links with another of the villages in the Armadale area, Westfield on the banks of the River Avon. While the people of Westfield travel regularly to worship at Torphichen Kirk, parish minister the Rev. Tom Crichton also holds regular monthly services in the village, and it is interesting that the setting for them is the hall of the paper mill, for it is to this industry that it looks for its livelihood. Westfield Mill, which is part of the giant G.P. Inveresk Corporation, has over its hundred years' existence developed

The old stable block at the long since demolished Polkemmet House now forms the headquarters for Whitburn's beautiful Polkemmet Country Park.

an excellent reputation for its special range of fine coated papers. 'Spartocote' and the other products in its range represent the top end of the process coated paper market and, as the name suggests, are produced from an esparto grass base, which makes them ideal for the high-speed printing of multi-coloured magazines, catalogues, book-jackets and brochures, either by traditional letterpress methods or by the latest litho techniques. The quality of the Westfield Mill's products, together with good marketing, including a steady export trade, has helped it to outlive the two other paper mills, Avonmill and Lochmill, which used to operate further down the Avon at Linlithgow Bridge, until it is now the last remaining paper mill in West Lothian.

Compared with its neighbour Torphichen, Westfield is very much a workaday place, but it does have some interesting historic links. It was for instance the birthplace of the nineteenth-century architect James Gowans, who was knighted by Queen Victoria. Gowans, who was born in 1821, was the son of a working mason and his ambition, he declared, was to see all working folk housed in decent homes. At the same time he insisted that there was no reason why artisan housing should not be artistic as well as efficient, and the first houses which he designed, Rosebank Cottages in Edinburgh, demonstrated this. In 1886 he was honoured by being made chairman of the Great Exhibition in Edinburgh.

On the outskirts of the village stands Bridge Castle. This typically Scottish fortified mansion was originally the home of the Earls of Linlithgow, and local legend has it that at the Reformation, when the Knights of St. John were forced to leave the Preceptory at Torphichen, their valuable and extensive library of medieval books, most of them handwritten, were taken and hidden in a secret room at Bridge Castle. It has never been found, but now after years as a country house hotel, Bridge Castle is being converted into flats, and there are hopes that the long missing books may be unearthed during the extensive renovations.

CHAPTER 9

The Union Canal, Almondell and Strathbrock

Walk along the narrow towpath of the Union Canal and you find yourself in the quietest of leafy green backwaters. Look, however, at the marks gouged deep in the stonework of the many old humpbacked bridges spanning its still waters by the thick tow ropes of innumerable barges, and you realise that this was not always such a quiet backwater, but was indeed for two decades during the 1820s and 1830s one of the busiest routes in the whole of Scotland and the fastest way to travel between Edinburgh and Glasgow.

When the Union Canal which flows right across West Lothian from the River Almond in the east to the River Avon in the west was first opened to navigation in 1822, it was indeed one of the wonders of the age. For its engineer, Hugh Baird, had succeeded in choosing a course which carried the canal all of the thirty-one miles from the centre of Edinburgh to Falkirk on the same level, thus avoiding the need for any of the costly and time-consuming locks which were a feature of every other canal. So impressed were the people of the time that they nicknamed the new waterway 'The Mathematical River', not only because it followed the two hundred and forty foot contour line for the whole of its course, but because it also maintained a constant depth of five and a half feet and a constant width of thirty-five feet.

Originally a route incorporating Linlithgow Loch, in the same way that Loch Ness was utilised in the building of the Caledonian Canal, was considered, but in the end Baird chose a line which carried his new venture along the hillside to the south of the old West Lothian county town, and the house in which he stayed to direct operations can still be seen at Manse Basin just up the hill from Linlithgow Station.

The reason for the digging of the canal was to transport cargoes of coal as cheaply as possible from the coalfields of Central Scotland to Edinburgh to fuel Auld Reekie's many fires, and in the days before the coming of the railways at a

The restaurant barge, *Pride of the Union,* lies alongside the quay outside the Bridge Inn at Ratho. Courtesy of Ronnie Russack.

time when Scotland's roads were nothing but muddy quagmires in winter and dustbowls in summer, canal barges were definitely the most economical way to move heavy loads. Thus the barges were also in demand to carry loads of stone for building the houses of the capital's New Town, and several quarries were opened along the banks of the new canal to supply this need. Nor did the barges return empty, because on the return trip they were just as heavy laden, but this time with cargoes of horse dung from Edinburgh's streets, which was sold to the farmers of West Lothian who used it to grow more crops, which in turn were shipped by barge to the city markets.

It was not only heavy cargo barges which plied the waters of the canal, but fast passenger boats also, because the Union and the Forth & Clyde were the express route between Scotland's two largest cities. For compared with the twelve-hour journey from Edinburgh to Glasgow or vice versa on a bumpy, uncomfortable and often dangerous stagecoach, the canal barges could complete the voyage from city centre to city centre in only eight hours of smooth safe sailing. Some of the fly boats as they were called were operated by the Union Canal Company itself, and these included the *Jeanie Deans* and the *Flora McIvor,* while others such as the *Appin* were run by licensed companies such as the Port Hopetoun and Port Dundas Shipping Company. So popular were these express barges, which maintained a very regular timetable departing from Port Hopetoun near Tollcross at 6 a.m., 8 a.m., 10 a.m., 12 noon and 2 p.m., with a 5 p.m. sailing to Linlithgow and Falkirk only, that intending passengers were advised to book in advance at the canal company's office at No. 20, Princes Street. From there also, ten minutes before each sailing, departed a special horse brake to convey passengers and their luggage up Lothian Road to the quayside at Port Hopetoun, but passengers were warned that they must not exceed the baggage allowance of 42 lbs per person. When booking, passengers also had the choice of travelling cabin class or steerage, which took its name from the fact that this cheaper accommodation was always situated in the stern half of each barge beside the rudder. When first introduced in 1822, first-class cabin tickets for the journey from Edinburgh to Glasgow cost seven shillings, while steerage cost five shillings, but by 1834 when no fewer than 121,407 passengers made the journey, the costs had gone down to six shillings and four shillings respectively.

To keep up their top rate of speed of over eight miles an hour each passenger vessel was pulled by a team of the best horses, and they were changed every four miles at canal-side stables, several of which can still be seen at various points along the route such as near Kingscavil on the road between Linlithgow and Winchburgh, and at Woodcockdale on the road between Linlithgow and Bathgate. In addition to the horses pulling the barge, a further horse was ridden by a scarlet-coated outrider, who rode in front of the team, blowing his horn to clear the towing path of any child or dog daring to get in the way of these royal mail barges.

Apart from all the excitement caused by the arrival of these express fly boats in each of their ports of call on the Union, which included Wester Hailes, the Bridge Inn at Ratho, Broxburn, Winchburgh, Linlithgow, Kettleston, Muiravonside, Brighton, Polmont, Redding and Falkirk, each of the express barges was very well equipped to ensure that the passengers, especially those in cabin class, were kept happily occupied during the whole eight-hour voyage. Meals were served in the dining saloon, the saloon bar was open throughout the entire trip, and for those who fancied trying to recoup the cost of

Striking a proud pose for the photographer is the Canal keeper, who controlled the flow of water into the Union at Linns Mill, where the Almond Aqueduct carries the canal high over the waters of the River Almond. Courtesy of Ronnie Russack.

their voyage, gaming tables were available. For both classes of passengers music was provided by fiddlers, amongst the most famous of whom were Willie Teenie and Blind Bob, and they were only too willing to strike up the latest strathspey or reel provided they were paid for it, just like the bands on the Clyde steamers of a later era. On fine days there was even room for dancing on deck, and dancing on the barges became so popular that in the evenings they were often specially chartered for private parties. From Edinburgh they sailed out as far as the Almond Aqueduct where they moored so that guests could admire the view down into the valley of the Almond with its pretty little Linn's Mill nestling on the river bank, but what the view down over two hundred feet must have done to the stomach of any partygoer who had had a glass or two too many is not recorded.

What is recorded is that for passengers who preferred a

quieter way of passing the time on the journey along the Union, each barge also had a small library which, as well as volumes to borrow, always had available for sale a very handy little volume called *The Canal Passengers' Companion*, which proclaimed that it gave 'A complete account of all the interesting objects that are seen along the line of the Union and the Forth and Clyde, such as towns, villages, gentlemen's seats, works of art, ancient structures and scenes of former wars; likewise an interesting description of the grand and beautiful scenery that is described on the shores of the Forth, the Clyde and the distant Highland Mountains, to which is added a table of reference for passengers from the west.'

In addition to the facts contained in the *The Companion*, cabin class passengers could also look forward to being regaled by tales of the canal by the barge skippers who loved to relate how amongst the navigators, or navvies for short, who dug the canal at a cost of £400,000, were two gentlemen more usually associated with other digging activities, namely the infamous body snatchers Burke and Hare. Even apart from Burke and Hare, the navvies, many of whom came over from Ireland, had a very evil reputation, and the people of Linlithgow were so worried for the safety of their homes, their money and their daughters that they insisted on a detachment of troops being based in the town, the last time that Linlithgow Palace was garrisoned. But it was the big-spending, hard-drinking navvies who had the last laugh, because as they dug the canal west beyond Linlithgow they either accidentally or perhaps deliberately cut through the pipes carrying the town's water supply.

West of Linlithgow too, for the barge passengers, came one of the highlights of their voyage, as they sailed out onto the impressive multi-arched Avon Aqueduct over which the canal is carried in a cast-iron trough. Beyond the aqueduct another engineering wonder awaited them in the shape of Scotland's only canal tunnel, which had to be dug through the hills between Polmont and Falkirk, because Colonel Forbes of Callender House would not allow the Union to spoil his view by passing in front of his mansion. When the canal first opened, this long, dark tunnel was a source of much worry to would be passengers many of whom feared that they might well suffocate in the depths of the hill. It was advertised, therefore, that the barges would always stop at the mouth of the tunnel, so that any ladies and others of a nervous disposition might disembark and be conveyed overland by horse-drawn landau, safely rejoining their travelling companions on the other side. Soon, however, the famous tunnel became just another excitement on the voyage and the *The Companion* described it as follows: 'At the 29½ mile, the mouth of the tunnel presents itself to view. Passengers on their way from Edinburgh will already have seen with surprise, the aqueducts and other various works, which have been constructed on the line of this canal, but when here they see the wide chasm, and the distant light, glimmering through the lonely dark arch of nearly half a mile in length, they are struck with feelings of awe and as they proceed through it and see the damp roof above their heads – feel the chill rarified air, – and hear every sound re-echoing through the gloomy cavern, – their feelings are wound up to the highest pitch. At the same time, there is something uncommon and interesting in the idea that there, secluded from the light of day, they are silently gliding through the bosom of a hill, whose surface is cheered by the enlivening rays of the sun, and covered with crops, cattle and the cheerful dwellings of man'.

Some canal passengers who were even more in the dark than those in the tunnel were those who chose to travel on the night express, which sailed every evening at 10 p.m., one barge departing from Edinburgh and the other from Port Dundas, near Cowcaddens in Glasgow. Equipped with bunk beds, this comfortable sleeper service allowed businessmen to be in either city early the following morning ready for the meetings and dealings of the day ahead. The overnight express was also a popular novelty with honeymoon couples who enjoyed spending the first night of their married lives sailing across Scotland on 'The Hoolets', as these night barges were affectionately nicknamed, because the lights in their bows made them look just like wee owls flying through the night.

Also in the bows of the passenger barges was a sharp blade with which they could slash through the tow rope of any slow-moving cargo craft which dared impede their progress. But that progress was abruptly halted in 1840 when the coming of the Edinburgh to Glasgow railway robbed them of their passengers and replaced them just as they had replaced the old stagecoaches. Cargo traffic on the canal did continue until the 1930s, but did not survive the Second World War, and in 1959 the Union was officially closed to navigation and was declared a remainder waterway.

Unfortunately this allowed West Lothian County Council and other local authorities along the route of the canal to culvert it to enable roads to cross it, thus making through navigation impossible. No sooner had this damage been done during the 1960s than canal enthusiasts began to organise themselves, and since the start of the 1970s the Scottish Inland Waterways Association and other local groups such as L.U.C.S., the Linlithgow Union Canal Society, have been campaigning to bring life back to the Union and even re-open it. Already these efforts to turn the tide for the Union have met with some success. As well as establishing Scotland's only canal museum in the old canal stables alongside the Manse Basin at Linlithgow and publishing guides for walks along the towpath, L.U.C.S. has raised sufficient money by charity efforts to purchase the replica nineteenth-century steam packet *Victoria*, and every Saturday and Sunday from Easter until Autumn this trim brightly painted little craft with her colourful awnings carries hundreds of passengers on short cruises, while on weekdays she is kept busy with school charters. In the evenings *Victoria* is also available for private supper cruises with catering provided, and each Christmas she makes a special voyage to bring Santa Claus to Linlithgow. L.U.C.S. also owns a fleet of smaller vessels available for members to set sail on their own, and many embark on picnic and barbecue cruises to quiet spots along the canal between Linlithgow and Winchburgh.

While L.U.C.S. concentrates its main efforts on the Linlithgow stretch of the canal, it also organises boat rallies at other points and is responsible for the now well-known Drambuie Marathon, which attracts competitors from all over Britain and from all of the services to negotiate the whole length of the Union and Forth and Clyde from Glasgow east in a variety of inflatable craft. As well as providing a great deal of fun for active sportsmen, it has also turned out to be an ideally peaceful setting for cruises for the handicapped, and these are operated regularly by the St. John Association and by the

The Bridge Inn at Ratho was originally a farm house, but by the time the navvies came to the district to dig the course of the Union Canal the 31 miles from Edinburgh to Falkirk, it had become one of seven ale houses in the village. Courtesy of Ronnie Russack.

Seagull Trust with barges specially designed and built by students at Telford College of Further Education in Edinburgh.

Most encouraging of all, however, has been the success of the luxury floating restaurant barge, *Pride of the Union,* the first commercial venture launched on the Union for half a century. The sleek sixty-five foot long *Pride,* which is the same length as the original express passenger barges, operates every day, all the year round, carrying up to forty-five guests on each of her lunch, afternoon tea and dinner cruises, which depart from the quay at the Bridge Inn, Ratho, where her owner, canal enthusiast Ronnie Russack, is the well-known mine host. It was in 1973 that Mr. Russack decided to turn his hobby of messing about on the canal into a business and placed his order for *The Pride of the Union* to be built by experienced barge-builders Meakin Marine, four hundred miles away in Atherstone, Warwickshire. Unfortunately 1973 was a very difficult year with the three-day week and a severe steel shortage, and for a

time the *Pride* was left with bows and midships completed, but
no stern. In the end, however, the hull was finished and the
engine was fitted. Then came the long haul north by road, and
Mr. Russack still shudders as he recalls the tension as *The Pride*
on a low-loader negotiated the final roundabout at Newbridge,
to the west of Edinburgh Airport on the boundary of West
Lothian, and painfully inched her way up the steep brae into
Ratho village. The launch of the twenty-nine ton *Pride* was
given wide coverage by both B.B.C. and Scottish Television,
and for the next two days the telephone at the Bridge Inn
never stopped ringing, and when eager diners could not get
through, they tried to book through the local post office and
even tried dialling Ratho Golf Club House.

With such an enthusiastic public response Mr. Russack's new
venture, which had been looked upon with such scepticism in
Edinburgh business circles, never looked back, but to begin
with the whole idea looked like being shipwrecked because
during the first few days Mr. Russack found himself spending
more time in the cold water of the Union than in the warm
saloon of *The Pride*. For as soon as she was launched it became
clear that something was wrong as she kept going aground, and
it was discovered that instead of the stipulated draught of one
foot nine inches she had a draught of two feet three inches,
and on the Union in 1973 these three inches made all the
difference between her floating and being stuck in the mud, so
silted up had the canal become. While British Waterways Board
was persuaded to start dredging the canal, Mr. Russack issued
his crew with wet suits as well as their chefs' hats and aprons,
and they had frequently to go over the side to free the
propeller from various entanglements. From the very first
dinner cruise, however, the motto of *The Pride's* crew has always
been that they sail not just come hell or high water, but come
ice, which often affects the canal in winter, and Mr. Russack
has gone to the extent of purchasing his own ice breaker, *The
Almond Queen,* which is a converted ex-army assault craft.

As well as her regular cruises, *The Pride* is also frequently
chartered for special wedding cruises, and on average three
couples a week are married aboard the barge. In a way this
revives the Victorian custom of holding wedding receptions
aboard the old passenger barges, but now the entire wedding

The towpath follows the north bank of the Union Canal as it flows through Winchburgh in this old picture postcard view. The chimneys of Winchburgh Brick Works dominate the scene. Courtesy of M.R. Meikle.

including the ceremony is conducted aboard *The Pride,* with Ratho minister, the Rev. S. Edwin P. Beveridge, usually officiating. For these wedding cruises *The Pride* is flag-bedecked and her main saloon is converted into a floating chapel, complete with organ and even a register signing area. The ceremony can be as formal or informal as the couple prefer. As usual at every wedding the bridegroom, his best man and the minister go on board first for final documentation. The congregation is then seated to await the arrival of the bride, who walks the entire length of the barge from the stern to where her husband-to-be awaits her in the forward section of the long main saloon. After the ceremony the bride and groom then walk down the aisle and disembark at the pier beside the Bridge Inn to jump the broomstick, an old tradition at bargees' marriages, two members of the crew holding an old sweeping brush at a low height as the couple leap into married life together. Reception drinks are served on the quayside, while *The Pride* is swiftly re-arranged from its role as a church back into its usual one as a floating restaurant. All the members of the wedding party then reboard the barge, which then casts off for a three and a half hour cruise, west from Ratho through attractive wooded farming country, while a full three-course meal and coffee, all freshly prepared and cooked aboard *The Pride,* is served. At the Almond Aqueduct, the third largest aqueduct in Britain, *The Pride* moors, just as the original passenger barges on their evening dance cruises used to do, to allow photographs to be taken, with the full sweep of the canal in the background, as a special souvenir of these unusual weddings.

Besides this increased interest in sailing on the Union, its use for many other leisure pursuits is being actively encouraged and it offers attractions for people with vastly different interests, from collecting wild flowers and studying wild life to industrial archaeology and from coarse fishing to model power-boat racing.

Wild flowers flourish along the banks of the Union, because unlike roadside verges they have never been sprayed with insecticide and for countless years have been left to grow quite undisturbed. Undisturbed to a large extent also have been the many fish which swim the waters of the canal, but coarse fishing enthusiasts are increasingly discovering that the Union offers excellent sport. The main species of fish found in the canal are pike, eel, perch and roach, but bream, tench, leather carp and mirror carp can also be caught. To fish the canal, it is necessary to obtain a season ticket, but these can be obtained free of charge from Lothian Region, which administers this aspect of canal life.

The long straight stretches of towpath which follow the north bank of the canal for the whole of its length are also ideal for people who either simply want to walk to enjoy the fresh air or those who aim to keep fit by jogging. Walkers who just enjoy the pleasure of strolling quietly along the towpath are often rewarded by coming upon wild ducks and swans, while long-legged herons are sometimes glimpsed. For those who care to use their eyes, apart from sighting other wildlife, interest can be added to walking the towpath by looking out for both the section stones erected by the old-time navvies to mark each section of canal dug and the milestones which they erected to provide a guide to the miles from Edinburgh to Falkirk. Another interest is to spot the numbers on the many bridges, while spotting the laughing and crying faces on the last bridge before the canal tunnel is considered a special find. It is interesting to note that the laughing face looks back towards Edinburgh, from which the canal had already been successfully dug, while the sad face looks west towards the tunnel which had still to be excavated.

There is so much of interest about the Union that it really forms a linear country park in its own right, and it is encouraging that its potential has recently been recognised by the appointment of an official canal ranger, who is based at Broxburn and who can provide help and information for all who want to use its facilities. Any fears that the appointment of such a ranger may rob the canal of its until now uncommercialised delights and pleasures will prove unfounded if the work is carried out in the excellent and tactful manner of the countryside rangers who already work in the Broxburn area at Almondell Country Park, which has been carefully developed since the late 1960s.

Almondell is in a way also a linear country park, because it follows the course of the River Almond from Mid Calder downstream to just beyond Linn's Mill and the Almond Aqueduct towards Broxburn. Like the canal, too, one of its attractions is its bridges. The oldest is the stone-arched Naismith Bridge, which was designed by the famous Scottish artist, who is better known for his portraits, and was built around the year 1800. It was followed in 1820 by the construction of an aqueduct needed to carry water required to feed the nearby Union Canal. It was constructed by the canal's engineer Hugh Baird and consists of a single cast-iron arch, about whose design it is believed Baird consulted master canal builder, Thomas Telford.

Most dominant of the country park's bridges is undoubtedly the massive nine-arched viaduct erected in 1885 to carry a branch of the North British Railway, which served a quarry, a neighbouring brickworks, a lime works at the village of Camps and James Young's Paraffin Light and Mineral Oil Company at Pumpherston.

In marked contrast to these three historic bridges is the country park's fourth bridge which was erected after the park was opened in 1970 in order to open up the east bank of the River Almond. It is a unique suspension bridge of A-frame construction. Great thought went into its erection, the deck being inched out across the river on rollers, while the A frame was flown in by helicopter in two sections and welded together on site before being hoisted into position to form one of Scotland's most unusual bridges, which bears some similarity to the Erskine suspension bridge across the Clyde.

In marked contrast to this streamlined bridge is the country park's headquarters and information centre, for it is housed in the original stone-built stables whose attractive facade has been carefully preserved. Sadly the stable block is all that now remains of Almondell House, which had been demolished before the estate became a country park. The mansion was built in 1789 for the Hon. Henry Erskine, who twice became Lord Advocate of Scotland – in 1782 and again in 1806 – and was known as 'The Poor Man's Friend' because it was said that as a young lawyer he never refused a case, even if he knew that the client was too poor to pay his fee. Born in 1746, Erskine was the second son of the 10th Earl of Buchan and brother of the Lord Chancellor Thomas Erskine, who became the first Baron Erskine of Restormel. During his time Almondell was the scene of many of eighteenth- and early nineteenth-century Scotland's most sparkling social occasions, for Erskine was reckoned to be the outstanding orator and wit of his day. His lively humour carried over into his court work, where his contemporary, Lord Jeffrey, declared that his added illustrations were always a delightful feature of every case, but were also always a material step in his reasoning of the matters before the court. Erskine retired in 1811 and enjoyed the quiet pleasures of his West Lothian estate, including fishing the waters of the Almond and its tributaries the Murieston Water and the Linhouse Water, until his death in 1817.

The house was inherited by his son, who had until then lived at Kirkhill House, which still stands on the north-eastern outskirts of Broxburn and which has recently been attractively restored. Later young Erskine became Lord Cardross and Earl of Buchan, and Almondell remained the family seat for over a century, the last member of the family to occupy the house being the Dowager Countess of Buchan, who lived there until her death in 1943.

The family vault for the Erskine family is situated at St.

Nicholas Parish Church, which stands on the hillside above what was formerly the village and is now rapidly becoming the town of Uphall, a place with a name which has often baffled radio announcers, but which is perfectly simple if both syllables are pronounced separately. In addition to the Erskine tombs and the many memorials to this distinguished family, the most interesting reminder of the Erskines' relationship with the church is the Laird's Loft, which they alone had the right to occupy as feudal superiors of Strathbrock, the Valley of the Badger as the surrounding area has always been known.

Old though the church of St. Nicholas looks, it is not in fact the first on the site, and the bell in the little steeple, which bears the inscription 'Campanum Sancti Nicholai do Strath-broke' and is dated 1441, has survived from the earlier one. Evidence of even earlier religious worship on this site comes from an old list of persons who held church lands in Scotland in 1296 and which reads, 'Ferquardus, parsona ecclesiae de Strathbroke, vicecomitatu de Linlidgo'.

Apart from the Erskines, Uphall and Broxburn's other well-known local family were the Shairps of Houston House, whose white-harled sixteenth-century mansion is now one of Scotland's most highly recommended country house hotels, its restaurant featuring in many good food guides. Houston, with its steep crowstep gables and its black-silhouetted windows, was built by Sir John Shairp, who was advocate to Mary Queen of Scots, but the family is known to have held lands in these parts since the peaceful Norman Conquest of Scotland during the reign of David I, when the King invited William E'scharp to come over from Normandy. Later, during the seventeenth century, the Shairps of Houston became well known in many different spheres of Scottish life including the army, medicine and the arts, while in 1707, Thomas Shairp, who was member of parliament for Linlithgowshire, and his brother-in-law, Murray of Livingston, who was also a Scottish M.P., were two of the leading opponents of the Union of the Parliaments. The Shairps, like their neighbours the Erskines, are remembered by a memorial at the Church of St. Nicholas.

From St. Nicholas the road winds over the hills to the little village of Ecclesmachan, which takes its name from another interesting church, 'L'Eglise de St. Machan', the Church of St.

Houston House began as a tall peel tower and developed into a traditional Scottish L-shaped mansion. With its white harled walls, black slate roof and steep crowstep gables, it is now one of Scotland's most attractive country house hotels.

Machan. According to Keith's *Calendar of Scottish Bishops*, St. Machan lived and worked during the first half of the ninth century, but what connection he had with this part of West Lothian is not known, and the present church dates largely from the beginning of the eighteenth century. According to its minister the Rev. John Smith, writing in the Second Statistical Account of Scotland, in April 1843 it was in excellent order, 'having undergone a thorough repair in 1822'. He continued, 'The church is neat and comfortable. It is provided with 153 sittings, which might easily be increased if required, to about 200. Considering the smallness of the population, the attendance is generally good. The manse is supposed to have been built about 1606; but an addition was made in 1800; and though the accommodation is not extensive, it is on the whole, sufficiently comfortable. The glebe and garden contain about four and a half Scotch acres of good ground. The stipend consists of 58 bolls, 3 firlots, 3 lippies of oatmeal; 58 bolls, 3 firlots, 3 lippies of barley; and £146..II of money'.

Most famous son of the Ecclesmachan manse was the

distinguished surgeon, Robert Liston, who was born in 1794 while his father was the parish minister there. A graduate of the Royal College of Surgeons, he became a surgeon at Edinburgh Royal Infirmary and later Professor of Clinical Surgery at University College, London. While there, he continued to practise as surgeon to the North London Hospitals. Later he published his *Principles of Surgery* and *Practical Surgery* and gained a wide reputation throughout Europe and the United States as the most successful surgeon of his day. He was noted not only for his skill, but especially for his swiftness, and in those terrible days before the discovery of anaesthetics this was of the utmost importance. Throughout his career Liston pioneered many new surgical techniques, including the invention of a thigh splint which was named after him, and as soon as anaesthetics became available he was amongst the first to use them. In Edinburgh he made surgical history at the Royal Infirmary by being the first surgeon to perform the major operation of amputating a leg through the thigh, while the patient was rendered unconscious using ether as an anaesthetic. In 1846 the future Lord Lister of carbolic acid and disinfectant fame came to witness one of the operations, which Liston carried out using the new anaesthetics. As well as being an expert on bone disease and amputations, Liston also led the field in his knowledge of aneurysms or enlargements of arteries, and it was therefore somewhat ironic that at the very height of his career in the following year 1847, when only 53 years old, he was himself struck down by an aneurysm of the heart.

Near Ecclesmachan stands Binny House, which has recently been acquired by the Sue Ryder Foundation for use as its first Scottish hospice. During Victorian times this fine nineteenth-century mansion house was the home of Captain Stewart, and he it was who in 1873 erected a mausoleum in the grounds. This struck the villagers of Ecclesmachan as very strange, but when they dared to quiz Captain Binny about why he had built a mausoleum, when the parish kirk had a perfectly adequate graveyard just down the road, he is said to have replied, 'Because on the day of the resurrection. I wish to rise from my own property!'

Today Ecclesmachan is best known as the home of the West

Lothian College of Agriculture at Oatridge, whose farm illus-
trates all of the most modern developments in Scottish farming. Annual open days also allow interested members of the
public to see all that is going on at Oatridge, and its family days
are very popular with children coming not only from neighbouring West Lothian towns but from Edinburgh and Glasgow.
Oatridge also always draws large crowds on a spring Saturday,
usually the last Saturday in March, when it plays host to the
Linlithgow and Stirlingshire Hunt's point to point race meeting. Point to point takes its name from the fact that the riders
originally raced from one local landmark such as a church spire
to another, but the events at Oatridge now follow a well laid
out set course, which allows the thousands of spectators an
excellent view of the start, the finish and all of the exciting
birchwood jumps in between. From early morning on Race
Saturday, the valley in which the point to point is held comes
alive as the horse boxes arrive, followed shortly afterwards by
the city bookies anxious to grab the best pitches from which to
lure the punters, many of whom arrive in plenty of time to
enjoy their first leisurely picnic lunch of the year before the
horses parade in the paddock. The colour of the jockeys' racing
silks and their multi-coloured caps is added to by the pink of
the huntsman's coat as he leads them out west along the foot of
the valley to the start, ready for the off. One of the attractions
of Oatridge is the fact that the horses, and the riders who
succeed in sticking on, make two complete circuits of the course
so that it is a true test of stamina of both horses and riders,
including the girl jockeys who always make the ladies' race one
of the most popular events on the card. By five o'clock
Oatridge is over for another year. Whether or not the departing racegoers have picked the winners seems to matter little,
for like the other hunt point to points which enliven the
Scottish spring, just being out in the countryside at Oatridge
seems sufficient reward to guarantee another equally large and
enthusiastic following next year.

   High above the farmlands of Oatridge and their cross
country racecourse rise the steep slopes of Binny Craig, on
whose rocks can still be found the elongated scratches or
striations left by the Ice Age when temperatures plummeted
and a thick blanket of ice covered the whole of Scotland and

Parasols and fairy lights bring a continental touch to the quayside bar at the Bridge Inn, Ratho, on the banks of the Union Canal.

left behind the typical crag and tail formations which form such a distinctive feature of the countryside to this day. This was caused when the sheet ice, which could easily sweep away the surface layer of soft sedimentary rock, came up against the hard igneous rock of a basalt plug, which today remains as a crag because the ice could not move it. Instead it swept to either side cutting even deeper valleys through the surrounding sedimentary rocks such as sandstone. At the same time the sedimentary rock immediately behind the plug was protected by it for some distance, thus forming a sloping tail, a geological phenonemon which can also be seen in the crag and tail formations at Edinburgh and Stirling castles and at Abbey Craig, Stirling, where the Wallace Monument crowns the crag. West Lothian's Binny Craig remains in its natural state, a nesting place for kestrels and a home for other wildlife, and it is interesting to wonder if it is this rugged hill which gave rise to the local place-name of Bangour, which means the Hill of the Wild Goats.

In the past Bangour was the home of the Scottish Jacobite poet, William Hamilton, whose ballad, 'The Braes of Yarrow', was praised by William Wordsworth. Now Bangour is famous as the home of one of Scotland's largest hospitals dating from Victorian times, when its peaceful rural site was considered particularly suitable for the treatment of patients suffering from mental illnesses. An entire village of separate villas was built among the trees on the hillside with, at its heart, a church, library, shop, tearoom, post office and even its own railway station. The station was served by a special branch line which connected it through Dechmont and Uphall with the main southern route between Glasgow and Edinburgh near Drumshoreland Station, where there was another isolation hospital for infectious diseases, and passenger trains brought both patients and visitors until 1921, when they were replaced by the new bus services which were spreading rapidly throughout West Lothian.

During the First World War the Bangour branch line had its busiest-ever period because it was used to transport injured servicemen brought by special troop trains direct from the Channel Ports. At Bangour the sidings into which the trains pulled and the platforms onto which the wounded soldiers were unloaded can still be traced in the grounds near the main entrance. The arrival of these army patients resulted in the creation of a temporary general hospital at Bangour. It has continued to the present day and looks like continuing for some time to come as more and more delays and financial problems plague the new general hospital which is being built in Livingston to replace it. During the 1930s Bangour Hospital's hilltop site resulted in its becoming a sanatorium for the treatment of the scourge of that age, tuberculosis, and to its fresh-air treatment were added fresh milk and other healthy products from its own home farm. During the Second World War hundreds of T.B. patients continued to be treated, but Bangour again gained fame for its treatment of injured servicemen, in particular airmen who had been badly burned in crashes, and to this day its burns unit continues to be famous.

Many of Bangour's surgeons and doctors have their homes in the neighbouring village of Dechmont, and their children go to the little infant school in whose logbook can be found an interesting mention of the old Bangour railway line, for it is recorded that the Director of Education for West Lothian gave special permission to one of the lady teachers to arrive late each morning, so that she could travel out from Edinburgh by the only available train.

Dechmont, Uphall and Broxburn make up Strathbrock, the Vale of the Badger, from which Broxburn also takes its name as brock was the Scottish name for badger, and it is good to know that these lumbering black and white beasts with their sharp noses and their broad rumps still frequent many parts of the neighbouring Bathgate Hills. Sadly, all too often one is killed on one of the narrow twisting hill roads which lead past farms such as Wester Binny and Tartraven, across to northern villages such as Three Mile Town, Bridgend, Philipstoun and Winchburgh, the last two of which are on the two hundred and forty foot contour line followed by the Union Canal.

Philipstoun owed its existence entirely to the shale industry and the shale mines and oil works of Messrs. James Ross and Company, whose petrol was marketed through hand-operated pumps topped with giant thistles bearing the one word 'Scotch'. At one time petrol from Philipstoun was shipped out on canal barges.

East along the Union Canal lies Winchburgh, which like Philipstoun owed its origin to the shale industry and especially to the influx of Irish miners during the 1850s and '60s. The strong Catholic influence in the growth of Winchburgh, whose name means the place at the bend in the river, can still be seen on the final Sunday each May, when the parishioners bring a touch of continental gaiety to the Scottish sabbath with their annual feast day. Each year one of the girls from the little Holy Family Primary School is chosen to be the May Queen, and in a ceremony reminiscent of many of the English Whit festivities, dressed all in white, makes her way in procession to the Church of St. Philomena.

The May Queen is preceded by one of the church's altar boys bearing a crucifix, and he is followed by the parish priest and all of the other altar boys wearing their white surplices. Two of the young 'queen's' classmates act as her ladies in waiting and another of her classmates acts as her crown bearer. At Winchburgh, unlike other West Lothian children's festivities, where the crown bearer is always a boy, the crown bearer is traditionally a girl, and the crown she carries is one of flowers with which to adorn the smaller of St. Philomena's two statues of the Virgin Mary. As during continental feast days in many French villages, the highlight of the Winchburgh procession is the appearance of the church's other and larger statue of the Holy Mother, which is borne high by two of the men of the congregation on this annual outing from the church. The remainder of the procession is made up of all the other girl pupils of Holy Family Primary, whose colourful dresses and bouquets of spring flowers bring a splash of colour to the walk to the church.

Once inside St. Philomena's, all of the children join in prayers to the Holy Virgin before singing a special flower hymn, 'We crown Her with blossoms'. During the hymn the climax of the day's celebration is reached, when the little crown bearer places the crown of flowers on the head of the smaller of the two statues of Mary, who in her blue gown overlooks the happy scene. Soon the statue of the Holy Mother is entirely surrounded with flowers as all of the flower girls parade around the church and lay their bouquets in special positions on the table at her feet. Then, the service over, the boys and girls leave the church, knowing that yet again they have kept alive one of the traditions of Winchburgh which is unique in this part of Scotland.

Winchburgh's neighbour to the east, Kirkliston, as its name suggests, also has an interesting church history, with connections with the Knights Templar. The fine old parish church is built in Norman style, and in its graveyard is the burial place of the Dalrymple family. One of the family who lies there is Elizabeth Dundas, wife of John, the first Earl of Stair, and she is said to have been the prototype of Lucy Ashton in Sir Walter Scott's *Bride of Lammermoor*. Newliston, the Stair family's mansion, is situated just outside Kirkliston, and the many plantations of trees in its grounds are said to be laid out as a plan of the battle of Dettingen, at which the second Earl distinguished himself.

Kirkliston is best known today as the site of the distillery which produces Scotland's most famous liqueur, Drambuie. The distillery is one of the most modern streamlined buildings in the village, but the liqueur is exactly the same as the drink whose secret recipe Bonnie Prince Charlie entrusted to the

MacKinnon of MacKinnon. For almost two hundred and fifty years the MacKinnons have jealously guarded the delicious secret of their whisky-based liqueur, and during many of these years the recipe was kept locked away at the family's home at Williamscraig overlooking the Union Canal a short distance to the west of Linlithgow. From there each week the matriach of the family, Mrs. Gina MacKinnon, made a special journey to the Kirkliston distillery to blend the ingredients which transform whisky into Drambuie. Sweet but with a warm glow, many people have suggested that Drambuie must be based on whisky carefully mixed with clear honey.

Local secrets of another kind may however soon be revealed, because work has started on the renovation of Niddry Castle, between Kirkliston and Winchburgh, and an archaeological dig is to be conducted to excavate the foundations, before it is converted into a private home and castle interpretation centre open to the public. The castle's main claim to fame is that Mary Queen of Scots received shelter and spent the night there after succeeding in escaping from imprisonment in Loch Leven Castle on 2nd May 1568. Niddry was the home of the Setons, one of whom was one of the Queen's Four Marys.

What can be done with careful restoration has already been demonstrated at another local castle, Ochiltree, to the west of Winchburgh on the ridge of the Bathgate Hills. It is known that there has been a fortified house on this prominent site since the thirteenth century, but the present castle dates from the early sixteenth century and, as was the fashion of the time, it was built as an L-shaped mansion with a newel or spiral turnpike stair in the angle of the arms. Three storeys high, including the attic, it was constructed of rubble and dressed stone.

Ochiltree was the home of the Stirlings, and the carved stone above the west door shows the arms of Sir Archibald Stirling and his wife Dame Grizel, daughter of James, Lord Ross. The Stirlings prospered during the seventeenth century, but at the start of the eighteenth they declared in favour of the Jacobites, and when that cause failed at the indecisive Battle of Sheriff-muir at which they fought on behalf of James Stewart the Old Pretender, their lands were forfeited.

Around the middle of the eighteenth century the Ochiltree

Estate was purchased by Neil Primrose, second Earl of Rosebery. He already had his home at Dalmeny, and so Ochiltree became a tenanted farm house, a role which it filled for over two hundred years until 1978. From then it lay empty until in 1980 it was purchased by Walter Goldsmith, an English portrait and landscape painter who had already had experience of restoring historic homes south of the border. He set about removing many of the modern alterations which had damaged the original structure, while the old house was used as a farm, and then with great flair and imagination he set about restoring it as far as possible to its original appearance as a fine example of a Scottish fortified mansion. Among its many attractive features are the newel stair, and the great hall and its gallery. Particularly intriguing is the Laird's Lug, a Scottish version of the English priest's hole, which was discovered during the restoration work. It consists of a small secret room tucked away behind the hall, from which the laird could eavesdrop on his guests.

For a short time after its restoration, Ochiltree was opened to the public, but since then Mr. Goldsmith has sold it to new owners, and it is once again a private home, but it can still be admired from the outside from the road which leads down from the Bathgate Hills to join the road to Linlithgow at Kingscavil, where there was once a similar L-shaped mansion, Kingscavil House, where Prince Charles Edward Stewart, the Young Pretender, is known to have spent the night, but it has long since disappeared.

Kingscavil is today a pleasant little hamlet with its church and lattice-windowed cottages clustered round their green lawns giving it a distinctly English appearance.

CHAPTER 10

Livingston: New Town with a Past

Livingston, West Lothian's New Town, which has yet to celebrate the official twenty-fifth anniversary of its foundation under the auspices of the Livingston Development Corporation, may not seem the most promising place to find local history, but such a first impression would be misleading. For the attractions of this sheltered site on the banks of West Lothian's eastern boundary, the River Almond, in the lea of the Bathgate Hills, were realised by Scotland's kings long before the modern planners.

The lands around Livingston stretching flat and even west over Blackburn Moss to Bathgate proved such good hunting country that it regularly attracted royal hunting parties. The only disadvantage, especially on short winter afternoons, was the long and sometimes dangerous ride all the way back to Holyrood. A royal hunting lodge was therefore established on a site just to the south of Livingston Village, where the king and his nobles could spend the night in warmth and safety, ready to resume the chase at first light the following morning. Lingering late at Livingston and spending the night with good food and good company at the hunting lodge must have had many attractions for the king rather than riding back to face all the worries and pressures of the court in Edinburgh, but King David I and the other Scottish monarchs who stayed at Livingston could not escape entirely from royal duties, because a tradition grew up that the famous royal touch was particularly effective in curing scrofula and other skin diseases, if administered with the liquid which flowed from a spring near the Livingston lodge. The site of this curative spring is still recalled by the local placename, Newyearsfield, so called because local lore maintained that when the monarch was in residence at Livingston for Hogmanay and administered the touch at the well first thing on New Year's morning this was the most effective time of all to be treated. Over the years some scorn has been poured on the whole idea of the effectiveness of the royal touch, but it is interesting to speculate if there just might possibly have been something in the treatment administered at Livingston, if the liquid which seeped out of the well in Newyearsfield was not water but oil from the shale seams discovered beneath it centuries later, because of course oil-based treatments are now favoured for many skin complaints.

During the peaceful Norman Conquest of Scotland during the reign of King David I at the start of the twelfth century, the lands of Livingston were granted by the King to a Flemish nobleman. His name was De Leving and he soon built a simple square stone tower on the slight rise to the north of Livingston Village, from which if necessary he could defend his new-found lands. As a nobleman, Leving acquired servants to wait upon himself, his wife and family, and as their cottages grew up around his castle, Levingstoun or Livingston got its name.

Leving and his relations spoke French, and this accounted for his home becoming known as Livingston Peel, from the Norman French 'piel' for a fortified fence or palisade. The local Scots, however, hearing this word 'piel', associated it with the small hill on which the castle stood, thus giving the word 'peel' its Scottish meaning, as is also seen at the famous royal Peel which surrounds Linlithgow Palace on the shores of Linlithgow Loch. In Livingston, Leving's peel tower has long since disappeared, but the old name is still remembered as a local place-name and has recently been adopted as the name for one of the New Town's latest primary schools, which has been built near to the original site.

The De Levings, or the Livingstons as they became known, prospered and went on to become the Earls of Linlithgow, keepers of Linlithgow Palace. Although they no longer lived there, the village of Livingston which they had founded also flourished, and as more peaceful times came to Scotland at the end of the sixteenth century farms flourished on the surrounding fertile soil. One early written reference to Livingston occurred in 1633, when the Scottish Privy Council issued a decree that its farmers should all send horses and carts to Holyrood Palace at dawn on the morning of 1st July to help carry the king's baggage from Edinburgh to Linlithgow, where Charles I was to spend the first night of his first royal tour of his northern kingdom since coming to the throne in 1625.

Howden House is now one of Livingston New Town's most popular community centres. Its coach house and stables have been converted into a fully equipped conference centre complete with a theatre. Courtesy of Livingston Development Corporation.

About the same time Sir Patrick Murray became Laird of Livingston and as an enthusiastic horticulturist transformed part of his estate into a garden containing many flowers, shrubs and trees never before seen in Scotland. West Lothian's earliest historian, Sir Robert Sibbald of Kipps Castle near Torphichen, who was also physician in Scotland to King Charles II, writing in 1710, described it as 'This curious garden, planted by a certain Baron Patrick Murray, in which he trained up many curious plants and herbs.'

To protect his rare specimens, Sir Patrick had constructed special dykes to provide shelter from the prevailing west wind, and adjoining the walled garden he established a well-stocked orchard. Sir Patrick made several journeys to the Continent to gather more flowers and shrubs, and while in Italy he was so impressed by a water garden complete with fountains, pools and waterfalls that he is said to have recreated it at Livingston, although no trace of it can be found.

Sadly it was on one of his trips to Europe to gather further specimens that Sir Patrick caught a chill, developed a fever and died. Fortunately his friends in Scotland included Sir Andrew Balfour, who was a keen botanist as well as a doctor, and together with Sir Robert Sibbald he travelled out to Livingston and carefully transplanted over one thousand specimens from Murray's garden. Back in the city they replanted all the flowers, shrubs and herbs in a garden at the Watergate at the east end of the old Nor' Loch on the site of what is now Waverley Station. Sibbald was particularly interested in Murray's herbs as he considered that if they were more widely cultivated they could provide the people of the capital with a ready source of medicines and drugs. As a result of his interest the collection became known as the Physic Garden, and with one of Scotland's earliest botanists, James Sutherland, as head gardener it flourished. Over the years it outgrew its site, until in the end the collection was transferred to provide the origins of Edinburgh's now famous Royal Botanic Gardens, which can thus trace its beginnings to Murray's seventeenth-century garden at Livingston Peel.

The Murray family subsequently moved to Blackburn House, and Baron Patrick is still remembered by the local place-name Murrayfield, where the primary school of the same

This view of Livingston Kirk shows the church as it was reconstructed in the 18th century. Its only external adornment is the little enclosed belfry. Courtesy of Livingston Development Corporation.

name has appropriately a sprig of yellow broom, the Murray clan's flower, as its badge.

Even after Sir Patrick's death, Livingston remained of interest to horticulrurists, because his nephew, who succeeded him as Laird of Livingston, followed the fashion of the time by deciding to have the whole estate landscaped and planted with clusters of oak trees and conifers to complement the elegant new mansion house which he had built to replace the original and by then old-fashioned and inconvenient peel tower.

Livingston Place, as the new house was called, soon changed hands and was bought by Sir James Cunningham, whose descendants lived there for many years. One of the most interesting of them was his eldest son, William, who succeeded him in 1767. The young Sir William was at first a captain in the Duke of Buccleuch's Southern Regiment of Fencibles and later, upon his retirement from active service, became Member of Parliament for Linlithgowshire as West Lothian was then

called. Duties at Westminster do not, however, appear to have
been so arduous as to interfere with Sir William's favourite
pastime of fox-hunting. In 1777 he was one of the twelve
founder members of the Caledonian Hunt, and he also built
new kennels on part of his Livingston estate for the hounds
belonging to the Linlithgow and Stirlingshire Hunt. Situated to
the west of the present road from Uphall to Midcalder, the
kennels soon became known to the local people as the Dog
Houses. Shortly after they were built the Dog Houses were the
scene of a most unusual tragedy. It appears that Sir William,
being eager that the hounds should be as well looked after as
possible at all times, included sleeping accommodation for the
huntsman adjacent to the dogs' pens. One night the huntsman
left the kennels to visit the neighbouring village of Midcalder
and returned in the early hours of the following morning, very
drunk indeed. In the dark and in his befuddled state he missed
the door of his own cubicle and stumbled on instead into the
kennels where he roused the dogs. Immediately they set upon
him and within minutes the defenceless man was ripped to
pieces. Next morning all that was found of the luckless
huntsman was two small fragments of his clothes and his
leather boots. All the foxhounds were put down.

Apart from hunting, Sir William Cunningham, who was
twice married, loved to entertain at Livingston, and often there
were as many as twenty or thirty carriages lining the long drive.
All this was soon to stop, however, for after Sir William's death
at his London home in 1828, his Livingston estate was
purchased by the 4th Earl of Rosebery, who already owned
large estates at Dalmeny and elsewhere in West Lothian, and
shortly afterwards, the 1845 Second Statistical Account informs
us, the mansion house was demolished.

Several other Livingston mansion houses however do survive. One of the most impressive is Howden House, where Dr.
Gregory of Gregory's Nursery Mixture fame and the Scottish
artist, Henry Raeburn, were both frequent visitors. An attractive whitewashed Georgian style building, it is now one of the
New Town's community centres providing an attractive setting
for many cultural activities and a home for many of Livingston's flourishing clubs. Its stable block has been converted into
the New Town's well-designed and excellently equipped con-

ference centre, and its spacious grounds are now a public park. Alderstone House, with its links with the Whitelaw family of Home Secretary fame, has also been well preserved and in its grounds the old doocot or pigeon loft has been beautifully restored.

The Alderstone Doocot or Dovecote is a reminder of the days when the lack of root vegetables for winter fodder meant that only cows, sheep and pigs required for breeding could be kept alive during the winter months. All other beasts had to be slaughtered in the autumn and their meat preserved by salting it away. Tasty fresh pigeon casserole or pigeon pie was therefore a very attractive alternative to salted and often rotten beef or mutton, and large country houses such as Alderstone carefully preserved their right to maintain a doocot with as many as two thousand birds crowded into its tighly packed stone or brick nesting boxes.

Like most Scottish doocots, the one at Alderstone House is stone-built and rectangular in shape, with a steeply sloping grey slate roof on which the pigeons loved to parade in the sun. Other features include a central circular window or light in the front wall, and just above it an external stone string or ridge. This ridge served both as a ledge for the pigeons to land on before entering the doocot by one of the eleven pigeon holes, but also more importantly it prevented rats and other vermin from climbing up and in through the same pigeon holes, as they could not climb past the overhang. Inside the doocot, for the same reason the first row of the eight hundred and three nesting boxes is set a foot and a half above the level of the floor.

As well as protecting the pigeons from attacks by vermin, the doocot also had to protect the birds from raids by human predators because some nice tender young pigeons, or squabs as they were called, were always a very tempting prize for either poachers or village laddies out to fill their wives' or mothers' pots, and at Alderstone security took the form of locked double doors, one of which was lined with sheet metal to further deter any illicit entry. At the same time access to all of the pigeon boxes had to be provided for the scullery boy to make his weekly selection of plump young birds for the cook in the kitchen, and so the doocot was equipped with a central pole to which was attached a tall revolving ladder from the top rungs of which even the highest of the boxes could be reached.

Interest in doocots declined after the agrarian revolution in Scotland in the middle of the eighteenth century made winter fodder available and with it the possibility of year-round fresh meat, and the Alderstone Doocot, like many others, was allowed to fall into disrepair. Now, however, it has been restored as a most attractive decorative feature by Livingston Development Corporation's architects, who have done their best to preserve the New Town's links with its historic past.

Most of the other historic buildings within the boundaries of the New Town are conveniently situated around Livingston Village, whose eighteenth-century inn, church and cottages make a pleasant contrast to the modern developments all around them. The old whitewashed inn is a reminder of the days when stagecoaches travelling the southern route through Whitburn from Glasgow to Edinburgh used to stop there so that their tired horses would be changed for fresh ones, while their weary passengers could snatch a quick refreshment. No doubt it was a very welcome one, because an advertisement of 1780 for the 'Edinburgh to Glasgow Flyer' boasted that the stage would complete the journey in just over twenty-four hours! Long Livingston Toll House at which the stage, like all other vehicles, had to pay to pass can still be seen to the west on the road to Blackburn.

Dominating the whole village is Livingston Kirk. A typically Scottish eighteenth-century church, it was built in 1732 but occupies the site of a pre-Reformation chapel where worship is known to have taken place as early as 1130, when it is recorded as being a sanctified site. The original chapel is believed to have been burned down and destroyed when Cromwell's troops occupied the area during the period of the Commonwealth in the 1650s. The communion cups in the present church bear the inscription 'Gifted by Sir Patrick Murray of Livingston, 1696'.

The present kirk is a plain grey stone rectangular building with a grey slate roof, the only external adornment being a small enclosed belfry at the summit of the west gable. Inside, as again was typical of Scottish eighteenth-century churches, the pulpit was set in the middle of the long wall rather than at either end so that the minister was surrounded by his flock.

On 23rd January 1823 the minister was apparently a worried man because he wrote to the local landowner, Lord Hopetoun, informing him that it was necessary to buy six mortsafes in order to thwart the Edinburgh bodysnatchers for whom the Livingston kirkyard was well within range. The heavy metal covers to place over freshly dug graves were purchased from Shotts Iron Works, just over the boundary from West Lothian in Lanarkshire, at a cost of £5.25 each.

Crime and punishment must often have been in the mind of the Livingston minister, because as well as the usual 'cutty stool' or seat of repentance found in most Scottish churches, Livingston Kirk also had a punishment stone like a finger pillory, where members of the congregation who had offended the elders of the session in some way had to stand beside the small entrance door as the other members filed into the Sunday service.

Amongst those who worshipped regularly at the little kirk must have been the labourers and their families who worked at nearby Livingston Mill and Farm. Both have now been skilfully restored as attractions for New Town residents and their families and are indeed well worth visiting. The mill, whose water wheel is driven by the River Almond, and which first came into production around 1770, is indeed possibly unique as its gearing is of a very complex nature, designed to drive a wide array of different machinery connected not only with threshing, but also with the more general chores of the adjoining farm, which was worked for almost two hundred years by the Buchanan family. Situated on the north bank of the river, water is led to the sixteen-foot wheel along an eight hundred yard, four feet wide lade. The wheel is of the undershot variety and is fitted with peripheral gearing to drive a threshing plant in a neighbouring building. The main machinery consists of a vertical drive shaft which turns three pairs of millstones on the first floor, along with a hoist in the loft, an elevator, a fanner or winnower and a sieve on the ground floor, where the grain arrived for bagging after being processed on the floor above. Adjacent to the main building there is also a drying kiln, used in the manufacture of oats, which was probably added in 1800.

Livingston Mill has been completely restored to full working order since this picture was taken in 1970. The awning in the picture was erected as a temporary measure to protect the sixteen-foot undershot mill wheel. Courtesy of John Doherty.

Even before then, however, it is clear that the mill had been added to and expanded, because an advertisement in the Edinburgh *Caledonian Mercury* of 12th August 1793 stated, 'The Mill of Livingston has just been rebuilt and fitted up with a new construction for the grinding of oats, peasemeal and making barley and with a view to adding a flour mill, to be driven by the same wheel'. As a final sales point the advert added, 'The mill is within two hundred yards of the Edinburgh to Glasgow turnpike road', so the salesmen of Livingston Development Corporation are by no means the first to capitalise upon the New Town's excellent setting for good communications.

Completing this interesting mill complex is the little stone-built buttery, where a smaller five-foot overshot cast-iron water wheel, utilising overspill water from the lade, used to provide power for two 'soormilk' or buttermilk churns, but they, like all the other machinery, had become disused and derelict by the time that the New Town began in the 1960s.

Fortunately amongst the New Town's very first residents there was a band of enthusiasts who were determined to find out as much about its past as they possibly could and to ensure that during its construction as much of this past as remained should be carefully preserved for their children and future generations of the new Livingston's inhabitants to appreciate. Amongst them were Forsyth Jamieson, Bill Turnbull and Alistair Weir, who came together when they attended a series of lectures on local history which they asked the Extra Mural Department of Edinburgh University to arrange at Craigshill High School. At the end of the course they decided to put their interest to practical use by investigating whether it might be possible to restore to working order the old mill on the shores of the Almond, which they could see from their office windows, and make it the focal point for a river walk which would bring the countryside right into the heart of the New Town.

They found out that the mill was the property of the then Earl of Primrose, now Lord Rosebery, and wrote asking him to meet them on the site. A meeting took place in October 1970. To their delight the Livingston enthusiasts found that not only did the Earl of Primrose support their ambitious restoration scheme, but went so far as to offer to supply them with timber from his estate at Temple in Midlothian to repair the huge mill wheel, about a third of which had rotted away.

With this backing Alistair, Bill and Forsyth persuaded friends at work and next-door neighbours to join them, and in December 1970 the Livingston Mill Restoration Group was officially formed. For over four years the members of the Group put in thousands of hours of backbreaking work every weekend and on countless evenings, digging out the long lade, sawing new timbers, shoring up the crumbling stonework and re-roofing the whole building. The help of students from West Lothian College of Further Education and Moray House College of Education in Edinburgh under the direction of their lecturers was sought to help with the more technical aspects, while offers of help from pupils at local secondary schools to assist with the labouring were warmly welcomed.

At last on Saturday 26th April 1975 Lord Rosebery was proudly invited back to set the wheel turning for the first time

Livingston Inn is one of the oldest buildings in Livingston Village which forms a historic oasis in the middle of the ultra modern New Town. Courtesy of John Doherty.

for many years. At that time the wheel was capable of turning one pair of massive grinding stones, a bruiser and some of the ancillary equipment, and since then, all thanks to voluntary efforts, more and more of the old machinery has been brought back into use. All of this success at the mill led the members of the Restoration Group to feel that if the mill was to have a proper setting and to be seen in its true context, the surrounding farmyard and steading simply had to be restored as well. When they had first acquired the mill the farm had still been tenanted by well-known local farmer Mr. Buchanan, but as the New Town's houses encroached more and more on his fields, he retired and moved out. The way was therefore clear for the creation of the Livingston Mill Community Farm Project so that New Town children now have a traditional Scottish farm which they are welcome to visit not only for school projects, but more importantly in their own free time in the evenings, at weekends and in the holidays when they are always welcome to help with the animals and the many other everyday chores which they would never otherwise have the chance to experience.

Like all really good stories, this one has a particularly happy ending, because it is one of the original enthusiasts, Forsyth Jamieson, who has been appointed farm manager and who with his family now lives in the old farmhouse. Emphasis in stocking the farm is being given to choosing traditional breeds of sheep, pigs and goats as well as a full range of farmyard fowls including hens, ducks and geese, but pride of place goes to the farm's big Clydesdale, who is appropriately known as Ben. Ben started life as one of the horses pulling St. Cuthbert Co-operative Society milk floats through the streets of Edinburgh, and when the Co-op abandoned its daily delivery service he was pensioned off to the green fields of Livingston Mill Farm, where he quickly became the children's favourite.

Many special events and countryside theme weekends are held as part of the community farm's very varied programme and on these occasions old Ben is harnessed up to pull one of the farm's collection of hay waggons, carts and floats. Most unusual of the collection of horse-drawn vehicles which Ben often pulls is a unique hundred-year old oil tanker, which used to provide a door-to-door delivery service of lamp oil for paraffin lamps. It is particularly appropriate that this last remaining horse-drawn oil tanker is in the Livingston collection, because the Mill Farm is at present the home of Scotland's Shale Oil Museum, where curator Simone Braithwaite has amassed an enormous collection of exhibits connected with the industry, which was so closely linked with Livingston, many of whose modern factories now in their turn produce supplies for the present North Sea oil industry.

Livingston had three shale mines at Alderstane, New Farm at Dedridge and at Deans at Livingston Station. All of the shale brought to the surface at Dedridge was carried by an elaborate aerial railway system to Oakbank Works in Midlothian where it was fed into the huge retorts and heated to produce the oil. The overhead carriageway, which was a well-known local landmark, was erected in 1910. It was specially designed and manufactured in Germany, and four years later in 1914 when war broke out it was feared that this might cause hostility amongst the workers, so the management gave orders that all of the maker's name plates should be discreetly removed.

As well as the Oakbank works, Livingston also had its own crude oil works at Deans next to the shale mines at Livingston

Livingston Village with its 18th-century cottages and its inn. Courtesy of John Doherty.

Station. It was opened in 1884 by the West Lothian Oil Company, who operated it until 1892, when the cheaper price of the rival imported crude from America forced its closure. In those days just as today the price of oil fluctuated, and the following year an increase in the selling price of foreign crude persuaded ex Royal Engineers officer James Henry Cowan that it would again be economical to produce oil from the Livingston shale, and so he purchased the Livingston Station complex and operated it successfully until he sold out in 1897 to the Pumpherstone Oil Company. The Pumpherstone company completely redesigned the site and installed new equipment, which continued to operate until the works finally closed down in 1953. By a coincidence the following year the disused site was purchased as a storage base by the Royal Engineers, the same regiment which its former owner James Henry Cowan had served in. The works were finally demolished in 1956, thus robbing Livingston of a familiar landmark and a link with the original Scottish oil industry, which thirty years later in 1986 would have been valued greatly as a site of industrial archaeological interest.

Even although the actual works have disappeared, many relics of them remain and many have now been lent for display at the new Shale Oil Museum. They range from phials of shale oil at various stages of its distillation, to the safety certificates issued to the mine deputies to show that they were qualified to fire the shots of gunpowder needed to dislodge the shale, and from the miners' safety lamps to special badges awarded to show proficiency in first aid.

The horses like big Ben who pulled the earliest oil tankers were not the only livestock employed in the shale industry, for just as at the West Lothian coal pits, the shale mines used thousands of ponies for underground haulage, and the Livingston museum has many certificates issued by the Scottish Society for the Prevention of Cruelty to Animals to show how well they were cared for. Despite popular belief, the pit ponies did not become blind because of the darkness of the underground workings, and many stories are told to show just how clever these animals were.

One-time President of the Shale Workers' Union and West Lothian County Councillor, the late John Wardrope, started his lifetime career in the shale industry as a pony lad in Livingston's Deans No. 4 mine at Livingston Station. Shortly before his death, he described his first job and the ponies he worked with.

'The twenty ponies we had in Deans No. 4 mine were all wise beasts. I left the school on a Friday and went straight underground on the Monday morning. My job was officially described as a boy pony driver and the overseer told me that I would have to be quick, because I had to cart out all the shale dug by three miners. Like all the pony lads, I was entrusted with my own pony. My first beast had been shipped over from Ireland, where they were bought for next to nothing at the livestock sales. When a pony first went down the mine his lad was allowed to christen him, but my beast was there before me and because he came from Ireland he was called Paddy.'

'Paddy sensed right away that I was new to the job and I had an awful job getting him harnessed that first morning, but at last all the trappings were on and I drove him up to the face for the first time. He stood right enough while the shovel fulls of shale were emptied into the hutch, but as soon as it was full and I tried to lead him out, he kicked the safety catch with his hind hoof, freed himself from the load and trotted off into the

The little buttery is one of the most interesting buildings at the newly restored Livingston Mill on the banks of the River Almond on the west side of Livingston New Town. Courtesy of John Doherty.

darkness. I chased after him but soon lost him in the pitch blackness of the workings and had to run half a mile, all the way back to the stables, where I found him settling himself down in his stall.'

'It took me ages to lead Paddy back through the dark and get him coupled up again to the hutch, but later I blessed the trick that Paddy had learned of how to free himself from the load, when he felt it was too heavy or that he could simply get away with it, because it saved my life. For on that occasion as the truck was being loaded, he suddenly kicked himself free and galloped forwards away from the face. Along with the miners, I dashed to grab him and the next second the roof behind us caved in. The hutch was crushed to matchwood and so too would we have been if it had not been for old Paddy. All of the ponies seemed to develop this sixth sense and the miners used to argue whether it was their keen hearing or what we used to call their "pit-eyes" that warned them of trouble long before the men were aware of any danger.'

'The ponies and the men were always very close. Every morning at ten o'clock all the miners downed tools and got their tin piece boxes out. They all contained the same thing, day in and day out, four slices of bread and jam, with a good thick hunk of cheese on top and of course they always spared a titbit for the ponies, but the beasts were never content with that. They would never give the men a moment's peace, until they got a drink, and I don't mean water. They wanted a good drink of hot sweet tea from out of the miners' vacuum flasks. They could smell the tea, before the tops were even off the flasks and one of the ponies became so addicted to tea that it learned how to unscrew the tops with its teeth. The only thing it couldn't manage was to lift the flask and drink it by itself.'

'Every year the ponies all had a week's holiday in July at the same time as the miners, but this wasn't the only time they came to the surface. Earlier in the summer on a Friday night in late May or early June the pony lads worked on late, long after the shift had loused. The ponies were groomed and groomed again and all their leather harness was polished until you could see your face in it, because the next day was the annual West Lothian Agricultural Show. First thing on the Saturday morning we all collected our ponies from their stalls, brought them to the surface and took them the ten miles across to Linlithgow where the show was usually held in one of Aitken's fields. There was always tremendous competition, for we had to compete not just with the beasts from the other shale mines, but with the pit ponies from the collieries in Bo'ness and Armadale and the Redding, but that made it all the better when we won and came home with a big red rosette to pin up in the stables at Deans.'

'This was only one example of the pride and rivalry which existed between the men who worked in the shale mines and the coal miners. The shale workers always considered themselves a cut above the colliery workers for several reasons. These included the fact that the shale mines were much cleaner, and so the men did not emerge black at the end of a shift. Then there were the better houses and the excellent sports and social facilities provided by the owners at the Miners' Institute at Livingston Station and all the other shale mining villages, but most important of all was that the shale mines had a much better health and safety record than the coal pits. Generally the shale mines were free from dust and gas, but one disaster did occur. This happened in 1947 when an explosion occurred at the Burn Grange Mine near Mid Calder. Fifteen miners, including two brothers, died underground. Several of those killed were particularly unlucky because they were only working temporarily at Burn Grange, while their own shale mine at Breich was closed to allow a new haulage system to be installed.'

As well as recalling these events at the Shale Oil Museum, visitors to Livingston can also follow the Shale Trail, which provides information boards at Limefield House, home of the industry's founder 'Paraffin' Young, at Young's Paraffin Light and Mineral Oil Company's Works which is still in production manufacturing British Petroleum detergents at nearby Pumpherstone, and at the Five Sisters shale bings on the road to West Calder, which dominate the scene looking west from the Livingston Development Corporation's headquarters at Sidlaw House.

While they take pride in remembering Livingston's industrial pasts, the officials of the L.D.C. are naturally even prouder of their many successes in attracting modern industries to the New Town since it was founded just under twenty-five years ago in 1962. First of the big-name firms to arrive was the American-owned Cameron Iron Works, and since then the range of goods made in Livingston has grown and grown to include everything from traditionally Scottish products such as oatcakes and shortbread to pipes for the North Sea oil industry. In particular Livingston is proud of its ability to attract pharmaceutical and high technology industries, and its Japanese-owned microchip factory has helped earn it a prominent place in Scotland's so-called 'Silicon Glen', Scotland's central belt now rivalling California's Silicon Valley in manufacturing importance.

With the growth in industries came a rapid growth in population from the original 2000 people who lived in the area, mainly in Livingston Station, when the district was designated as a New Town in 1962, to the present 40,000. This makes Livingston the largest town in West Lothian, and although it is already almost three times the size of any other

The restored Alderstone House Doocot is a reminder of the days when pigeon provided fresh meat in winter when most stock had been slaughtered and salted. Courtesy of Livingston Development Corporation.

community in the county, it is still only half complete as it is estimated that it will eventually achieve a population target figure of 80,000.

Most of the first influx of newcomers came from Glasgow under an overspill agreement, and so it was appropriate that it was the Lord Provost of Glasgow who was invited to hand over the keys of the first of the new houses completed by Livingston Development Corporation on 18th November 1964 and that the first house was occupied by the Pickering family from Glasgow. By Hogmanay they had seven neighbouring families with whom to welcome in New Year 1965, but apart from these first residents of the first housing development at Craigshill, Livingston was still virtually a greenfield site. Already, however, the New Town's officials were making plans which have been turned into reality today with the Almondvale Shopping Centre with its huge undercover shopping mall, blocks of multi-storey offices, and four secondary schools, including two of Scotland's first community high schools amongst its eye-catching landmarks.

In its religious development too the idea of one community has been stressed and the Livingston Ecumenical Experiment has resulted in the opening of the Lanthorn Centre, where members of all faiths share this one purpose-built building for acts of worship and social events connected with their churches. Social facilities too have grown with the population until Livingston now has its own cinemas, discos, restaurants, pubs and hotels. Sports facilities include several indoor swimming pools, while outdoors, as well as the usual games pitches, the New Town's young population is catered for with several unusual attractions including a jogging track and trim course, a skateboard park and an autocross B.M.X. cycle course. There are also good facilities for the more traditionally Scottish pursuits of golf and bowling.

With such a range of excellent new modern facilities Livingston's much vaunted excellent transport links are now working in both directions bringing many people from other West Lothian towns to shop and to enjoy the leisure pursuits which it has to offer. From the original once-hourly bus service which ran from Livingston Station to Bathgate, Livingston's public transport system operating from the streamlined coach terminal at Almondvale now links it direct with Edinburgh, Glasgow and London as well as providing services to all parts of the New Town itself and all of the surrounding towns and villages. Livingston residents also have the choice of travelling by rail, as the New Town's two passenger stations provide fast trains to Edinburgh, Glasgow and Bathgate as well as to several other local destinations. With the M8 motorway on its northern boundary Livingston's private car owners are equally well catered for and the New Town is only ten minutes' drive from Edinburgh Airport at Turnhouse.

It is not surprising therefore that Livingston has become a

very cosmopolitan community with as many families from England and overseas as from Glasgow and other parts of Scotland. Many efforts have been made to give them a sense of community in their new home town including the encouragement of more clubs and organisations than any other place of its size in the country, but one method which has proved particularly successful has been the deliberate revival of traditional place-names both in the New Town's own corporation housing developments and in the new private housing estates at Murieston and Deans. Ladywell is a reminder of the well originally dedicated to the Virgin Mary, while Knightsridge recalls that these lands belonged originally to the Knights of St. John at Torphichen, and Harrysmuir indicates exactly what the countryside was like before the New Town took it over.

Best indication of all, however, of the New Town's success is that when its residents are asked where they come from, they no longer reply Glasgow or England, but simply Livingston, for Livingston is now firmly placed on the West Lothian map and looks set to dominate the scene in future decades.

Index